Good
Housekeeping
BASIC
GARDENING
TECHNIQUES

Good Housekeeping BASIC GARDENING TECHNIQUES

Ralph Bailey
EDITOR-IN-CHIEF

Elvin McDonald
EXECUTIVE EDITOR

Compiled under the auspices of
the Editors of Good Housekeeping

Book Division,
Hearst Magazines, New York

Table of Contents

About This Book   🌺   6

1   The Good Earth   🌺   9

2   Design with Purpose   🌺   23

3   How To Propagate All Kinds of Plants   🌺   39

4   Keys to Successful Planting   🌺   81

5   How To Prune Almost Everything   🌺   98

6   Forcing Plants Out of Season   🌺   119

7   How To Grow Flowers   🌺   129

8   Gardens for Eating   🌺   175

9   Gardens for Seasonings and Fragrance   🌺   191

10   Container Gardening Outdoors   🌺   201

11   Gardening the Organic Way   🌺   215

12   Gardening Techniques for Artistic Expression   🌺   225

13   Basic Garden Construction   🌺   245

14   How To Cope with Garden Problems   🌺   263

15   Indoor Gardening   🌺   281

16   Gardening Under Glass   🌺   299

17   Tools for a Better Garden   🌺   309

Index   🌺   315

About This Book

Whether your gardening thumb is bright green or just the opposite this book can be your growing partner. Even seasoned and successful gardeners forget, or like to brush up on their technique, but if you are that know-nothing beginner, the text and how-to illustrations will be equally understandable and useful to you. Essentially this is a book of the basic gardening techniques—the sort of things you need to know to grow one pot plant or an acreage of vegetation—everything from flowers to fruit, ground covers to towering trees, vines to vegetables.

As editors, it has been our goal to make Good Housekeeping Basic Gardening Techniques to a gardener what a good dictionary is to a writer. Or, in the same way a good cook can cook without slavishly following a recipe, this book can make you a good gardener who doesn't always have to be dependent on an expert to answer every question that arises in day-to-day gardening.

In 1972 the 16-volume Good Housekeeping Illustrated Encyclopedia of Gardening was published, and from its more than 2500 pages, we have edited these basic gardening techniques. Where appropriate we have updated the material, but mostly this is information that is tried and true, always timely—and timeless. This single volume is the perfect companion for the 16 earlier books, for it is of a size convenient to carry into the garden or to travel to a weekend or vacation house.

Good Housekeeping Basic Gardening Techniques, like the 16-volume Good Housekeeping Illustrated Encyclopedia of Gardening, is a direct outgrowth of the life's work of the late Ralph Bailey who was for more than a quarter of a century garden editor of two distinguished magazines, House Beautiful and House and Garden. He not only loved gardening but brought to it and to his editorial work an irreplaceable knowledge, a warm sense of humor and a brilliant talent for prose that made gardens bloom on paper and gardeners-at-heart of all his readers.

Unfinished at the time of Mr. Bailey's death, the earlier 16 volumes, and now Basic Gardening Techniques, have been completed and edited

6

under the auspices of the Good Housekeeping *staff, by Elvin McDonald, the Senior Editor and Garden Editor of* Good Housekeeping's *sister publication,* House Beautiful. *Mr. McDonald has been an avid practicing gardener and garden writer since his early teens when he wrote articles published in virtually every gardening and home service magazine. In 1949 at age 13 he founded the American Gloxinia and Gesneria Society. Today, as author of more than 20 books on the subject, he brings to* Basic Gardening Techniques *practical dirt-gardening experience on a ranch in arid western Oklahoma, suburban landscapes in Kansas City and Long Island and windswept terraces of New York's high-rise apartments. In his apartment alone there are more than 300 different plants growing at the windows and under fluorescent lights.*

For sharing their expertise in specialized areas, the editors would like to acknowledge the contributions made by Betty Ajay, Dr. John Philip Baumgardt, Dr. R. Milton Carleton, Mary Deputy Cattell, Marjorie J. Dietz, Montague Free, Jacqueline Heriteau Hunter, Dr. Roscoe Randell, Dr. Malcolm C. Shurtleff, George Taloumis and Dr. Cynthia Westcott. Line drawings have been prepared by Dale Booher, Kathleen Bourke, Home Garden, *Andre LaPorte, Lord & Burnham, John W. Stewart and Alice Uchiyama. The photographers whose work appears include Morley Baer, George de Gennaro, Jeanette Grossman, J. Francis Michajluk, Oldale International Features, O. Philip Roedel and Roche.*

The Editors
Good Housekeeping

TOP, LEFT: *Soil sample collected on an auger. Shake soil loose, and stir with auger; do not touch with your hands.*
TOP, RIGHT: *For lime test, fill test tube ¼ full of dry soil, then ½ full with lime solution. Shake. When color clears, match against colors on lime chart for information on lime needed.*
LEFT: *To test for phosphorus, combine chemicals as the kit instructs; pour the mixture over the soil sample; then filter into another test tube.*
BOTTOM LEFT: *Stir 30 seconds with tin rod; then allow to settle.*
BOTTOM, RIGHT: *Matching chart color gives soil's phosphorus percentage; tells how much your soil requires.*

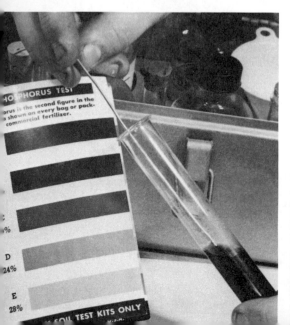

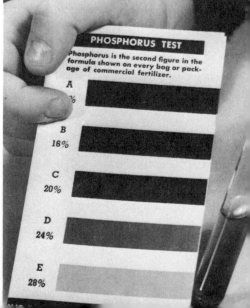

1. The Good Earth

The single most important fact to understand about soil is that it is neither a reservoir nor an inert mass, but a living biological community of such proportions as to stagger the imagination. Pick up a handful of soil and within your palm you hold billions of living organisms. The secret of building garden loam in which these can thrive is to maintain the organic content of the soil at a high level. Because it is spongelike in structure, organic matter will absorb water without crowding out air, and will supply nutrients even when the supply of applied chemical fertilizer elements runs low.

For years, natural manures were the basic fertilizers of both agriculture and horticulture, with a history going back to the early days of Greece and Rome. In the era of the horse and the backyard poultry flocks, gardeners did not have to look far to find raw materials.

Today the answer is to strive for a balance between chemical fertilizers and whatever organic materials are available. We can convert weeds, fallen leaves, garbage, wood shavings, sawdust, disease-free faded annuals and perennials and countless other organic substances into an important basic material for gardening. The purpose of composting is to provide for the soil bacteria a culture medium in which they can attack complex organic wastes and break them down into simpler plant foods. (See Chapter 11 for how to build and utilize a compost pile.)

The most important substance in compost is humus. It contains the remnants of organic matter, yet is resistant to further rapid breakdown by bacteria. Humus serves as a soil conditioner. If you mix liberal amounts of it with garden soils, you can produce a true garden loam.

Humus lightens clay that might otherwise make a soil too tight.

9

In sandy soils, humus has the opposite effect; it contains a gluelike substance that sticks the sand grains together and fills the spaces between the grains with spongelike matter. This results in a soil that will hold more water. Also, the addition of humus stimulates the growth of bacteria and the roots of higher plants. Even in loams that owe their character to the presence of organic matter, the addition of more humus is never injurious and is often beneficial.

This does not mean that you can sit back and expect to feed your plants entirely from the nutrients in organic matter. Most soils need additional supplies of fertilizer elements, at least during certain times of the year. Of these, nitrogen is the most frequently in short supply.

The activities of bacteria and fungi in the soil fluctuate at an amazing rate—from day to day or even from hour to hour. As temperatures rise, microorganisms increase their attack on organic matter to the point where excessive heat weakens or kills them. At temperatures below 60 degrees they slow up. At 42 degrees and below most of them are in a state of suspended activity.

Because of this effect of temperature, you must rely on chemical plant foods at certain seasons of the year. To apply natural fertilizers like raw sewage sludge, pulverized sheep or shredded cow manure in early spring would have little or no effect, for the soil bacteria, inert and dormant in the cold soil, make no effort to break them down. Any free nitrogen that might have been in the soil the previous autumn would have been blotted up by these same bacteria and locked away in their cells, not to be released until soil temperatures had risen above 60 degrees.

In areas north of the Ohio River, for instance, soils don't warm up to 60 degrees until June in most years. (Soils warm up much more slowly than does the air above them.)

Many early plantings, such as onions from sets, early peas, radishes, early lettuce, corn-salad and rhubarb, may have to be harvested before the soil is warm enough to release nitrogen freely. For this reason it pays to apply chemical plant foods to even the richest soil. Nutrients must be in a form immediately available to plants, such as nitrate of soda, ammonium nitrate or potassium nitrate. Early crops will extract plant foods that enable them to make as vigorous growth in early spring as they could make later without this stimulus.

Similar lack of nitrogen exists in autumn after soil temperatures have fallen below 60 degrees. Kale, lettuce, cabbage, spinach and other cool-weather crops have been known to double in weight during the growing period after a heavy frost, when fed with a form of nitrogen quickly available to the roots. A late planting might not mature at all without such a boost. In the home garden, this may mean an extra crop.

Fertilizer Basics

Strictly, a fertilizer is any material containing concentrations of chemical elements used to increase the fertility of a growing medium. But through long usage the word has been restricted to materials of organic or inorganic origin that will increase the available supply of nitrogen, phosphorus and potassium (sometimes abbreviated N.P.K.) when applied to soil and dissolved in water.

By this definition, fertilizers are derived from a variety of sources. For example, nitrogen is derived chiefly from the following:

Sodium nitrate (nitrate of soda), containing about 16 per cent nitrogen; ammonium nitrate, containing about 35 per cent nitrogen; and ammonium sulfate, containing about 20 per cent nitrogen. These are inorganic materials which become quickly available to plants once they are in solution. Their effect is fairly short-lived.

Urea: slow-acting but very rich in nitrogen, containing about 38 to 42 per cent nitrogen.

Cottonseed meal: containing about 7 per cent nitrogen as well as some phosphorus and potassium. It is moderately slow-acting.

Dried blood: containing 12 per cent nitrogen; moderately fast-acting.

Bone meal: containing 1 to 4 per cent nitrogen and 20 to 30 per cent phosphorus. It is very slow-acting.

Phosphorus is derived chiefly from:

Superphosphate: by far the best source of phosphoric acid; available concentrations contain 16 per cent, 20 per cent, 32 per cent and 44 per cent phosphoric acid.

Bone meal: as noted above. (Bone meal is a relatively expensive source of nitrogen and phosphoric acid.)

Potassium is derived chiefly from:

Muriate of potash (containing about 60 per cent potassium) and sulfate of potash (about 50 per cent potassium). Both are readily available to plants.

Wood ashes contain about 5 per cent potassium and considerable lime.

Complete, or balanced, fertilizers are available in many combinations of the three essential elements. The formulas are represented on the container by three numbers, the first of which indicates the percentage of available nitrogen; the second, the percentage of phosphorus (often expressed as phosphoric acid); the third, the percentage of potassium (often expressed as potash). Common combinations are 4–12–4, 5–10–5, 8–6–6.

No one of the balanced fertilizers is perfect for all plants, but 4–12–4 and 5–10–5 approximate all-purpose formulations. Other mixtures are formulated to suit specific types of plants. For example, 8–6–6 is good for lawns; 6–10–14 for broadleaf evergreens; 0–20–20 for potatoes. In the most general sense, nitrogen promotes leaf growth, phosphorus hastens flowering and potash is needed by root crops. The formula you need depends not only on the plants you wish to grow but also on the nature of the soil in which you will grow them. This means that if you seek maximum growth you should make a chemical analysis of the soil before selecting a fertilizer; your State Experiment Station will do this free or for a nominal fee. Bear in mind that phosphoric acid is largely lost in surface applications; it should be incorporated in the soil for full effect.

Most standard commercial fertilizers are fast-acting, and the nitrogen they contain may burn plants badly if they are allowed to stand for long in direct contact with the foliage. Many modern lawn formulations, however, are slow-acting and harmless to foliage no matter what the weather or mode of application.

When to fertilize: The basic rule is to make the first application of fertilizer at the time when plants start to make growth or at the time seeds are planted. This is usually in the spring, though many house plants start growing in the fall. Additional applications are made, as necessary, up to about Aug. 1 in the North, Sept. 1 in the Deep South. Thereafter, fast-acting fertilizers should not be used (except on lawns, vegetables and annuals) because they are likely to encourage growth which will be too soft to survive the winter. Slow-acting fertilizers, however, may be applied to all types of perennials in fall and winter.

How to apply fertilizer: On lawns, for even distribution, it is best to use a spreader. In vegetable gardens, for the sake of economy, apply fertilizer in a line down each row about 3 in. from the plants. In flower and shrubbery borders, make a ring of fertilizer around each plant (also about 3 in. or more from the stems) or sprinkle it more or less evenly, in broad bands, between plants. Whenever possible, and always when the soil is exposed, scratch or dig the fertilizer in. In all cases, after the fertilizer has been applied, water well. This not only helps to prevent it from burning the plants, but also makes it more immediately available to the plants.

To feed trees (except in orchards, where the fertilizer is scratched into the soil), make a ring of holes around each tree under the tips of the branches. Use a crowbar. The holes should be about 18 in. deep and 24 in. apart. Half fill each hole with fertilizer; add soil and water well.

How much fertilizer to use? A precise answer is impossible because plant needs and soil conditions vary so widely. Here, however, are the rule-of-thumb application rates per year.

Commercial fertilizers: follow manufacturer's directions, which are almost always given for lawns. If directions are not also given for other

ABOVE: *The second season after planting, feed trees. One system is to make holes 6 inches deep and 12 inches apart about a foot from the trunk. Fill them with tree fertilizer or a 5-10-5 garden fertilizer. As branches begin to spread, make these holes in a circle at approximately where the drip line occurs.*

BELOW: *Spread sifted compost from drip line to trunk in fall as tree begins to reach bearing age, if fruit. This also benefits shade trees.*

plants, use 2 to 3 lb. of fertilizer containing up to 5 per cent nitrogen per 100 sq. ft. For fertilizers of high nitrogen content, reduce the application rate about one-quarter for each 5 per cent rise in the nitrogen content.

Sodium nitrate, ammonium nitrate, ammonium sulfate: ½ lb. per 100 sq. ft.

Urea: ⅓ lb. per 100 sq. ft.

Organic nitrogenous materials: 6 lb. per 100 sq. ft. However, in the case of dried blood, use 2 lb.

Superphosphate (20 per cent grade): 5 lb. per 100 sq. ft.

Potash: ½ lb. per 100 sq. ft.

pH Degree Is Important

Before adding fertilizers or other conditioners to garden soil, an understanding of the term pH is necessary, for it is the key to adjusting the soil's fertility and alkaline-acid balance so that plants can grow better. Briefly, these letters stand for "power of hydrogen," and they indicate by an arbitrary scale the relative amounts of hydrogen in a substance. The pH scale runs from 0 to 14, with 7.0 the midpoint, representing neutrality. Acid and alkaline elements are in balance at 7.0. From 7.1 and up, there are relatively more alkaline elements present, and from 6.9 down, more acid elements. Thus the pH scale tells us when to add lime to soil to counteract the acidity caused by excess hydrogen (and thus raise the pH), or when to add sulfur, which will increase the acidity and thus lower the pH. Other substances you may add to the soil have a pH of their own that may need to be taken into account. Peat moss, for instance, usually has a pH of 4.5.

Changes in the pH of a soil are important because they affect the availability of food elements to your plants. If the soil is too acid, calcium, phosphorus and magnesium are changed into forms that plants cannot use, and the plants may suffer from a deficiency of these elements. If, in an attempt to correct this condition, you apply too much lime, such elements as potash, iron and manganese may be locked up in similar fashion. Juggling the soil reaction may make food elements available again. For example, in Midwestern soils, phosphorus (which can be locked up by both too high and too low alkalinity) may become insoluble soon after it is applied. I have seen lawns that were almost low-grade phosphorus deposits because they were oversupplied with this element. However, the lawns showed marked improvement when fed for three or four years with ammonium sulfate, which not only supplied nitrogen but also unlocked both phosphorus and iron present in insoluble form.

This kind of manipulation is possible and desirable only if the element in question is actually present in the soil. And, of course, unless the particular element is present in excess, it will be more quickly exhausted, because it will be taken up by the plants in much greater quantities once it becomes more readily available to them. A case in point is iron, usually present in alkaline soils in small amounts. If the soil is acidified, iron is set free and used by the plant. A temporary greening takes place, but the limited amount of iron available is used up more quickly than necessary. If the soil had not been acidified, this iron would have become available only when small pockets of decaying organic matter created an acid condition, and thus released a little locked-up iron. In this way, the small amount available would last for a considerable time. Thus, while changing the pH is not a substitute for proper feeding, it is a means of getting the most from the elements present.

For the majority of garden soils, a reading of 6.0 to 6.9 is best suited for most plants. This applies to all plants that use nitrate forms of nitrogen better than they do ammonia. Some plants, such as the broadleaf ornamental evergreens, blueberries and oaks, prefer their nitrogen as ammonia. These plants thrive best in a pH range of 4.5 to 5.9. Within the 6.0 to 6.9 range, all the food elements needed by plants are available. This is alkaline enough to allow liberal amounts of calcium, magnesium, and phosphorus to remain available, yet not so alkaline that iron, manganese and potash are locked up.

To determine the pH of your garden soil, use one of the inexpensive kits available for the purpose, or consult with your State Experiment Station (for address, write U.S.D.A. Information, Beltsville, Md.).

Following are four classifications of plants, according to their pH preference. It is not complete, and is intended only as a guide. Most

---

pH CLASSIFICATIONS

CLASS I
pH 8 to 6 (including all common annuals, perennials and vegetables—unless otherwise listed—as well as most species of genera listed, but not all)

Abelia	*Crataegus*	*Pyrus*
Acer	*Forsythia*	*Rosa*
Aesculus	*Hedera*	*Syringa*
Berberis	*Ligustrum*	*Taxus*
Buddleia	*Lonicera*	*Thuja*
Buxus	*Malus*	*Ulmus*
Celastrus	*Philadelphus*	*Wisteria*
Cotoneaster	*Prunus*	*Yucca*

pH CLASSIFICATIONS (continued)

CLASS II
pH 7 to 6

Acanthus mollis
Aesculus pavia
Amelanchier
Aquilegia caerulea
Coreopsis
Cornus florida
Fuchsia x *hybrida*

Iberis sempervirens
Lagerstroemia
Monarda didyma
Petunia x *hybrida*
Phlox drummondii
Prunus persica
Vitis

CLASS III
pH 6 to 5

Azalea
Calluna vulgaris
Ceanothus americanus
Chionanthus virginica
Clethra
Convallaria
Cytisus scoparius
Dicentra eximia
Erica
Gardenia
Hydrangea macrophylla
Ilex

Ixora
Juniperus horizontalis
Kalmia latifolia
Lupinus hartwegii
Magnolia
Picea
Pinus
Podocarpus
Rhododendron
Solanum melongena
Solanum tuberosum
Stewartia

CLASS IV
pH 5 to 4

Calopogon pulchellus
Cypripedium acaule
Dionaea muscipula
Drosera

Epigaea repens
Galax aphylla
Leiophyllum
Pieris

common garden plants grow in a neutral to slightly alkaline or slightly acid soil. They will adapt themselves downward to the more acid requirements of plants in Class III, but the reverse is not true. Common garden plants (azalea, holly, rhododendron) that *need* acid soil do not adapt to neutral or alkaline conditions. In other words, the farther plants get away from each other in the pH scale, the less compatible they are.

It is not fully understood why acid-loving plants prefer their special environment. There is some evidence that this is due to their needs for larger amounts of iron and possibly manganese than other plants. Tests show that when a special form of iron (called chelated iron) is used, these acid-loving plants can be grown at higher pH for at least a year or so.

How To Make Garden Loam

Every dedicated gardener wants to increase the depth of good soil in his garden. The best method for accomplishing this is by "double digging" or trenching. This involves turning the entire area upside down, inverting soil and subsoil. When the job is finished, the soil that formerly was 12 to 24 inches below the surface will be on top, while the old topsoil will be 12 to 24 inches below the surface.

As complicated as this sounds, it calls more for manual labor than juggling skill. Before you start, decide where you are going to finish. Your first step is to dig out a strip of topsoil one "spit" deep—the depth of a spade. Wheel this soil to the other side of the plot, where you plan to finish. Next, dig out the soil from the bottom of this trench, also to spade depth. Wheel this also next to the topsoil. You now have a trench across one side of the garden 18 to 24 inches deep. Into the bottom of this trench throw 3 to 4 inches of well-decayed compost or fresh organic

Trenching is a cultivating procedure that improves soil's upper layers. At one end of area, dig a trench 1 foot wide, 20 inches deep. Transfer this soil to other end of area. Dig second trench adjoining first, 1 foot wide, 10 inches deep. Toss this soil into first trench and enrich it with compost. Dig bottom half of second trench; pile soil in first one. At end of area, place soil from first trench into the last trench.

matter. (If the latter is used, a liberal "sugaring" with a complete fertilizer will speed up its decay.) Then spade the bottom of the trench, working the organic matter at least 6 inches deeper. Finally, dig the topsoil from the second trench and throw it in the bottom of the first trench, with the subsoil on top of that. Thus, the original trench is filled. Work this way all across the plot, until the piled soil at the far end is reached. Now the topsoil is thrown into the bottom of the last trench, with its subsoil over it, and the whole operation is complete.

This leaves the rich soil buried 12 inches down. Roots may take some time to reach it, so for good early growth it is essential to enrich the new top layer with liberal amounts of compost and chemical fertilizer. Within a year or two, it should assume the appearance and quality of the original topsoil.

Double digging improves drainage, increases the amount of rich soil available to roots and eliminates the zoning that occurs between the original topsoil and subsoil. Movement of soil water both up and down is improved. Double digging is not always the answer to poor drainage, however. It may even increase the tendency of the soil to become waterlogged after heavy rainfall. A loose, well-tilled soil surrounded by compacted clay becomes a drainage dump into which water may run. Where water does not drain away from the garden quickly, it may be necessary to put tiles under the plot, and provide a runoff with an outlet below the 24-inch level.

Double digging the perennial flower border is possible only when the original bed is made or during a complete replanting. Such preparation is particularly important where you are going to grow deep-rooted perennials such as lupines, poppies and peonies. Although you can usually dig in sands and lighter loams at any time, heavier loams and

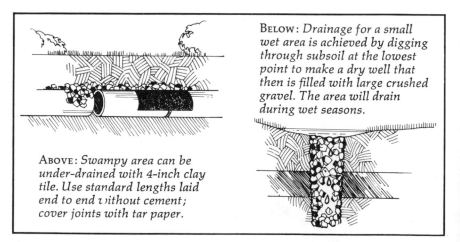

BELOW: *Drainage for a small wet area is achieved by digging through subsoil at the lowest point to make a dry well that then is filled with large crushed gravel. The area will drain during wet seasons.*

ABOVE: *Swampy area can be under-drained with 4-inch clay tile. Use standard lengths laid end to end without cement; cover joints with tar paper.*

clays are often damaged by working them when they are too wet. In the spring, or after heavy rains, they are often so filled with water that they cannot be handled without compacting them almost to the consistency of concrete. Before you dig, try the "mud-pie" test: press a handful of soil between your palms. If it crumbles readily into loose soil again, it is in condition to dig or cultivate. If it stays in a lump, let it dry out further before working it.

On the other hand, sometimes clay soil can be too dry to dig. When you water to correct this condition, avoid heavy continuous watering or you will puddle the surface and cause excess water to run off before it can sink in and soften the clay. A mulch of leaves, compost, peat moss or straw, kept moist for several weeks, will condition a soil that is too dry for digging.

Maintaining Garden Loam

The experienced gardener knows that no soil treatment will produce permanent improvement. Every force of nature strives to impoverish it. Rains leach out nitrogen; bacteria burn up organic matter; plants exhaust food elements; and compaction destroys structure, pounding together the particles you separated at a high cost in labor and materials. Soil improvement is a continuing routine.

The use of compost has already been described. Unless you have a constant outside source of suitable organic matter, you can hardly expect to maintain tilth without a compost heap. Cover-cropping and "green manuring" are tricks for stealing fertility from the air and adding it to the soil. Rows in the vegetable garden can be seeded as they are vacated. In summer, almost anything that will produce a mass of green growth (I have used everything from cabbage to corn) will work. The one plant that grows well universally is winter rye. This is not rye *grass*, but the cereal grain: planted in the fall, it remains green all winter. (Sown in September, it may be 3 feet tall by spring.) When spaded or plowed under, it decays quickly. Its root mass is astonishing, blotting up in short order any unused fertilizer left by other crops. Since fertilizer elements will be locked securely in the rye tissues, they cannot be lost but will become available again in spring on the decay of the plowed-under crop.

Do not despise weeds. Their contribution to good tilth is considerable. A plant like giant ragweed, for example, can contribute several tons per acre to good humus-forming material, at no cost. True, its seedlings are annoying, but normal tillage should control them. A weedy garden in the fall is better than one bare of all plants.

Occasionally, the gardener must bring in additional soil to fill in low spots or top-dress lawns. Such soil should be introduced into the garden

This is winter rye planted over dahlia beds. The rye, sown in October and plowed under in spring, will add humus-forming materials to the soil and is one of the crops recommended for use as "green manure." This is one of the least expensive ways to add organic content to poor soils.

or lawn with considerable caution and skepticism. Claims made about "good, rich, black dirt" usually turn out to be wrong. Most "black-dirt" fields are worn-out farms from which have been scraped half a century's accumulation of weeds and plant diseases. If you must buy additional soil, use it as a compost base.

Once you approach your ideal soil, the routine of yearly renovation, renewal and preservation becomes easier, and its rewards become more apparent.

Recipes for Potting Mixes

Home gardeners often go to an extraordinary amount of trouble to make up special soil mixtures for the various plants they grow. This is unnecessary. You can save much work and worry by starting with one good basic potting soil which can be changed to suit plant requirements.

The following is a basic mixture which has proved highly satisfactory for house plants, greenhouse plants, plants grown in containers of all kinds outdoors, and seedlings.

Basic Potting Mixture
4 parts coarse builder's sand (not ocean sand)
2 parts sedge peat (moist) or peat moss (the coarse brown kind)
1 part dried cattle manure
1 part vermiculite
Add to each bushel (32 qt.)
   8 level tb. superphosphate
   8 level tb. cottonseed meal
   4 level tb. sulfate of potash
   4 level tb. ground limestone (omit for acid-loving plants)

For succulents and to increase drainage
   double the sand
For bromeliads
   increase sand 1½ times
   double the vermiculite
For acid plants and to increase moisture retention
   double the peat and omit limestone
For lime-loving plants (though not necessary)
   double the ground limestone
For all potted plants
   every three to six weeks, apply liquid plant food diluted according to manufacturer's directions

If plants require pasteurized potting soil (as do African violets), you can either (1) moisten the soil mixture slightly with water and bake in an oven for two hours at 200°; or (2) fumigate in a tightly closed garbage can with chloropicrin or another fumigant.

If for some reason you find it difficult to prepare the Basic Potting Mixture (above), use the prepared, sterilized potting soils sold in garden centers.

In a pinch, a reasonably satisfactory potting soil can be made with 2 parts garden soil, 1 part peat and 1 part coarse sand.

Charcoal is unnecessary in potting mixtures except when plants are in containers without bottom drainage holes but helps tremendously when city water is used. In such cases, mix ½ to 1 teaspoonful of crushed charcoal (not the barbecue type, but one obtained from a garden center or druggist) into each pot.

LEFT: *Concrete masonry for steps, walks and retaining walls and a symmetrical design make this bank rising from the terrace of a city house inviting. The treatment holds up the bank and provides gardening spaces.*

ABOVE: *Railroad ties, anchored firmly with wooden stakes (see cross-section drawing), hold up a moderately inclining bank, attractively landscaped with boulders and plantings of low hardy perennials, such as iberis, creeping phlox, dwarf iris and dwarf asters. This treatment might be used in a flat, suburban landscape where a change in grade is needed to please the eye, and to provide a place for growing rock-garden plants that require perfect drainage.*

RIGHT: *Steep bank with existing rock outcroppings at top, is stabilized with railroad ties placed vertically at ground level and dry-laid stone walls above. The steps also are railroad ties.*

2. Design with Purpose

A well-thought-out and carefully executed landscape design will give you grounds that are attractive to look at, comfortable to live in and easy to maintain. Today more and more of family life is lived outdoors, so the size of your family, its hobbies, habits and general way of life will play a large part in landscaping plans. Other elements to take into account in planning your grounds are local climate, topography, the general style of the community and your own sense of style and taste.

A plan on paper makes it possible to avoid mistakes and to tie all these requirements into a pleasing and unified whole. It may be amateur or professional, but a drawing ought to exist. The necessity for a plan is most obvious on a brand-new property where everything is still to be done. It is just as valuable, however, where a garden is to be remodeled, either for a new owner or for a change in family size or way of life.

Advantages of Hiring Help

Professional advice is an economy in working out a long-range plan. There are parts of the country where landscape advice is not available; other owners feel they cannot afford the fee of a competent professional or mistakenly think their needs are too modest for such help. Actually, a small property may have greater need for the guidance of a landscape architect or landscape designer. The small spaces and low budget, intrusive neighboring houses and garages of the small lot make it more difficult to design to satisfy the need for beauty, comfort and efficiency. And any mistake here is more apparent and correcting it may take a discouraging amount of time and money.

The services of a professional landscape architect range from consultation only to the purchase of a complete set of plans, cost estimate and supervision of work. Fees depend on the type of plan and help required. On preliminary visits to the site, existing conditions will be evaluated. The trained designer takes into account the neighborhood in general, the architecture of the house, the existing plant material, soil conditions, prevailing wind at various seasons and views in all directions, either desirable or undesirable.

A survey of the property as it exists will be necessary. You can take these measurements yourself, or hire an engineer. Without an accurate plot plan or survey, accurate drawings are impossible. Include on the plot plan buildings, existing driveways, plant masses, trees, walks, fences, property lines and, if possible, the location of cesspools, septic tanks, electric and water lines and other utilities. For most newer properties there already exists a title survey made in small scale. It shows property lines and buildings. Photostated to a larger size, this makes a starting-point drawing on which other information can be traced by you or the professional surveyor.

Prepare a Questionnaire

If you have engaged a professional landscaper, this person will require additional information about you, the size of your family and its lifestyle. A professional may present a questionnaire that includes:

1. How many in the family—adults, children, and their ages?
2. Is it a year-round house? If not, what month or months is the family likely to be away?
3. How many cars are likely to be coming in and out daily—family or guest drivers?
4. What is the local provision for garbage and trash collections—daily, weekly or on infrequent order?
5. Is outdoor laundry-drying rare, daily, weekly; large or small?
6. Are most deliveries made by truck or by the family?
7. Is street traffic heavy and is street parking permissible?
8. Where are tools to be kept?
9. Is entertaining usually in small groups, large groups, frequent or infrequent, formal or informal?
10. Who furnishes the gardening labor—the family or hired gardener—how much time of either, or each, is available?
11. Are any special areas desired now or later for flower borders, a rock garden, a greenhouse, a vegetable garden, a play yard, a swimming pool, special game courts?
12. Has the client or have members of the family any particular preferences in materials, colors, styles, plants?

With an accurate survey and answers to these questions in hand, the professional landscape architect proceeds to make a general overall plan which shows paved areas, walks, general plant masses, service yard and the shape and size of all areas. While this plan is to scale, it can have very few details and is really only a picture of space allotment. From there the landscaper can go on to detailed working drawings either immediately, or as you are ready to commission or undertake the work yourself. A master or overall plan alone is helpful, but like any partial service it is only a start in the right direction.

Do-It-Yourself Planning

If you are not planning to have professional help, proceed in much the same way as the landscape architect. He does a survey or has it done, and fills out his, own questionnaire before starting work. Without professional help, you must analyze your own problems, desires, necessities, assets and liabilities; the more exhaustive the analysis, the more likely is the final result to be both practical and interesting.

The problems of grading and drainage are the first considerations; they make or mar the beauty and the livability of a property. If the site is perfectly flat, there should be relatively few problems. If, however, it is rolling country or very steep hillside property, grading and drainage must be taken into account in placing the house and in designing or redesigning overall landscape and service areas. The sharper the slope, the more complex the problems and the more expensive the solutions. Also, the more interesting the layout in the long run.

In gently rolling property, it is often possible in initial planning to improve drainage and grading by accentuating existing grades, a solution that may also create interesting variations in levels. Such plans must be studied very carefully, however, to avoid a too man-made appearance. Steep banks, for instance, are more artificial-looking than long, gradual slopes. More or less flat areas, as garage courts, terraces and areas immediately adjoining the house, should be fitted into the landscape with as little disturbance to natural grades as possible.

In rolling land, the terraces, gardens and lawns can pitch at a rate of about 1 foot in 25. They will then look level in comparison with slightly steeper slopes nearby. If the garden slope is more gradual, it is likely to look tilted in the opposite direction or stick out of the landscape in an artificial fashion.

Problems of Hilly Land

On hilly land, grading is a major problem and must be planned with great care. An accurate topographical survey by an engineer is imperative, otherwise plans will be inaccurate, estimates impossible to get and the final results will have none of the drama and attractiveness such properties can afford. Careful preliminary planning can save hundreds of yards of fill or excavation, many feet of wall and a great proportion of the budget. On such properties, retaining walls are more economical than banks. The walls may be of concrete, brick or stone, according to the architecture of the house and the materials locally available. Retaining walls are particularly important on small properties, because a wall takes up a fraction of the space of a bank of the same height. Even a heavy stone wall takes up no more than a foot and a half of ground space, while a drop of four feet, if the bank is to be mowable, takes up twelve feet.

The second step in landscape design is to work out successful solutions to the need for utility areas and good traffic patterns. The driveways, garage courts and entrance court are of first importance in comfortable daily living. Most of us begrudge the room that is necessary for paved surfaces that motor cars take up, yet no one factor can cause more irritation, more repair or correction than inefficiently planned motor approaches. The driveway must be planned so that access from the street is both comfortable and safe.

Planning Traffic Patterns

Where no street parking is permissible, room must be found on the property itself for parking two or three cars without completely blocking all other traffic. On a straight driveway, nothing less than 18 feet wide allows one car to park and another to pass. The all too common twelve-foot driveway is an extravagance. It is not wide enough for two cars and too wide for one. It spends unnecessary money to achieve no useful purpose. Where cars or trucks must turn on the property itself in order to get to the street, two or three feet in length can make all the difference between safe and comfortable maneuvering and encroachment on adjacent planting, lawns, fences or buildings.

Family preference and climate may also play a very large part in planning the driveway and entrance courts. In areas that can expect heavy snowfall, provision should be made for piling up snow as the plow comes through. Where there is a great deal of inclement weather or the family habits demand, the driveway may have to go directly to the front door, or at least to some door without exposure to the weather. If cars cannot reach the front door directly, their relation to it should be carefully studied; otherwise, the owner is likely to receive deliveries at the front door and guests in the kitchen.

Planning Service Areas

The next most important area is the collection point for garbage and trash. The most attractive garden in the world does not gain from trash barrels, garbage pails or baskets awaiting disposal. In communities where there is no regular collection service, provision for disposal of these materials should be planned for on the property itself. This means an efficient incinerator or out-of-sight storage for trash that is called for infrequently or on special order. The truckman or the family station wagon should be able to get very close to the place of storage. Usually it is better to make provision for trash cans close to the kitchen door or service entrance where they are accessible from house and grounds and from the driveway. This can prove to be a design problem that affects all the surrounding area and should be solved in the planning stage.

Outdoor laundry also plays a role in landscaping design. Even with a dryer in the house, most families do some outdoor drying. It may be occasional hand laundry, wet bathing clothes or bedding. If the family does not hang out large laundries, the drying area can be reduced.

Outdoor Work Areas

Other utility areas that may be wanted include space for compost piles, cold frames and garden work areas. They depend on the gardening enthusiasm of the family. The compost pile need not be completely unpresentable, but neither it nor cold frames are objects of art. They should be in inconspicuous places, easy of access, but not featured. A small orchard, an ornamental hedge, a low stone wall, a specimen shrub are some of the landscape elements that can be used to camouflage these less-than-beautiful features.

Storage space for tools can prove to be a major problem later, if not provided for in the original plan of the property. Probably the most economical place to store them is in or near the garage.

Recreational Areas

When all the utilitarian spaces have been analyzed and at least partially planned, the outdoor living areas can be designed. They depend on the desires of the individual family, on the budget and on the climate. First, there must be access to all parts of the property with paved surfaces where there is to be either frequent foot traffic or a considerable amount of furniture and congregation of people. Direct and obvious access to the front door and the kitchen door is mandatory. Both of these entrance walks should be of some hard material, durable, easy to clean and more or less impervious to weather. Brick, flagstone or textured concrete is satisfactory. If other materials are used the house is likely to be tracked with mud or snow because the walks cannot be cleaned properly. It is important for the walk to the front door to be wide enough for two people to walk abreast—four feet at least. If the size of the garden allows, five feet is more comfortable. If grass is worn down along the sides of a walk, the walk is too narrow. A path worn into a shortcut indicates the walk is in the wrong place. The shortest distance between the point of arrival and the front door is usually the attractive and efficient place for an entrance walk. People will not detour along curves arbitrarily laid out for no apparent reason.

The next important paved areas are one or more terraces. Most families spend time outdoors and need surfaced living areas that are easy to maintain, attractive and convenient. The size, location and material of an outdoor living room are dictated by the architecture of the house and grounds and by the general landscape plan. Since outdoor furniture is larger in scale than indoor, it is wise in planning a terrace to err on the side of over-generosity. Sixteen feet minimum width is advisable for the main terrace and is particularly important if this terrace is raised above the level of the lawn. The outdoor living room should be adjacent to the living quarters of the house and accessible from one or two doors, preferably the living room and the kitchen or dining room. As far as space and layout permit, it adds greatly to family enjoyment of the outdoors if there are one large living terrace and two or three smaller ones where seasonal conditions of sun and wind can be used to advantage, terraces planned for the morning, the afternoon, or for spring, summer, fall or even for winter.

Surfacing Materials

The surfacing material of the paved area where there is to be furniture should be easy to clean and even enough for furniture to be level. Brick or flagstone can be laid without cement in the joints—it is more attractive that way. The joints, however, should be very tight so that there is no space for grass that will have to be clipped by hand, or for furniture or feet to catch. Concrete is usually less expensive and very easily maintained but gives an industrial feeling. It can be used in combination with brick, flagstone or wood. With careful addition of color and texture, it is particularly appropriate with contemporary houses.

As the plan of the garden develops, certain other areas may need to be paved. If there are big trees where neither ground covers nor grass will grow, it may be wise to have brick or stone set under the trees.

Most people think of landscape design only in terms of plant materials—lawns, shrubs, trees and flowers. These are important and integral elements of the overall design, but probably should be the last to be considered in detail. Certainly, nothing enhances the beauty of property more than a well-designed and well-cared-for lawn. Unfortunately, nothing can take a larger proportion of the budget of time and money and be more of a disappointment if it is not properly planted and executed. As a generalization, grass should be restricted to areas where it will grow well, usually in good sunlight, and should be as free as possible of edges that need hand-trimming. It is as important to design shape and boundaries of turf areas as to plan paving, flower gardens or any other defined area. Bits and pieces of grass, hard of access, not well unified, add nothing to the appearance of the landscape and demand a great deal in hours of upkeep needed. The test of a well-designed lawn is that it can be fertilized, mowed and raked with power machinery with a minimum of hard work of any sort. There are always times when lack of labor or time or bad weather leaves ragged edges, so that instead of being an asset, the lawn is a detriment. Reducing this to a minimum takes forethought.

Designing a Lawn

The lawn is undoubtedly the largest solid green area in the garden, so its pattern should be well proportioned and have pleasant lines. Where grass adjoins any sort of paved area (driveways, paved terraces, walks)

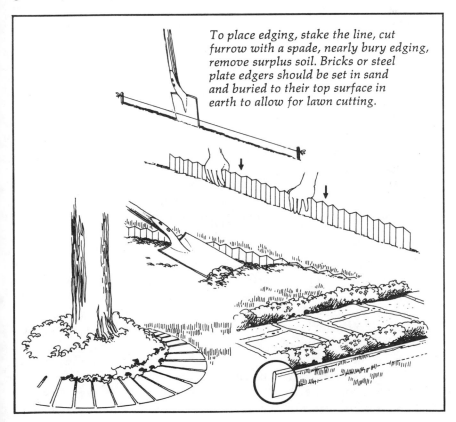

To place edging, stake the line, cut furrow with a spade, nearly bury edging, remove surplus soil. Bricks or steel plate edgers should be set in sand and buried to their top surface in earth to allow for lawn cutting.

there should be a definition created by steel curbing, brick, concrete, stone or other hard edges. Where turf is adjacent to shrub borders, flower borders or other plant masses, the same care should be given to establishing a pleasing curve or straight line that can be maintained. Without an edging, flowers grow over the margins of grass paths, shrub borders get to be scallops instead of free-flowing curves and the garden loses the quality of repose that is essential to good garden design.

Next in importance after lawn areas and flower borders are the woody plants—trees and shrubs. On small- or medium-sized property each mass of shrubs and each individual tree must serve two or three purposes. Plantings of evergreens and deciduous plants should provide a background to flower gardens, screen out a neighbor's house or garage and provide material for cutting for the house. One tree may have to shade some of the house windows, frame the house from the street and make a tall neighboring house less intrusive. Trees and shrubs are the most permanent of all the plantings and must be considered in terms of present and future effects. They should be selected to provide year-round beauty or effect, not just one season of bloom. They must be in proportion to the size of the house and the size of the property. In a spacious garden large shade trees such as linden, Norway maple and beech will be appropriate, while on the small property dogwood, flowering crab apple or a shade tree with high, light branches—a sycamore, for example—can give the same effect without taking up ground room.

When planning shrub borders good design includes plans not only for combinations of flowers but, more important, for combinations of texture, seasonal effect and growth habit. When vertical growth habit is combined with horizontal growth habit, small leaves with large, there is an interesting pattern throughout the year. Without this discrimination, shrub borders are likely to look monotonous and indeterminate, whether they are broadleaf evergreens for year-round effect or deciduous shrubs with no particular character except at flowering time.

Landscaping with Trees

Each tree, whether it is a giant oak or a small flowering cherry, should be allowed its own sphere of influence. Other trees that encroach are bound to give a cluttery effect. If you are about to plant a tree, you can readily determine its sphere of influence—or how much space to allow around it.

Find the ultimate height of the tree you want to use. Then calculate that tree's sphere of influence as a circle with a radius equal to the ultimate height of the tree. Thus, a 35-foot tree, such as one of the flowering crab apples or cherries, has a sphere of influence of 35 feet in any direction from the trunk of the tree. Say that the next tree you might want to use has an ultimate height of 20 feet. Then the minimum

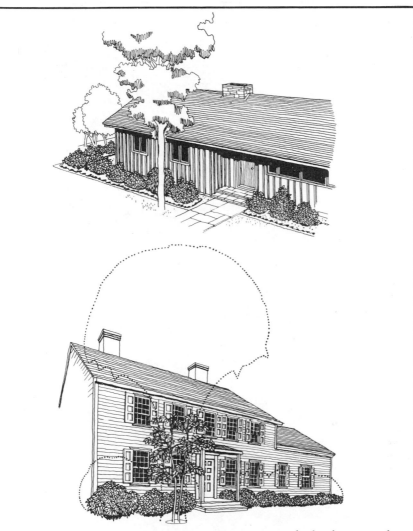

A tree is one of the most important accent points in the landscape, and for this reason a small yard can have only a few. The relationship between the overall size of the garden, the house and the trees must be harmonious. At the same time, the professional landscaper uses the fact that the scale, or size, of trees can better help the house fit its environment. For instance, a small house, upper, fronted by a giant tree seems dwarfed. The same house set off by several smaller trees will look more impressive. A house that may seem too tall or too large for its setting, lower, can be made more attractive if it is dominated by a very large tree: the scale of the tree set against the scale of the house will soften the boldness of the overpowering architectural mass.

UPPER: *The tree's clearly defined trunk makes it an accent point in contrast with shrubs, whose many-branched base creates an effect of mass but not an accent point. Here, a large home with a large entrance easily accommodates the demand for attention made by the little Japanese maple planted in the shelter of the overhang. The shrubs' irregular mass and flow conceal the building's foundation, but the tree is the planting that visitors will notice.*

LOWER: *Smaller home isn't of a scale to have a tree at its doorstep, is in better proportion with mass of similar flowering evergreen shrubs.*

distance from the trunk of the 35-foot tree to the trunk of the 20-foot tree would be 55 feet, or it might be preferable to have them even farther apart.

Choosing the Trees

Once you are committed to using only a few trees you will need to have some way of narrowing down the wide range of enchanting and dramatic trees from which you can choose. The first important design factor to consider in making your choice is scale. Scale is the relationship between the dimensions or sizes of the different elements in a design. The size of a tree sets the scale of your garden picture.

When you choose the trees for your garden, notice the relationship between (1) the size of the total area of the garden, (2) the size of the house (which is usually part of the garden scene) and (3) the size of the trees. Suppose your house seems too large for its setting and you want to give it a more gracious aspect. A very large tree will dominate the scene and reduce the apparent size of the house, soften and, at the same time, hold its own against an overpowering architectural mass. Or if you have a modest little cottage that you want to make more impressive, use several smaller trees. Watch, though, that you do not choose too tiny a tree. If you do, you will find that it will look smaller than it actually is, diminutive and out of scale.

How Many Trees To Use

An assortment of little trees tucked around a larger one clutters its sphere of influence, upsets the scale and takes away the feeling of restful spaciousness that is essential to a pleasing design. On the average-size suburban lot, you can't very well use more than four or five trees effectively. And if one of the trees which you do use is a large one, you might find yourself limited to two or three, or possibly even one if the tree is a huge old specimen. In other words, if you have a 100-foot tree on a 100-foot lot, its sphere of influence will cover the entire lot.

There is an exception to this rule which might at first glance seem to be a contradiction. Suppose your house is situated in a little piece of naturalistic woodland and you have had the good sense not to chop down all the native trees. Perhaps there are 20 or 30 trees in a comparatively small space. They are mostly of one kind and have grown together for a number of years. Their tops have formed a canopy overhead, but the trunks are bare of branches to a considerable height. Here you have a woodland area which is an integrated unit. Instead of being conscious of the trees as separate and distinct accent points you find the trunks are more like pillars holding up a ceiling. Trees which grow together in this way in a happy natural association form a simple naturalistic unit. You lose this simplicity and get an effect of spotty accentuation if you introduce other trees that are not related in character or in scale to the existing growth. It is better to supplement this native growth with shrubs rather than other trees.

Basic Principles

Working out the choice of trees for your garden along these lines, you can readily see that the selection and placing of trees is based upon a few fundamental principles, and that instead of making a random choice you let your decision be governed by the following principles of design.

First, keep prominently in mind that every tree is an accent point. Then you will be careful not to use too many of them.

Second, choose the trees that are just the right size to be in scale with the scene in which you plan to place them.

Third, do not let any tree encroach upon another's sphere of influence. The number of trees which you can use in building the garden structure is thus automatically determined. One tree might dominate a whole garden. Another garden the same size might have two or three slightly smaller trees, and another have as many as four or five, some of moderate size and some quite small. In other words, there is considerable freedom of choice within the framework of these simple basic rules.

Here are examples of universally grown trees in different sizes:

Large trees (60 feet or more tall)
Beech (*Fagus* species)
Honeylocust (*Gleditsia triacanthos*)
Sweet gum (*Liquidambar styraciflua*)
Tulip tree (*Liriodendron tulipifera*)
Buttonwood (*Platanus occidentalis*)
Red and white oaks (*Quercus* species)

Medium trees (35 to 60 feet tall)
Norway maple (*Acer platanoides*)
Ohio buckeye (*Aesculus glabra*)
European birch (*Betula pendula*)
Saucer magnolia (*M. soulangeana*)
White mulberry (*Morus alba*)
Chinese elm (*Ulmus pumila, U. parvifolia*)

Small trees (15 to 35 feet tall)
Redbud (*Cercis canadensis*)
Flowering dogwood (*Cornus florida*)
Hawthorns (*Crataegus* species)
Flowering crab apples (*Malus* species)
Flowering cherries (*Prunus* species)

The Modular Approach to Landscape Design

To design a modular garden, a simple shape of a specific size is selected, usually a square or a rectangle, and this shape is repeated, using two or more materials in various combinations, to form the surface pattern of the garden. The modular method almost invariably produces an attractive garden even when it is used by an inexperienced gardener with no particular training in design, for it remedies the most common fault in amateur gardens; namely, the absence of a coherent design of any kind. This unfortunate and widespread lack is responsible for the disappointing appearance of thousands of well-tended gardens filled with beautiful plants. The modular method is the simplest way to introduce a unified pattern into the garden. Far from being the strait jacket that some gardeners fear it to be, use of the module brings clarity and crispness to the garden and, within its firm structure, allows the complexity of plant material to show to full advantage.

The first step in designing a modular garden is to choose the shape and size of the modular unit. If a square is chosen, and it is the easiest to use, the size should be between 2 by 2 feet and 5 by 5 feet. Only in exceptional circumstances should the unit be smaller than 2 by 2 feet or larger than 5 by 5 feet, and in most gardens 3 by 3 feet or 4 by 4 feet will be the most desirable size. In choosing the best dimensions, the size of the garden is of primary importance, but other factors, such as the size of the house and other structures and the size of the existing trees, should also be considered. If the garden is small but surrounded by a large house and tall fences and overhung by a large tree, a small module

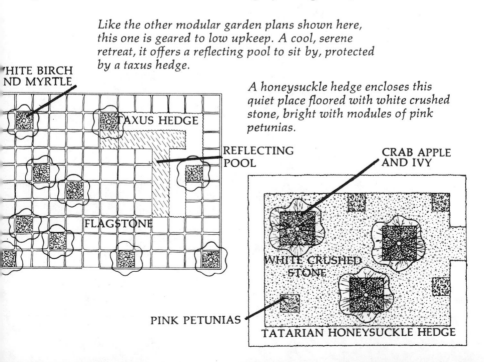

Like the other modular garden plans shown here, this one is geared to low upkeep. A cool, serene retreat, it offers a reflecting pool to sit by, protected by a taxus hedge.

A honeysuckle hedge encloses this quiet place floored with white crushed stone, bright with modules of pink petunias.

WHITE BIRCH
ND MYRTLE

TAXUS HEDGE

REFLECTING POOL

FLAGSTONE

CRAB APPLE AND IVY

WHITE CRUSHED STONE

PINK PETUNIAS

TATARIAN HONEYSUCKLE HEDGE

would probably be overwhelmed by the scale of the other elements, and a more satisfactory result would be obtained by using a 4-by-4-foot or 5-by-5-foot modular in spite of the limited space. In a large garden a large modular unit is nearly always the best choice.

Materials To Be Used

When the shape and size of the module have been decided, the next step is to determine the materials to be used in the modular units. In most gardens a place to sit and a place to walk will be required, and, therefore, a permanent surfacing material such as flagstone, brick, poured concrete or crushed stone should be one of the materials selected. The other materials can be water, trees, shrubs, flowers, ground covers, tan bark, sand or any other material the gardener can think of.

However, while the choice is wide, the selection should be limited. If a few materials are used, it is much easier to produce a unified design than if a wide assortment of different materials is used. The specific choices should depend on the personal preferences of the gardener, not only in the limited sense of which surfacing materials and plants are preferred, but in the larger sense of what kind of garden is wanted. If a cool, restful, low-maintenance garden is desired, stone, water, trees and a ground cover would be logical choices. If a profusion of color and texture is wanted, brick, flowers and herbs might be selected.

After the materials have been chosen, the basic pattern into which the modular units will be fitted should be designed. The pattern will be

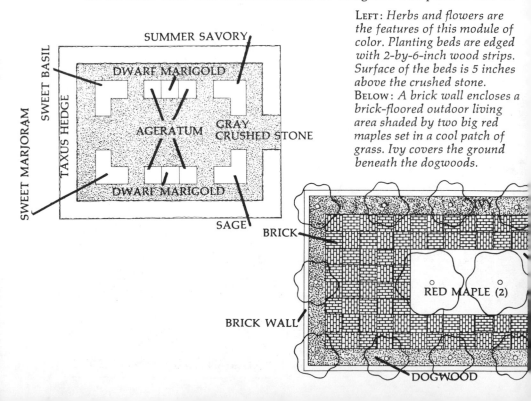

Left: *Herbs and flowers are the features of this module of color. Planting beds are edged with 2-by-6-inch wood strips. Surface of the beds is 5 inches above the crushed stone.*
Below: *A brick wall encloses a brick-floored outdoor living area shaded by two big red maples set in a cool patch of grass. Ivy covers the ground beneath the dogwoods.*

determined by the available space, the materials which have been selected and the ingenuity and skill of the gardener. The only requirement to be met is that the allotted space must be level, with just enough pitch for adequate drainage. The modular concept does not work on sloping land, since a discernible pitch distorts proportions. If the land is not level, it must be leveled by cutting or filling or both, and the necessary retaining walls must be built before a pattern is laid out.

The sketches here suggest a few of the infinite variations in pattern and materials which can be worked out in an area 30 by 39 feet, using a 3-by-3-foot modular unit.

If trees are omitted so that sun-loving plants can be grown in all parts of the garden, the horizontal plane should be broken by raising the planting beds. In addition to breaking the monotony of the flat plane, this change in elevation will create interesting shadow lines.

The last step in designing a modular garden is to enclose it. If the garden is directly adjacent to the house, the enclosure should surround three sides; but if the garden is not adjacent, it should be enclosed on all four sides, with appropriate openings for entrance and exit. The enclosure can be a wall, a fence or a hedge; it can be high or low, formal or informal. It can be one material throughout or a mixture of several materials, but it should never be omitted. Without it the garden will be incomplete, for a sense of containment, desirable in all gardens, is vital to a modular garden.

BELOW: *Flagstoned outdoor living room is sheltered by a fieldstone wall.*
RIGHT: *A garden that is colorful in spring, shady and cool in summer, features laurel, azaleas, rhododendron and a dogwood. Pin oak shades one corner. Concrete floor has wood dividers.*

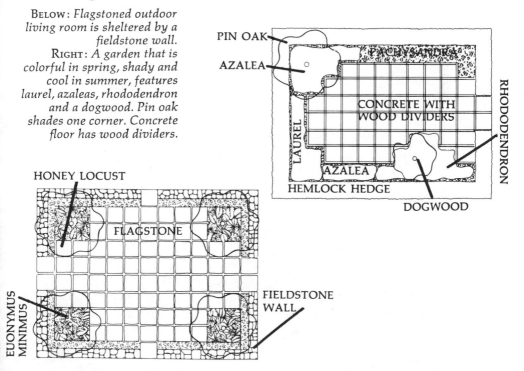

PIN OAK
AZALEA
PACHYSANDRA
CONCRETE WITH WOOD DIVIDERS
LAUREL
RHODODENDRON
AZALEA
HEMLOCK HEDGE
DOGWOOD

HONEY LOCUST
FLAGSTONE
EUONYMUS MINIMUS
FIELDSTONE WALL

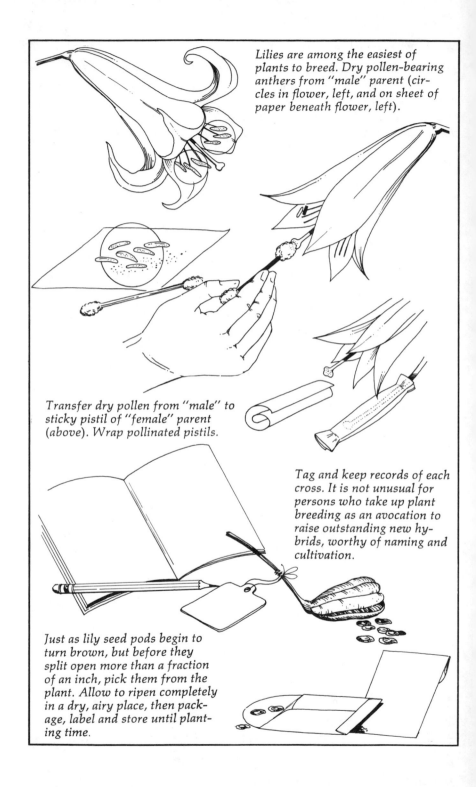

Lilies are among the easiest of plants to breed. Dry pollen-bearing anthers from "male" parent (circles in flower, left, and on sheet of paper beneath flower, left).

Transfer dry pollen from "male" to sticky pistil of "female" parent (above). Wrap pollinated pistils.

Tag and keep records of each cross. It is not unusual for persons who take up plant breeding as an avocation to raise outstanding new hybrids, worthy of naming and cultivation.

Just as lily seed pods begin to turn brown, but before they split open more than a fraction of an inch, pick them from the plant. Allow to ripen completely in a dry, airy place, then package, label and store until planting time.

3. How To Propagate All Kinds of Plants

The art and practice of raising new plants by means of old ones is called propagation. There is a score of ways by which plants are propagated, some of natural origin, some adapted or improved upon by man. The commonest in nature, and therefore the method most widely understood and practiced by gardeners, is sexual propagation by means of seeds and spores. But while all plants may be increased by sexual means, in actual practice many of the gardener's most prized plants may be exactly reproduced only by asexual or vegetative means; that is, new plants are produced from living parts of old ones. Most annuals, which grow, flower, produce seeds and die in a single year, are grown from seeds. Most biennials, which spend the first year in vegetative growth, producing flowers and seeds before dying the second year, are also seed-grown, though other means may be used. Perennials, which live indefinitely, are propagated in various ways, both the herbaceous species, in which the tops die down each year, and the woody trees and shrubs.

Propagation by Seeds Outdoors

Growing flowering plants from seeds sown in the open ground is a quick and easy way to bring beauty and color into the garden. Most seeds sown outdoors do not demand a great deal of soil preparation, and usually their cost is negligible. Hundreds of plants can be raised from a 35-cent package.

Seeds of hardy annuals are usually sown outdoors in the spring as soon as the ground is fit to work (when it can be raked without lumping or sticking to the tool). There are some annuals, however, that benefit from late-summer or early-fall sowing. Some of these seeds ripen in late summer, germinate in fall, survive the winter as seedlings. Among them are rocket larkspur (*Delphinium ajacis*), love-in-a-mist (*Nigella damascena*), shellflower (*Molucella laevis*), cornflower (*Centaurea cyanus*) and California poppy (*Eschscholtzia californica*). Others, such as spiderflower (*Cleome spinosa*), snow-on-the-mountain (*Euphorbia marginata*), flowering tobacco (*Nicotiana* species), petunia (*Petunia* x *hybrida*) and *Portulaca grandiflora,* go to seed in the fall, survive the winter as seeds and germinate in the spring. Most biennials are propagated by seeds planted outdoors in summer.

Although most gardeners prefer to start their perennials from seeds early in the year (April or May), there are some species that germinate more freely if sown soon after they have ripened—delphinium and globe flower (trollius), for example. If you have seeds from the seedsman, by planting them early in August you may expect to gain considerable time over seeds sown the following spring. In many cases the plants become large enough to produce flowers the following year. Some seeds may germinate before the advent of cold weather; some may lie dormant over the winter; all germinate or grow in the spring earlier and with greater vigor than would be the case if sowing were delayed. This is especially true of certain rock-garden perennials whose seeds are benefited by exposure to low temperatures. In regions of cold winters, some perennials are grown as annuals or biennials and, in general, may be raised from seed to flower in a season or two.

Let alone, many plants seed themselves. But too often gardens are kept so meticulously tidy that self-seeding is impossible. Consequently, if you want these plants, you must rear them by hand, so to speak. For example, dig up three or four dozen forget-me-not plants early in June when beds of spring flowers are being replanted with summer bedding material. Heel these plants (temporarily transplant) in an out-of-the-way place. After a month or two, a crop of self-sown seedlings will appear around the heeled-in plants, and you can dig as many as you require and transplant them to neat, tidy rows, where they can grow until fall. Then transplant to provide a groundwork of blue bulbs the next spring.

To prepare the soil, spread a 2-inch layer of leafmold or peat moss and to each square yard add 4 ounces of a fertilizer with a high phosphorus content, such as a 4-12-6 formula. Dig to a spade's depth and mix the organic matter and fertilizer thoroughly. Rake the surface to make a fine seedbed. (Over spring-flowering bulbs, the only soil preparation that is safe is the mere scratching of the surface with a hand cultivator.)

Seeds may be sown in rows, or broadcast in patches of irregular shape. Small seeds such as petunia, poppy and portulaca may be sown on the surface of newly raked soil and then patted down to bring them in close contact with the soil. Larger seeds and most biennials should be

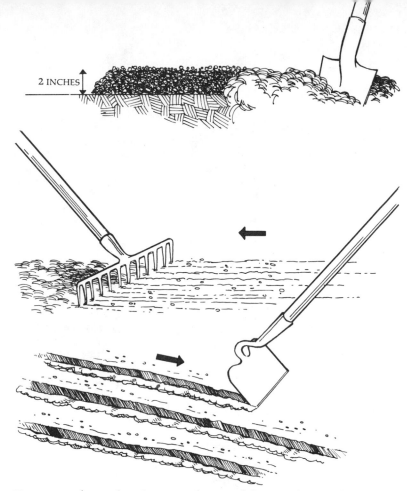

2 INCHES

To prepare the garden, first spread a 2-inch layer of leafmold or peat moss, with 4 ounces of high-phosphorus fertilizer added to each square yard. Then, as in upper sketch, dig in to a spade's depth; mix thoroughly. Rake the surface, as in center sketch, until granules of soil are fine and bed is smooth. A hoe may be used to scratch trenches, bottom sketch, for planting.

covered to a depth of two or three times their diameter. Very large seeds such as sunflower or castor-oil plant may be planted about half an inch deep in "hills" spaced from 1 to 4 feet apart. You can make depressions with a trowel, and mark the extent of the patches by making a groove in the soil around each patch. When seeds are grown chiefly to supply flowers for cutting, it is better to sow the seeds in rows.

It is important to thin out the young seedlings so that those that remain can develop properly. The distance apart is determined by the size of the mature plants. Small plants like torenia can stand 6 inches apart, stronger growers like ageratum from 6 inches to a foot apart, snow-on-the-mountain, 12 to 18 inches apart, cleome and sunflower, 2 to 3 feet apart.

Since perennial and biennial seedlings may be small at frost time, it is desirable to put them in an open cold frame, in which they can be

Top sketch shows place-
ment of seeds in drills or
furrows. Large seeds and
most biennials should be
covered to a depth of two
or three times their diameter, while very large
seeds, such as sunflower
or castor-oil plant, may be
planted about half an inch
deep. When seeds have
been sown, cover the fur-
rows, as shown in center
sketch. Bottom sketch
shows how to broadcast
seeds. This is the method
for sowing very small
seeds, such as petunia,
poppy or portulaca. They
are scattered over newly
raked soil and then are
patted down firmly.

Trowel is used to make
planting holes in a patch-
shaped bed, and patch is
circled by a groove. Bot-
tom sketch shows amount
to thin young seedlings:
Thin small plants to 6
inches apart, strong growers 6 to 12 inches apart;
medium plants 12 to 18
inches apart; and big
plants, such as sunflower
and cleome, 2 to 3 feet
apart.

properly protected over winter. A frame affords shelter from drying winds in summer and early fall, enabling you to shade the seedbed and seedlings conveniently, and saves the seeds from being washed out by drenching rains. (For how to build cold frames and hotbeds, see Chapter 13.) Seedlings of biennials especially should be shaded in their early stages. Then gradually remove the shade and transfer the plants to their winter quarters not later than the middle of September so that they may become established before winter. Pansies, English daisies, wallflowers and Canterbury bells are usually best cared for in cold frames; foxglove, hollyhock, sweet William, forget-me-not and mullein usually will come through the winter without trouble if planted in the locations where they are to bloom the following year.

Propagation by Seeds Indoors

In the North the growing season is not long enough to enable the half-hardy, tender annuals such as ageratum, China aster, verbena and Madagascar periwinkle to make much of a show before they are cut down by early frost. Consequently, they are often started in late winter or early spring under glass in the house, or in a greenhouse or closed-in cold frame, then hardened off prior to placing them where they are to bloom. And by sowing some biennials indoors early in March, it is possible to get flowers the same year instead of the year following.

It is best to sow seeds in pots or flats, depending upon the number of plants you want. Flats may be of plastic, metal or wood, approximately 3 inches deep, and of any size that is convenient to handle (usually not more than 12 by 18 inches). Wooden flats should be pretreated with a wood preservative. Clay pots of from 3 to 5 inches in diameter are convenient to handle. Or small peat-and-pulp pots may be used for both starting seeds and raising seedlings to transplanting size.

Many soil mixtures will do for starting seeds in pots or flats. A standard formula (1-1-1) consists of equal parts of loam, sand and sifted leafmold or peat moss. Other starting mediums are vermiculite, perlite, chopped sphagnum moss, sand, peat moss and combinations of these. They are essentially sterile and do not need any treatment against fungi or soil pests. In pots, insure drainage by putting a piece of plastic window screening or a fairly large piece of broken flowerpot over the hole in the bottom, adding half an inch of pot pieces and a small pad of sphagnum moss to prevent the soil from sifting through the clogging the drainage. Sift the soil through a ¼- or ⅜-inch sieve. Fill pot or flat more than full with soil mixture, strike it off even with the rim and then, with a tamper, press it down half an inch. For pots, the tamper may be improvised—a tumbler, a section of tree branch or a smaller pot. When a flat is used, a "float" made of a piece of board 6 inches wide and 8 inches long, with a handle on the top, is convenient for pressing down the soil.

The pot size may be from 3 to 5 inches, depending upon the number of plants required. Sow the seeds thinly and cover them with about ⅛ inch of sand or soil. A small ⅛-inch-mesh sieve makes it easier to cover the seeds evenly. As in the open, when the seeds are very small (African violet, begonia, calceolaria, petunia and gloxinia), no attempt should be made to cover them; merely press them in with a tamper. Water them either with a very fine spray or, better still, by standing the pots in a baking pan containing 1 or 2 inches of water and leaving them there until moisture shows on the soil surface.

Sterilizing the Soil

If you have experienced trouble in the past from damping-off disease, play safe and sterilize the soil. The easiest way to do this is to put 1 or 2 inches of water in a pan, bring it to a boil, then put in the soil. Keep it cooking for half an hour. Allow to cool, then empty the soil into a sterile receptacle, such as a new plastic garbage bag, until you want to use it. Clay pots should be boiled before use. Plastic pots can be cleaned when you are doing the dishes. Another way to pasteurize the soil is to put it

Equipment for propagation indoors. Top row, sketch at left shows a homemade tamper, used to firm soil. Center sketch shows a sieve for pulverizing soil. Wooden flat, right, is used for growing seedlings. Center row, left, clay pots in various sizes, and, right, plastic flats for sowing seeds. Sketches in bottom row show Jiffy pots and peat pots, which can be planted in the ground without removing seedlings from the containers.

in pots or flats and water it with boiling water several times in quick succession. Seeds may be sown when the soil has dried out sufficiently.

Damping-off fungi can also be controlled by mixing 2½ tablespoon-fuls commercial 40 per cent formaldehyde with a cup of water, sprinkling it over a bushel of soil, then mixing it in thoroughly. Cover the soil with plastic to retain the fumes for two days. Then remove the cover and stir the soil. When there is no longer any odor of formaldehyde (usually about two weeks), it will be safe to use the soil.

Chloropicrin (tear gas), sold as Larvacide, may be used to control weed seeds, nematodes, soil insects and some fungi. It is sold in a special dispenser with full directions for use.

You may also avoid damping-off by sowing in sphagnum moss or vermiculite, applying liquid fertilizer as the seedlings develop to compensate for the lack of nutrients in the medium. Or use a standard 1-1-1 soil mixture surfaced with a 1-inch layer of sphagnum moss or vermiculite, in which the seeds are placed.

When To Sow Seeds

Seeds of poplar, willow and those maples that ripen their seeds in spring are short-lived and must be sown just as soon as they are ripe. Some

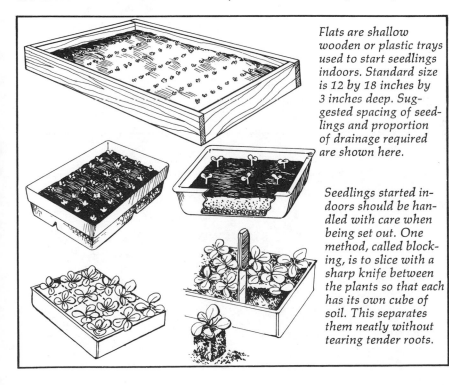

Flats are shallow wooden or plastic trays used to start seedlings indoors. Standard size is 12 by 18 inches by 3 inches deep. Suggested spacing of seedlings and proportion of drainage required are shown here.

Seedlings started indoors should be handled with care when being set out. One method, called blocking, is to slice with a sharp knife between the plants so that each has its own cube of soil. This separates them neatly without tearing tender roots.

All drawings on this page show various ways of starting tiny, dust-sized seeds—for example, begonias, gloxinias, African violets and hybrid petunias. One of the easiest ways, especially for a sizable quantity, is to fill a small flat with starting medium (for example, milled sphagnum moss or horticultural vermiculite), moisten, dust seeds across the surface (but do not cover them), then enclose the flat in a plastic bag.

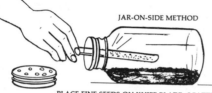

JAR-ON-SIDE METHOD

PLACE FINE SEEDS ON KNIFE BLADE; SCATTER INSIDE JAR ON MOIST MEDIUM.

The jar-on-side method has been used for many years, long before the advent of plastic film and bags. Place an inch of moist milled sphagnum moss or horticultural vermiculite in the bottom. Level with the blade of a knife. Sow seeds as indicated by the sketch.

If medium shows signs of dryness, either before or after seeds sprout, add water of room temperature, gently dropping it in from a spoon. Avoid adding so much water the growing medium or seedlings float away.

HOLES IN LID PROVIDE NECESSARY AIR. TRANSPLANT WHEN LARGE ENOUGH TO HANDLE.

POT-IN-POT METHOD

CORKED CLAY POT WATER RESERVOIR.

SOW SEEDS IN SPACE BETWEEN TWO POTS

KEEP POT IN CENTER FILLED WITH WATER.

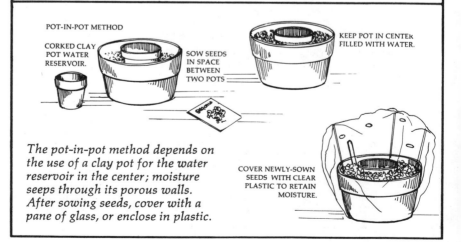

The pot-in-pot method depends on the use of a clay pot for the water reservoir in the center; moisture seeps through its porous walls. After sowing seeds, cover with a pane of glass, or enclose in plastic.

COVER NEWLY-SOWN SEEDS WITH CLEAR PLASTIC TO RETAIN MOISTURE.

other species produce what the nurserymen call "two-year seeds," which do not germinate for a year or more after they are planted. In this group are included some roses, hawthorn, cotoneaster and dogwood. Instead of being planted in the normal way, these should be mixed and stratified (placed in layers) in a moist medium such as peat moss, vermiculite, sand or sawdust for a year before being planted. Many seeds require an "after-ripening" period at fairly low temperatures to insure success. For this, the pulp should be removed from the seeds by first breaking the outer skin and then soaking them in water for a few days. Usually the pulp comes off quite easily if the water is stirred. The good seeds will drop to the bottom; the pulp and the immature seeds will float and can be skimmed off. Stratify the good seeds by mixing them with moist peat moss in small glass jars and then covering them with either glass or plastic film. Place the seeds so that some of them are visible from the outside. The jars can be put in the refrigerator and looked at from time to time. As soon as signs of germination are seen, remove the seeds and plant them in a mixture of equal parts of loam, sand and peat moss and put in a greenhouse or cold frame.

Rhododendron, heather (*Calluna*), heath (*Erica*), enkianthus, leucothoe, oxydendrum and many others can successfully be sown in sphagnum moss during January or February in the greenhouse. The dry sphagnum should be rubbed through a ⅜-inch hardware cloth sieve and placed in a flat that has drainage holes. The openings in the bottom of the flat may be covered with plastic window screen or with pieces of broken flowerpot. The moss should be moistened, packed firmly in the flat and thoroughly watered. An additional *thin* layer of sphagnum is then put on the surface before sowing the seeds.

Prepare the soil in a cold frame by adding a 1-inch layer of coarse sand and 1 or 2 inches of granulated peat moss or sifted leafmold. Mix these with the upper 3 inches of soil. A thorough raking will break up lumps and leave the surface level.

Sow the seeds thinly (20 to 30 per foot) and at a depth of two or three times the diameter of the seed in furrows spaced about 6 inches apart. Cover the seeds with soil and pat it gently over them. Water well with a very fine spray and cover with glass sash as a protection from heavy rains. Shade the bed by putting a coat of whitewash or two thicknesses of cheesecloth on the glass, and ventilate freely at all times. When the seeds have germinated, gradually reduce the amount of shade by covering them only during the hottest part of the day. When the seedlings seem strong enough to withstand rain, remove the sash entirely and do not replace it unless there have been several hard frosts. If seedlings are to be held over the winter, mulch them with about 3 inches of salt hay, excelsior or pine needles, and put the sash on for the winter.

If a cold frame is not available, the open ground will do if protective measures are taken. Drive heavy stakes (2 by 2's are good enough) into the ground at each corner of the bed (which may conveniently be 6 by 4 feet) to project about 1 foot above the soil surface. Make a frame to match of 1-by-2-inch wood furring strips to which cheesecloth or burlap is tacked, or make a lath screen by nailing builder's lath half an inch apart on furring strips. Fasten the lath, burlap or cheesecloth screen to the stakes with hooks and screw eyes to prevent it from sailing away during a summer gale. It not only will serve to shade the seedlings but also, to a large extent, will prevent damage from heavy rains.

If neither of these measures is possible, a cold frame can be improvised. Plant the seeds in a box about 1 foot high (such as a bushel apple box) into which you have put an inch of coarse sand and 2 or 3 inches of rooting mixture pressed firmly down. Cover the box with a pane of glass. Or, a better method, if there are numerous species or varieties to be dealt with, is to rest 3- or 4-inch pots directly on the sand in the box.

Propagation by Spores

Although botanically they are vastly different, spores serve the same purpose as seeds as far as the gardener is concerned. Ferns are the only spore-producing plants the gardener is likely to be interested in raising. Ordinarily spores are not offered for sale by seedsmen, so you will have to gather them yourself. Usually they are produced on the underside of a fern frond. It is important to secure them at the right time—when the spore cases are beginning to open. Close observation with a magnifying glass will enable you to see when the spore cases are opening. You can lay the fern fronds underside down on paper for a day or two and let the

Ferns are propagated by means of spores, usually produced on the underside of the frond. When spore cases begin to open, cut fronds; lay, spore side down, on soil. Seal loosely in plastic bag with a little water in it. When fronds appear, loosen plastic to harden them off. After a week or two, uncover pot entirely.

spores drop off, or you can cut the fern frond into convenient-size pieces and lay them on the surface of the growing medium. The medium can be the standard 1-1-1 mixture, which should be pasteurized by pouring boiling water on it after it has been put in pots. The air, as well as the growing medium, must be kept moist. A convenient way of doing this is to put the pots in a plastic bread container with a little water in it. When the prothallia (the equivalent of seedlings) are visible, gradually harden them by tilting the cover. After a week or two, uncover the pots entirely.

Propagation by Parts of Plants

Vegetative asexual propagation is necessary in some cases because the plant has lost its ability to produce seeds—examples are the navel orange and the edible banana. In other cases it is desirable because the ancestry of the plant is so mixed that seedlings cannot be relied upon to be exactly like the parent plant.

When raised from seed, garden varieties of such plants as chrysanthemum, peony, phlox and iris cannot be relied on to reproduce true to their parents. Consequently, unless new varieties or a diversity of forms are desired, such varieties should be propagated by division of established plants or by cuttings of plant parts. Among the methods for reproducing plants vegetatively are dividing (rootstocks and rhizomes); planting stolons, layers, runners, offsets, suckers, bulbs, tubers, corms or cuttings; and, finally, grafting part of one plant upon another.

Division. Many garden varieties of herbaceous perennials, and a few shrubs, can be propagated by division of the rootstocks. Usually the best time to make the division is when the plant is dormant. In general, plants that bloom early in the spring are best divided in fall, whereas those that bloom in late summer or fall should be divided in spring. There are some exceptions, primroses for instance, that can be divided immediately after the flowers fade, provided that the divisions can be kept watered and in part shade throughout the summer months. There are a few plants which are most nearly dormant in early summer or August. These include Oriental poppies (roots) and Madonna lilies (bulbs). Tall bearded iris (rhizomes) can be dug up and divided any time from June until September.

Early spring division is advisable for late-flowering plants such as hardy chrysanthemums and perennial asters. Cannas also can be propagated by division of the roots in the spring. About the middle of March, the rootstocks of cannas that have been carried over winter in a frost-free place are divided by cutting the short stocky rhizomes into pieces, each containing at least one growth bud. These should be put into 4-inch pots and kept in a sunny window or in a greenhouse for about three or

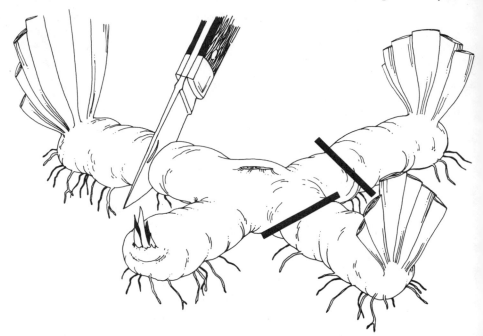

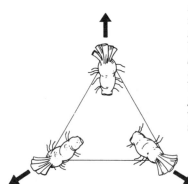

ABOVE: *Sketch shows correct division of mature iris rhizome. Discard old center section; transplant new rhizomes.*
LEFT: *Planting iris in clumps promotes good air circulation, keeps leaf fans growing outward for best appearance and health.*
BELOW: *Angle rhizomes on mounds to guarantee good drainage; cover scantily with soil, as shown. Late summer is ideal time to divide.*

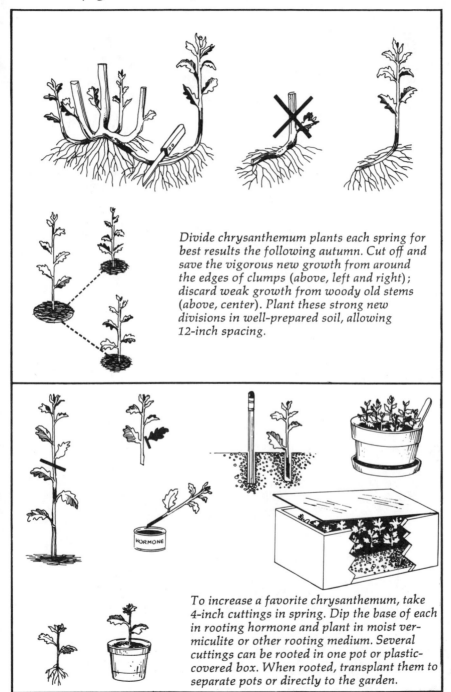

Divide chrysanthemum plants each spring for best results the following autumn. Cut off and save the vigorous new growth from around the edges of clumps (above, left and right); discard weak growth from woody old stems (above, center). Plant these strong new divisions in well-prepared soil, allowing 12-inch spacing.

To increase a favorite chrysanthemum, take 4-inch cuttings in spring. Dip the base of each in rooting hormone and plant in moist vermiculite or other rooting medium. Several cuttings can be rooted in one pot or plastic-covered box. When rooted, transplant them to separate pots or directly to the garden.

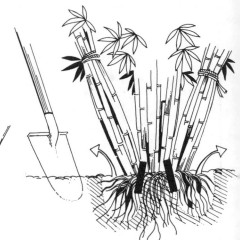

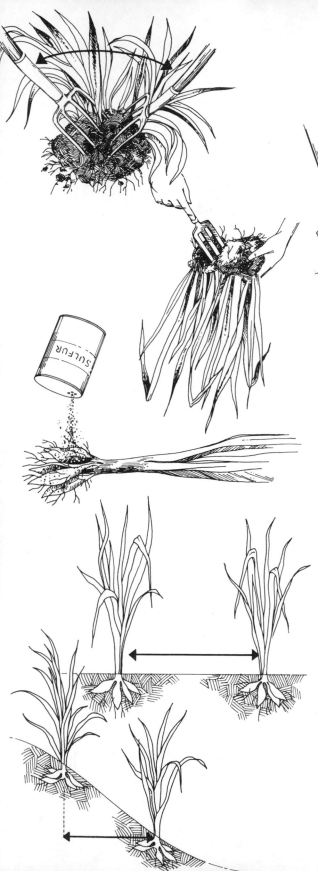

ABOVE: *Clump-forming bamboos may be divided as a chrysanthemum. Remove enough soil around rootball to determine growth pattern. Then cut apart as indicated by the dark slash marks.*

LEFT, *beginning at the top: Daylilies* (Hemerocallis) *can be divided and replanted at almost any time the soil can be worked, but late summer or early autumn, after the annual flowering season, is a favorite time. Use two spading forks to split apart a large, old established clump. Do final division with a smaller hand fork or sharp knife. Dust each division with a fungicide to prevent disease. When replanting, allow 12 to 15 inches spacing between each division, as indicated by the arrows on the drawings. Daylilies make excellent bank binders on steep hillsides.*

four weeks before it is safe to put them outdoors. Or they can be hardened off in a cold frame; keep the sash on for a few days, and then gradually admit more air.

Most of the hardy plants propagated by division do not demand any special soil or treatment, and divisions may be planted where they are to grow permanently. Much depends upon how closely the divisions are made. Japanese irises, for example, if divided into individual shoots solely for propagating purposes, need more attention (they should be put into a cold frame) than those divided into clumps, each containing five or six shoots.

Stolons and layers. Stolon is the name given to a branch which originates above the soil level and takes root when it comes in contact with the soil. Examples are *Cornus sericea*, forsythia and black raspberry.

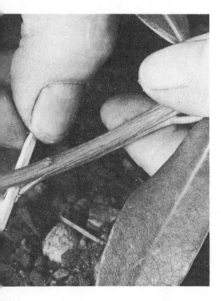 

ABOVE, LEFT: *Almost any shrub stem will send out roots if it is buried, and most shrubs may be propagated by this method, called layering. For rhododendrons, select one-or-two-year-old stems, near the ground, with flexible and greenish bark. Make an upward slit 1½ inches long and one-third through the stem. Insert a matchstick to hold pieces apart.*
ABOVE, RIGHT: *Press cut stem under the soil; cover and peg down firmly.*
LEFT: *Root formation of layered rhododendron. Without digging up, sever from mother plant when rooted. Dig and transplant next season.*

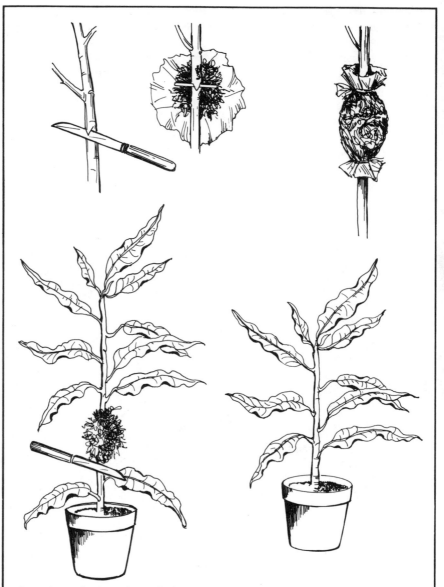

Layering, which is also called air layering, is a technique used to root plants above ground level, as shown here.

UPPER ROW: *Notch stem, and dust with rooting hormone. Prop notch open with toothpick; wrap in wet , wrung-out sphagnum. Wrap sphagnum tightly in plastic; tie firmly above and below.*

LOWER ROW: *When roots appear through sphagnum, cut through stem just below new roots and pot up the new plant.*

Any of these rooted stolons can be cut from the parent plant, dug up and planted in the spring to lead an independent existence.

Essentially, layering is the making of an artificial stolon. It can be applied to almost any shrub having branches that can be bent down and brought into contact with the ground. Make a split in the stem at the point where roots are to be formed. Then peg the stem to the earth so that the wounded part is covered with soil. Layers should be made in the spring. In most cases they will be ready to be cut free and transplanted the following spring.

Air layering. When suitable branches may be too far from the soil, so that it is not possible to bring them down to earth, air layering comes into the picture. Formerly, air layering often failed because it was difficult to keep the rooting medium moist enough under outdoor conditions. But with the advent of polyethylene plastic film, which can retain water vapor but admit air, the practice has become easier and more popular. Remove a cylinder of bark about an inch wide from the place on the stem where roots are to be formed. Then dust the wound with a root-inducing hormone powder and cover it with a generous handful of moist sphagnum moss (soak the moss in water and then sueeze out the surplus), which is then held in place by wrapping a sheet of polyethylene film around it and fastening the film top and bottom with strips of plastic or rubber. It is essential to put the fastenings on so that rain cannot get in to the moss. When new roots are visible, the rooted top may be cut off and planted, preferably in a shaded cold frame until sufficient roots are formed.

Runners. Runners are specialized shoots that run along the surface of the ground, making buds at intervals, and from them producing roots and leaves. Strawberry is an example. New plants produced on strawberry runners can be dug up and cut off from their runners and planted when they are about 3 inches across or they may be guided into 3- or 4-inch flowerpots filled with good soil. (The pots are sunk to the rims in the earth around the mother strawberry plant, and the runners are held in place with stones or pegged down with bent wire.) It is good practice to prevent the runners from going on to make additional plants. Treated in this way, they can be moved to a new strawberry bed in August or early September without any disturbance of their roots. Another familiar plant that behaves in the same way is the so-called strawberry-begonia, which is, incidentally, neither strawberry nor begonia but is one of the rockfoils, *Saxifraga stolonifera.*

Offsets. Offsets are short side shoots that grow from the base of a plant

ABOVE: Ananas comosus, *the pineapple of
commerce, may be propagated by rooting the
leaf rosette that forms on the mature fruit.
Slice off the top; scrape away the fruit; air-dry
24 hours. Plant in a pot of soil. Keep barely
moist until top growth indicates the new plant
has rooted. Fruiting will occur in about 18
months to 2 years.*

*Mature bromeliad plants, including
the pineapple of commerce (see
above) usually send out a sucker from
the base at the time they flower, or
not long afterwards. After the sucker
is making obvious growth it can be
cut from the mother plant as sketched
here and potted up separately. Suckers
handled in this manner do better than
those left in the original pot, even if
the parent plant is destroyed when it
goes into decline.*

and produce roots of their own. Houseleek (*Sempervivum*) is a good example. Offsets can be taken from the parent plant any time after they are half-grown, and planted in sandy soil.

Suckers. Shoots that originate beneath the soil and form roots are called suckers. Familiar plants that sucker freely are lilac and plum. It is often

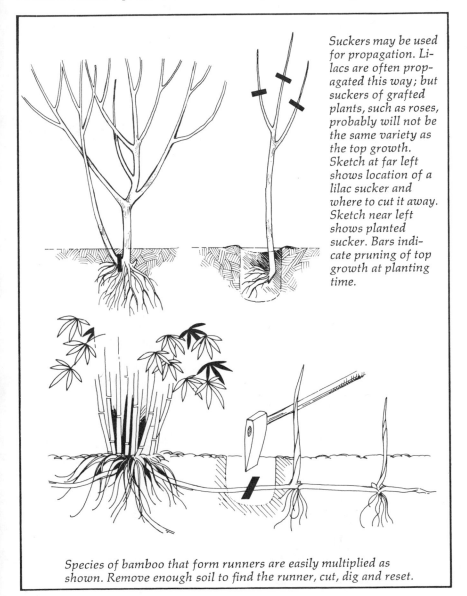

Suckers may be used for propagation. Lilacs are often propagated this way; but suckers of grafted plants, such as roses, probably will not be the same variety as the top growth. Sketch at far left shows location of a lilac sucker and where to cut it away. Sketch near left shows planted sucker. Bars indicate pruning of top growth at planting time.

Species of bamboo that form runners are easily multiplied as shown. Remove enough soil to find the runner, cut, dig and reset.

possible to stimulate the formation of suckers by injuring the roots, as is often done to Lombardy poplar, or by severe pruning of the top. Suckers may be dug up and planted in the spring or fall. (But with grafted plants, most roses, for example, remember that suckers probably will not be the same variety as the top growth.)

Rhizomes. The most familiar example of a plant commonly propagated by rhizomes is the bearded iris, which can be dug up, separated and replanted any time from mid-June until September. Another example is Solomon's seal (*Polygonatum*), which can be separated in the spring or fall, when the plant is dormant.

Slips. Popularly the term "slip" is used as a synonym for cutting. In a more restricted way it is applied to side shoots of pineapple and sweet potato. Slips or "draws" of sweet potatoes are produced by putting the root tubers in moist peat moss or vermiculite (or a mixture of these)

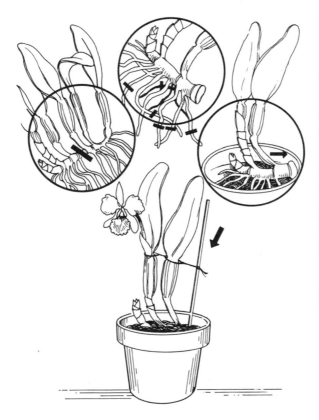

Orchids are usually repotted every two or three years, and that is the time to divide them. Cut the rhizome to form clumps of three to five pseudobulbs. Sketch at top left shows division of rhizome, undertaken just as new roots are growing. Use sharp, sterile knife. Black bars in top center sketch show where to prune back the roots. Sketch top right shows placing of the cut rhizome on top of potting mixture. Bottom sketch shows how to stake and tie plant as it develops.

about six weeks before the last frost is expected. They are kept preferably in a greenhouse with a temperature around 70°. So treated, they produce a forest of shoots, which should be hardened in a cold frame when they are about 6 inches long. Then they can be pulled off with the roots attached and planted in the field.

Bulbs. Some bulbs, such as those of tulips, produce new bulbs every year. These may be big enough to bloom the following spring, but if too many of them are produced, they may not be strong enough to produce flowers. Undersize bulbs should be dug up while dormant and planted 4 inches apart in rows a foot apart in rich soil. If conditions are favorable, they may grow to blooming size in two to three years. Shallow planting is believed to favor the production of bulblets.

Some bulbs can be induced to make bulblets by mutilating the bulbs. This is done with hyacinths by either "scooping" or "scoring" the basal plate, thus killing the terminal scale bud and forcing the growth of many of the surrounding lateral buds. The ideal tool for this purpose is a potato- or melon-baller. If you have difficulty in getting this gadget, a teaspoon will serve if you file it sharp enough to do the job. Or you can score the bulb by making three cuts through the basal plate, extending about one-third of the way into the bulb. This should be done as soon as possible after the leaves have faded. Then place the bulbs upside down in moist peat or sandy soil at a temperature between 70 and 80. After two or three months, each will have produced between ten and 50 bulblets that are ready for planting in September or October. The entire bulb should be planted, still upside down, about 3 inches deep. Dig it up the following year and plant the bulblets separately about 3 inches apart in rows 6 inches apart. They may be expected to grow into flowering-size bulbs in from three to five years.

Many lilies can be propagated by means of bulblets or bulbils produced in the axils of the leaves. Others make bulblets on the underground parts of the stem. In some species the bulblets are larger and more of them are produced if the flowers are removed in the bud stage (*Lilium sulphureum* and *L. umbellatum*, for example). Another method of propagating lilies is by scale leaves. You can pull off up to a dozen scales from the main bulb at planting time. Bury them ½ inch deep in a flat containing a mixture of peat moss and sand and keep them in a cold frame over the winter.

Dahlias can be propagated by division of the rootstock. It is essential to cut the rootstock apart so that an "eye," or growth bud, is retained in each division—the roots themselves are not able to produce growth shoots. Another way of propagating dahlias is by cuttings. To do this, plant a clump of roots in damp sand or peat moss in April or

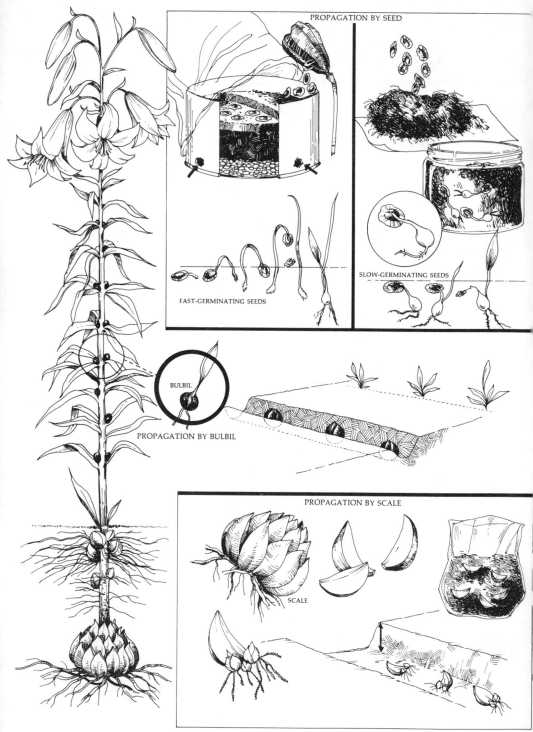

PROPAGATION BY SEED

FAST-GERMINATING SEEDS

SLOW-GERMINATING SEEDS

BULBIL

PROPAGATION BY BULBIL

PROPAGATION BY SCALE

SCALE

OPPOSITE, TOP, LEFT: *Many popular lilies—trumpets, Aurelians, Mid-Centuries—produce fast-germinating seeds that grow well planted outdoors. For a head start, sow indoors in gravel-lined containers of garden soil under ¼ inch sphagnum.*
TOP, RIGHT: *Slow-germinating seeds of other species do poorly outdoors. Plant in plastic container, and keep moist at room temperature two or three months until bulblets form. Then refrigerate in tight container two or three months longer. When first leaves appear, transplant to the garden.*
CENTER: *Bulbils produced by lilies such as* L. bulbiferum *and* L. tigrinum *may be planted in the garden in fall and will produce good-size bulbs in a year or two.*
BOTTOM: *To propagate by scale, store in sphagnum in plastic at room temperature till bulblets form; transplant to cold frame.*

RIGHT, *this page: Divide and plant dahlia tubers at about the time lilacs bloom. Shake away soil, then divide, being sure each tuber has a part of the stem with a growth bud attached. Set each tuber in a hole 6 inches deep. For tall-growing varieties, set a sturdy stake about 2 inches from the growth bud. Cover the tuber with 2 or 3 inches of soil at planting time; fill in the rest as growth begins. When 12 inches tall, begin tying to stake. Bold slash marks on flower stem suggest the disbudding technique. Reading clockwise, flower forms shown are decorative, collarette, cactus and anemone.*

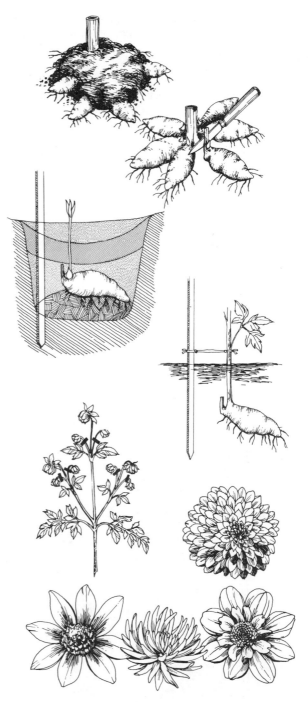

May with their eyes at surface level. Keep the clump in a sunny location in a window or greenhouse with temperature of at least 60°. When the shoots are about 4 inches long, they can be cut off and inserted as cuttings.

Tubers. Tuberous begonia, gloxinia and potato can be propagated by dividing the tubers. With begonias and gloxinias it is advisable to wait until the shoot growth is started, so that you can be sure of getting a growth bud on each division. The cut surface should be dusted with a fungicide such as 10 per cent fermate and 90 per cent dusting sulfur, and the division planted as any whole tuber would be planted.

Corms. Gladiolus propagates itself by corms, which are produced on top of the one that was planted the preceding spring. The old corm shrivels and dies. In addition to two or three sizable corms, many varieties produce an abundance of cormels. These are small and pelletlike. They may be sown in the spring much as you would plant peas. Some corms may be large enough to produce blossoms the following year.

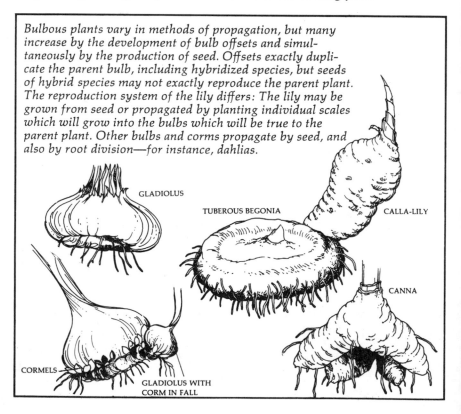

Bulbous plants vary in methods of propagation, but many increase by the development of bulb offsets and simultaneously by the production of seed. Offsets exactly duplicate the parent bulb, including hybridized species, but seeds of hybrid species may not exactly reproduce the parent plant. The reproduction system of the lily differs: The lily may be grown from seed or propagated by planting individual scales which will grow into the bulbs which will be true to the parent plant. Other bulbs and corms propagate by seed, and also by root division—for instance, dahlias.

GLADIOLUS

TUBEROUS BEGONIA

CALLA-LILY

CANNA

CORMELS

GLADIOLUS WITH
CORM IN FALL

Cuttings. Cutting is the name applied to a portion of a plant severed from its parent and so treated that it may form roots and produce a new plant. Cuttings may be made of stems, leaves, portions of leaves, tubers or roots.

Among the materials used for rooting cuttings are: coarse sand, peat moss, sphagnum moss, vermiculite, perlite, powdered glass and powdered pumice. The glass and pumice are used for their abrasive effect, which, by wounding the cutting, stimulates root formation.

Cuttings should be placed for rooting in an environment where their tissues will not dry out or their foliage, if they have foliage, will not wilt or die from excessive moisture loss. This environment may be provided by a case or box, which may be enclosed as desired, by a propagating case in a greenhouse, in a cold frame, by flats or boxes enclosed with polyethylene plastic or glass, depending upon the nature and number of the cuttings involved and the time of the year when they are to be placed in the rooting medium. In general, it is necessary to provide shade for the cuttings by means of slats, cheesecloth or other light-retarding material, and to control humidity while also providing fresh air both to prevent rotting and to cool the cuttings in hot weather. For the amateur this may be largely a matter of individual improvisation, which is fine as long as the basic requirements are met and the cuttings' needs understood.

During recent years among experienced amateurs, as well as professionals, there has been great interest in rooting cuttings under mist, either the constant or the intermittent type. Misting allows cuttings to be in full sun so that photosynthesis is not hindered, yet it prevents the leaves from becoming too hot, and prevents loss of moisture from the leaves by keeping them constantly moist. Hardwood and evergreen cuttings benefit considerably from mist treatment, and rooting of softwood cuttings is also speeded up.

When I first used constant mist, the only place close enough to the water supply, and in full sun, happened to be a windy one. I felt that some protection was necessary to prevent the mist from blowing away, so I made a square "corral," using 4-foot high 2 by 2's for corner posts. To form the side panels, I ran, from post to post on each of the four sides, a 6-inch board at ground level, and a 1-by-1-inch strip of board along the top. Then I nailed several pieces of builder's lath vertically between these two horizontal boards, and tacked polyethylene film to this framework. The two panels that were opposite each other I made movable by building them separately and holding them in place with broom-clamp fastenings. These panels can be slipped up and out.

Boxes for the cuttings were 12 by 12 by 6 inches, though 4 inches deep would have been enough. The boxes were made with a crack at the bottom to allow for the escape of water. All of the boxes had a 2-inch layer of coarse sand at the bottom, to provide good drainage, and a strip of window screen under the sand to keep it from sifting through. They were placed on a grating of 1-by-1-inch wood strips to avoid danger from standing water. The rooting medium varied from plain sand to a mixture of sand, peat moss and vermiculite. The fog nozzles (two) were mounted on a length of ¼-inch copper tubing attached to a hose connected to the water supply. The tubing was bent so that the nozzles were supported about 2 feet above the cuttings. Each nozzle pointed downward and was adjusted to give off 1 gallon of water per hour. The water was turned on about the middle of June and allowed to run night and day until about the middle of September.

It has since been established that intermittent mist is generally preferable to constant mist, although this constant-mist setup worked very well for me with some species.

One interesting fact about mist is that comparatively large cuttings rooted with greater facility than small ones. For example, rose daphne (*D. cneorum*) and early broom (*Cytisus praecox*) cuttings that consisted mostly of wood formed the preceding season rooted more quickly than those that had wood of the current season. Surprisingly, the cytisus rooted 100 per cent. From my previous experience using conventional methods, only shoots of the current season were successful.

One would think that fungus diseases would be rife with so much moisture present, but there was no trouble whatever when I used mist, not even from mildew on the lilacs or black spot on the roses.

There are some drawbacks to this system. One is the difficulty of carrying the fully rooted cuttings through the winter—they will rot if left too long under the mist but will often die without the moist atmosphere. I think this difficulty can be overcome by using intermittent mist, and after roots have started, gradually increasing the length of the dry periods. The rooted cuttings should be potted as early as possible and kept under mist for a few days. Also it would seem to be desirable to keep them under glass until the following spring, either in a cold frame or, preferably, in a cold greenhouse—40° to 45°.

Various methods have been used to insure that the mist is adequate without being wasteful of water. Apparently, the most satisfactory one right now is a so-called electronic leaf—a device which is placed among the plants, and which, when wet, completes an electrical circuit that in turn causes the misting mechanism to turn on. Another method is a timing device that can be set to turn on the water for one minute and then off for ten minutes, more or less. With this method, however, the rapidity with which the leaves dry out may fluctuate considerably because of the weather.

Deciduous hardwood cuttings. Many shrubs and some trees can be propagated with ease by cuttings which are made soon after leaf fall. Shoots including the preceding season's wood should be cut into lengths of 6 to 9 inches. Tie each kind separately in a bundle with the butts even and pointing in the same direction. Pack them in moist sand, sawdust or peat moss in a box that is not too large to be handled easily. Store them in a temperature between 50° and 55° for about a month and then at 35° to 40° until spring. Most amateurs do not have the facilities to provide these temperatures; instead they can put the cuttings outdoors before hard frost, burying them in a sandy place and being sure to mark the spot so that the cuttings can be found in the spring.

James S. Wells, in his book *Plant Propagation Practices*, tells of the excellent results he had when he wounded stems of cuttings. The wounds varied from light ones made by drawing the tip of a sharp knife down the stem, and heavy ones (cutting a thin slice from one side of the base of the cutting). This should be done before cuttings are stored for the winter.

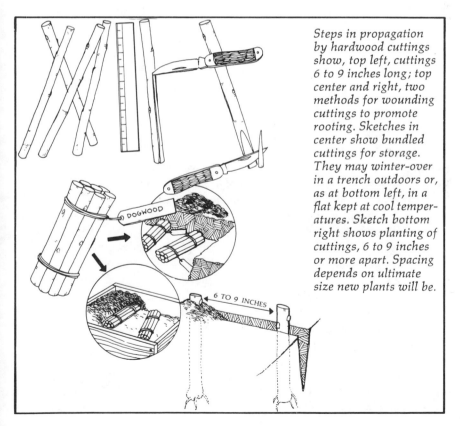

Steps in propagation by hardwood cuttings show, top left, cuttings 6 to 9 inches long; top center and right, two methods for wounding cuttings to promote rooting. Sketches in center show bundled cuttings for storage. They may winter-over in a trench outdoors or, as at bottom left, in a flat kept at cool temperatures. Sketch bottom right shows planting of cuttings, 6 to 9 inches or more apart. Spacing depends on ultimate size new plants will be.

DOGWOOD

6 TO 9 INCHES

As soon as the ground is fit to work, cuttings can be set in the open. A slitlike trench should be made with a spade and the cuttings dipped in root-inducing powder and then put in right side up with about an inch or two of the cuttings above ground. The distance apart will vary according to the vigor of the species. The average would be about 6 inches apart in rows which are 2 to 3 feet apart.

Plants which can be expected to root fairly easily include buttonwood, catalpa, poplar, willow, Russian olive; fruits such as fig, blueberry, currant, gooseberry, quince and grape; and ornamental shrubs such as barberry, shrubby dogwood, deutzia, diervilla, euonymus, forsythia, hibiscus, kolkwitzia, privet, philadelphus, rose, willow, spirea and tamarix. Some kinds will succeed even when planted directly in the spring, notably privet, forsythia and multiflora rose. In general the following are not successful from hardwood cuttings: ash, oak, beech, birch, apple, pear, cherry, maple, most nuts, linden, lilac and witchhazel.

Evergreen cuttings. Fall or early winter is generally the best time to put in cuttings of evergreens. The broadleaf evergreens such as boxwood, barberry and rhododendron can be put in during September or early October; also easy-to-root conifers such as yew, chamaecyparis and arborvitae. Fir, pine and spruce are difficult to root from cuttings. While a greenhouse is definitely preferable, a sun porch where the temperature does not fall below 45° or rise much above 60° may give good results. Even if you have nothing better than a well-lighted window in a cool room, you can expect some success.

Cuttings should be gathered preferably when the temperature is above freezing. Select healthy young branches bearing a number of young shoots. With a sharp knife, remove the shoot and cut down to 4 to 6 inches. If you wish, shoots of a suitable length can be pulled off with the heel attached to them and any shreds trimmed off afterward. Success is most certain if the cutting is treated with root-inducing hormones before insertion. Indolebutyric acid in powder form, obtainable under various trade names, including Hormodin and Rootone, is probably the most convenient. Take about half a dozen cuttings, dip 1 inch of the butts in water, shake off the surplus and then dip them in a container of the root-inducing powder and tap the cuttings on the edge of a dish to remove the surplus. Insert cuttings immediately and make sure that the bases are in contact with the rooting medium by thrusting a dibble or trowel down beside the cutting. Thoroughly soak the medium to settle it further.

Heat supplied from below the medium is desirable, although not absolutely necessary. It is generally believed that it is an advantage if the rooting medium can be maintained 5° higher than the air temperature. There are available plastic-covered heating cables with thermostats, which will heat about 20 square feet. If you do not wish to devote this much space to propagating, you can make a box 5 inches deep and whatever length and width you desire. This can be fitted with a transparent superstructure of glass or clear plastic film and set on a radiator in your home, preferably in a water-tight tray. The radiator supplies the bottom heat.

Softwood cuttings. Softwood cuttings of herbaceous plants such as chrysanthemum, phlox and delphinium are taken from the plant and inserted in a rooting medium in early spring, or at any time during the growing season when young shoots about 3 inches long are obtainable. Softwood cuttings of woody plants are made between May and late July. It is imperative to prevent softwood cuttings from wilting. Gather materials from which cuttings are to be made early in the morning. Put them in a plastic bag or in a container such as a clean garbage pail lined with wet newspapers. Working in the shade, make your cuttings from 2

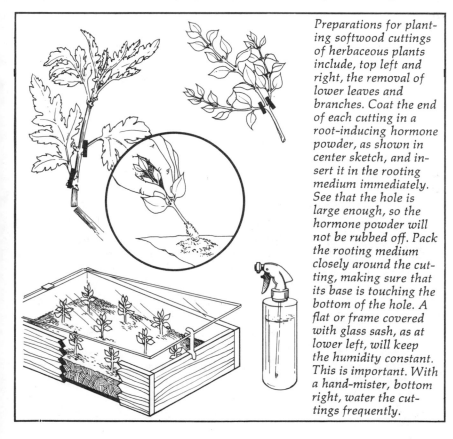

Preparations for planting softwood cuttings of herbaceous plants include, top left and right, the removal of lower leaves and branches. Coat the end of each cutting in a root-inducing hormone powder, as shown in center sketch, and insert it in the rooting medium immediately. See that the hole is large enough, so the hormone powder will not be rubbed off. Pack the rooting medium closely around the cutting, making sure that its base is touching the bottom of the hole. A flat or frame covered with glass sash, as at lower left, will keep the humidity constant. This is important. With a hand-mister, bottom right, water the cuttings frequently.

to 8 inches long. Make the basal cut just below a joint and remove the lowest leaf or leaves. Treat the cuttings with a root-inducing hormone powder, insert them in the rooting medium without delay and water well. Make the holes large enough so that the rooting powder is not rubbed off. Pack the rooting medium in close contact with the cutting, making sure that the base is touching the bottom of the hole (except in vermiculite, which should not be compacted). When only a few cuttings are to be rooted, it is advisable to put cuttings one to a 3- or 4-inch pot. The advantage of this is that those which root quickly can be removed from the frame without disturbing the slower ones.

It is important to keep the air continuously humid. With this in view, sprinkle the cuttings several times each day. Shade the frame with a coat of whitewash supplemented by lath shades or a double thickness of cheesecloth tacked on to the furring strips. Keep the sash on to maintain high humidity, although ventilating may be necessary to prevent the temperature from rising too high.

Usually it is a good plan to coddle the cuttings during the first winter by keeping them in a cold frame. When cuttings are rooted, they should be potted separately in individual pots or spaced out in flats of soil or put into wood-veneer bands or peat-pulp pots for the rest of the growing season. If they are set in individual pots, plunge them in peat moss, sawdust or coal ashes in the frame, which should be left open to the air until there have been several frosts. Before winter really sets in, the cuttings should be mulched lightly with excelsior or salt meadow hay, and the sash put on. During very severe weather, an additional covering of salt hay, old quilts or such should be put on. During periods of mild sunny weather, tilt the sash to admit air. Maintain the cold frame without violent fluctuations in temperature.

Leaf cuttings. Leaf cuttings of some plants root with great ease. Among them are begonia, gloxinia and African violet. Plants such as croton (*Codiaeum*), while they will root readily (from leaf cuttings), never make productive growth. When making leaf cuttings of rex begonia, cut off a mature leaf, leaving on it 1½ inches of leafstalk. Before inserting it into the rooting medium, which can be a mixture of sand and peat moss, make a cut through each of the main veins, just above the point where the veins join each other. Usually a new plant grows wherever a cut is made. Insert the stalk so that the blade lies flat on the rooting medium. If necessary, weight the leaf down with small stones. Christmas begonias are treated differently because you may expect only one plant per leaf. Make the cuttings in late December or January. Medium-size leaves are preferred. The stalks should be cut 3 inches long, dibbled into the propagating bed and kept at a temperature of 70°. Leave them there

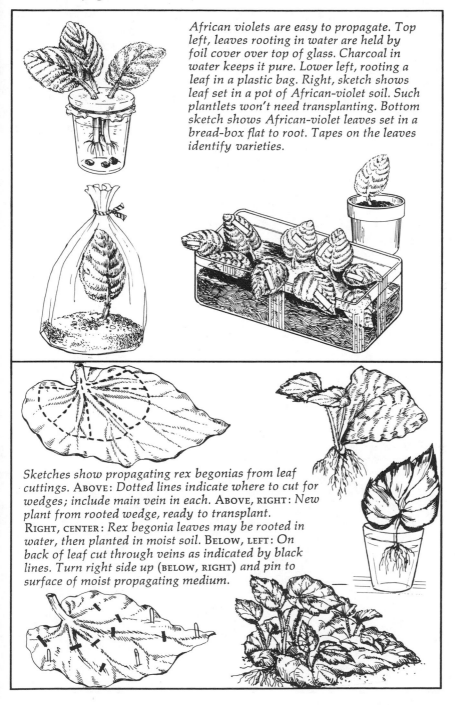

African violets are easy to propagate. Top left, leaves rooting in water are held by foil cover over top of glass. Charcoal in water keeps it pure. Lower left, rooting a leaf in a plastic bag. Right, sketch shows leaf set in a pot of African-violet soil. Such plantlets won't need transplanting. Bottom sketch shows African-violet leaves set in a bread-box flat to root. Tapes on the leaves identify varieties.

Sketches show propagating rex begonias from leaf cuttings. ABOVE: Dotted lines indicate where to cut for wedges; include main vein in each. ABOVE, RIGHT: New plant from rooted wedge, ready to transplant. RIGHT, CENTER: Rex begonia leaves may be rooted in water, then planted in moist soil. BELOW, LEFT: On back of leaf cut through veins as indicated by black lines. Turn right side up (BELOW, RIGHT) and pin to surface of moist propagating medium.

until the roots and shoots begin to form, when they may be removed and potted in 2-inch pots in the standard 1-1-1 mixture.

Undoubtedly the ease with which they can be propagated is one of the chief reasons for the popularity of *Saintpaulia* (African violet). There are many ways of starting African violets from leaves. One is to root them in water by cutting the leafstalks about 3 inches long, putting them in an inch of water in a small glass, and, when they are rooted, potting them into 2-inch pots. Another way is to insert them in vermiculite, sand or a mixture of both in a plastic bread box. More than one plant may be expected from each leaf. Plantlets usually develop into replicas of the parent, but they may sport or mutate and be entirely different.

Leaf-bud cuttings. One way of overcoming the inability or reluctance of some leaves to make growth shoots is to take the leaves off the plant with a portion of the stem to which the leaf is attached. The important thing is to include a growth bud. Dr. Henry Skinner of the National Arboretum was successful in rooting rhododendron hybrids by this method. He made the cuttings late in July and put them in a mixture of

Propagation of rhododendron by leaf-bud cutting may succeed when other methods fail. Sketch top left shows suitable locations for cutting. Center sketch shows leaf with its growth bud and portion of the stem, ready for rooting. Treat cutting with rooting hormone; then plant as in sketch at bottom. For rhododendrons, some experts use rooting mixture of three parts sand to two parts peat moss.

three parts by bulk of New Jersey quartz sand and two parts peat moss. He also treated them with a root-inducing chemical, indolbutyric acid. *Ramonda*, a relative of *Saintpaulia*, may be rooted by leaf cuttings provided the leaf is pulled off so that the entire leafstalk with the bud attached to its base is used.

Root cuttings. Many plants, including Oriental poppy, horseradish and sea kale, can be propagated easily by root cuttings. Dig the roots up in the fall and cut them into lengths of 2 to 4 inches. Then put these cuttings horizontally into flats containing 3 inches of a 1-1-1 soil mixture and cover them with an inch of sand or vermiculite and water thoroughly. They should then be put in a cold frame and after a few frosts mulched with 3 to 4 inches of salt hay, excelsior or oak leaves. Finally, put the sash in place. In the spring the mulch and sash should be removed, and shoots will soon appear. When they have grown 3 or 4 inches high, they should be planted in nursery rows and kept shaded for a few weeks.

Oriental-poppy roots may be dug in August when the plants are dormant, then cut into pieces about 3 inches long and about as thick as a

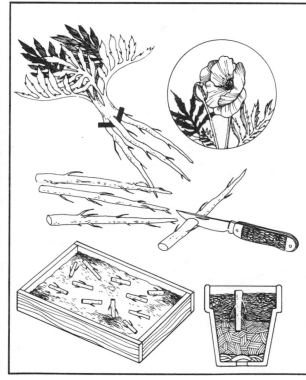

Propagation by root cuttings. Sketch at top left shows Oriental-poppy root division. Center sketches, left and right, show poppy roots cut into lengths 2 to 4 inches long, and sketch at bottom left shows how to lay these on rooting mixture. Place in cold frame through frosts; then mulch and cover for winter. They'll produce shoots in spring. Sketch at lower right also shows rooting of Oriental poppy. By this method, 3-inch root pieces are set singly in 4-inch pots of sandy soil. Plunge pots into sand in a cold frame. Transplant to garden in spring, when leaves appear.

pencil. Insert pieces singly in 4-inch pots of sandy soil, keeping them right end up. (They are put into individual pots because poppies are notorious for resenting root disturbance.) The pots should be plunged in sawdust, peat moss or sand in a cold frame and the cuttings transplanted to their permanent locations when they have made a few green leaves in the spring.

Viviparous plants. Several species of *Kalanchoe* (*K. daigremontiana*, *K. verticillata* and *K. pinnata*), sold under the name "bryophyllum," form small plants in the notches on the leaf margins (in *K. verticillata* they are produced only at the tips of the leaves). *Tolmiea* and several varieties of tropical water-lilies (notably the one known as *Nymphaea daubeniana*) produce plantlets at the junction of leafstalk and blade. There are also ferns and begonias that sprout plantlets on leaf surfaces. To propagate any of these viviparous species is simply a matter of transferring the plantlets to a suitable rooting medium, such as a mixture of sand and peat, or vermiculite and perlite.

Grafting and budding. Grafting and budding are terms used to designate the placing or insertion of a portion of one plant (bud or scion) upon another plant (the understock) so that they grow together. Budding and grafting are essentially the same except that budding is done while the plants are in active growth and grafting is done when plants are more or less dormant; and in budding, as a rule, only one bud is inserted, while in grafting, the scion normally contains at least two buds. The chief use of grafting is in the propagation of plants which do not "come true" from seeds and those that do not readily or quickly root from cuttings. In general, a grafted plant reproduces the parent exactly. In some instances, the understock may modify the grafted plant's growth. For example, apples can be dwarfed by grafting them on a specific variety of apple understock known as Malling IX. Pears can be dwarfed by grafting them on quince.

Many of our most valued plants, such as some varieties of hybrid tea roses, do not make satisfactory growth on their own roots; therefore nurserymen propagate these plants by budding or grafting them to hardier stock. Because some of the named forms of lilac can be made into salable plants more quickly when they are grafted, it is common practice for nurserymen to bud or graft them either on cuttings or plants of privet, or, preferably, on roots of the common lilac.

Grafting may be used to adapt plants to various soil conditions. Plums, which thrive best in a clay loam, are sometimes budded on peach, which enables them to grow in a sandy soil. Grafting apples on rootstocks of greater winter hardiness may help them to withstand a severe climate. This also works in the opposite direction. European nurserymen were in the habit of grafting many varieties of rhododendron on seedlings of *R. ponticum*, a somewhat tender species. Undoubtedly, this accounts in part for the high mortality of these plants in the northern part of this country. In some cases, grafting may help the plant to be more resistant to insects. For example, if grape varieties of Eurasian origin are grafted upon understocks of grapes of American origin, they are better able to resist attacks of the grape phylloxera, a louse which causes galls to form on roots and leaves, and root eel worms (nematodes), which attack peaches, are much less injurious when the peach is grafted on Marianna plum.

Grafting is also used in making plants of special form. Examples are the dwarf catalpa, weeping mulberry, the Chinese scholar tree (*Sophora japonica*) and weeping cherries. "Tree" roses are commonly made by budding or grafting them on a single stem of the desired height.

The chief reason why grafting is not more popular with amateurs is that they seldom have access to suitable understock material. A good understock must be easy to raise from seeds or cuttings and it must be botanically related to the scion. While it is feasible to graft a lilac on ash (they belong in the same plant family), it would be just a waste of time to attempt to graft an apple on ash. You must be foresighted and start raising understocks either by seeds or cuttings a year or two in advance.

But it may be that you have a usable understock on hand. For example, privet may provide cuttings on which lilac can be budded during the growing season, or roots which can be dug up in the fall and used as understock during the winter; apple roots of pencil thickness may be obtained from any apple tree; roses can be budded in canes of easy-to-root *Rosa multiflora* or many climbing varieties.

Bud grafting. The most important type of bud graft is the T or shield method, and it is easiest for the beginner. The method gets its name from the shape of the cut on the understock and the shape of the piece that bears the bud. To make a T, first cut horizontally through the bark of the understock. An upward vertical cut starting an inch or so below completes the leg of the T. When the knife reaches the horizontal cut, turn it to right and left to raise the flaps of bark.

The bud to be grafted on the understock is cut from a "bud stick," a shoot of the current season prepared by cutting off all the leaf blades and leaving ½ an inch of the leafstalk (petiole) to serve as a handle when inserting the bud. The bud is taken from the shoot by cutting slightly into the wood about ½ an inch below the bud, and continuing upward for ½ an inch or so beyond the bud. The flaps of bark should be

BUD
GRAFT

WHIP
GRAFT

This is the technique used
for grafting nursery
stock and small limbs.
Scion and stock are
cut through at a long angle
and a tongue is cut
into each surface. Tongues
are pressed together
until they interlock. Graft
is wrapped firmly to keep
pieces pressed together.

SIDE
GRAFT

INLAY
GRAFT

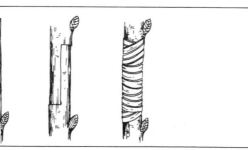

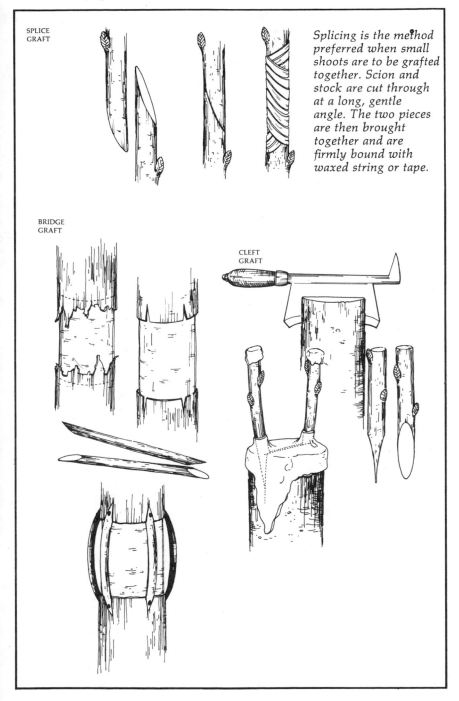

SPLICE
GRAFT

Splicing is the method preferred when small shoots are to be grafted together. Scion and stock are cut through at a long, gentle angle. The two pieces are then brought together and are firmly bound with waxed string or tape.

BRIDGE
GRAFT

CLEFT
GRAFT

lifted carefully, and the bud, on its "shield," slipped in beneath them. If the upper part of the shield projects above the top of the T, it should be cut off flush with the top. Tie the bud in place with a rubber budding strip, which can be improvised by cutting a ⅛-inch-broad rubber band. Rubber is preferred to raffia (the older method) because it "gives" with the expanding stock, and there is no danger of strangling the bud.

The understock most commonly used for roses is a one- or two-year-old plant of *Rosa multiflora*. Budding of roses can be done in June, July, August or whenever the bark separates easily from the wood. Since the understock will later be made into cuttings, you should space your grafted buds far enough apart to allow for at least two leaves on each cutting. After two or three weeks the inserted buds will have "taken," and canes may be cut up into pieces and put as cuttings in a cold frame, where they may be left until the following spring. In spring, the understock above the inserted bud is cut off, and the cuttings thus produced should be rooted and planted in the rose bed or in the nursery row. The growth bud that would be underground after planting should be cut out to lessen the danger of suckering.

In all forms of budding and grafting it is essential that the cambiums of stock and scion touch. The cambium is a single layer of actively growing cells just underneath the bark. Thus it encircles the inner wood. When the diameter of the scion and the stock are not the same, it is necessary to put the scion to one side of the cut edge of the understock so that the two cambiums meet.

Scion grafting. The most important scion-grafting methods for the amateur are cleft, whip or tongue, saddle, wedge, side and veneer. All grafts are best done in late winter or early spring, either indoors or outdoors. Cleft grafting is used to make a young tree of an undesirable variety into a preferred one. First, when the buds begin to swell in the spring, the branches are cut back to stubs one to three inches in diameter. Then, with a grafting chisel or a strong pruning knife, a cleft is made in a branch stub. A club or wooden mallet is used to drive the chisel into the wood. The scions are cut to a long wedge shape. The cleft is held open by the wedge of the chisel, the scions are slipped in, the wedge is removed and the "spring" of the wood holds it in place. All scions should be completely dormant (usually cut in the fall and buried outdoors in the coldest spot available). All cut surfaces should be covered with grafting wax. Usually two scions are put in each cleft. Be careful to match the cambium layers. The following year, if both scions have started, one of them can be removed.

Whip or tongue grafting is used chiefly to propagate fruit trees. The understock commonly used is a root of a one- or two-year-old

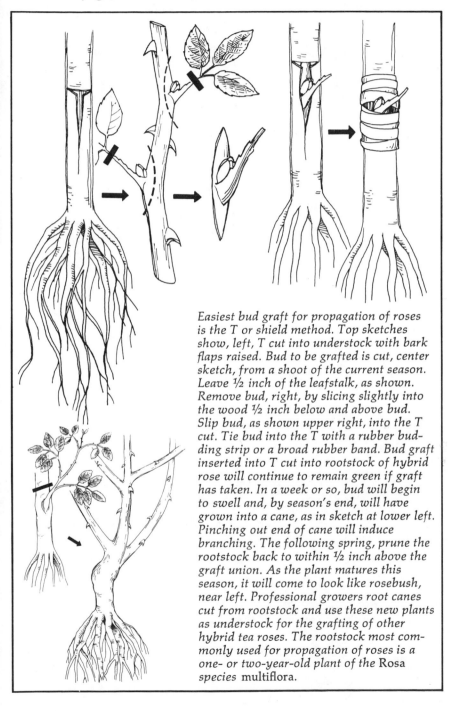

Easiest bud graft for propagation of roses is the T or shield method. Top sketches show, left, T cut into understock with bark flaps raised. Bud to be grafted is cut, center sketch, from a shoot of the current season. Leave ½ inch of the leafstalk, as shown. Remove bud, right, by slicing slightly into the wood ½ inch below and above bud. Slip bud, as shown upper right, into the T cut. Tie bud into the T with a rubber budding strip or a broad rubber band. Bud graft inserted into T cut into rootstock of hybrid rose will continue to remain green if graft has taken. In a week or so, bud will begin to swell and, by season's end, will have grown into a cane, as in sketch at lower left. Pinching out end of cane will induce branching. The following spring, prune the rootstock back to within ½ inch above the graft union. As the plant matures this season, it will come to look like rosebush, near left. Professional growers root canes cut from rootstock and use these new plants as understock for the grafting of other hybrid tea roses. The rootstock most commonly used for propagation of roses is a one- or two-year-old plant of the Rosa species multiflora.

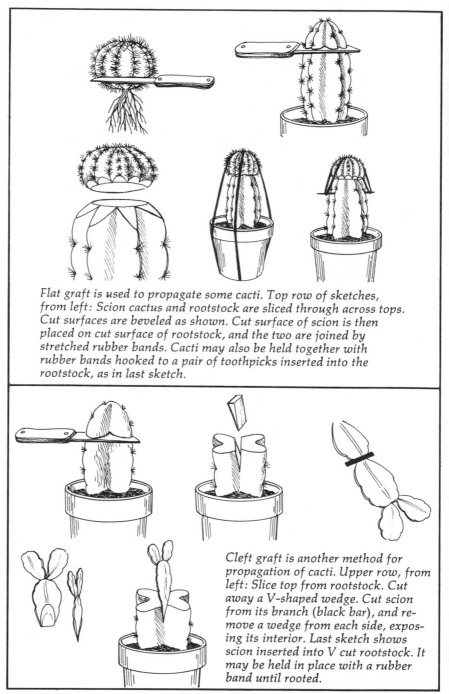

Flat graft is used to propagate some cacti. Top row of sketches, from left: Scion cactus and rootstock are sliced through across tops. Cut surfaces are beveled as shown. Cut surface of scion is then placed on cut surface of rootstock, and the two are joined by stretched rubber bands. Cacti may also be held together with rubber bands hooked to a pair of toothpicks inserted into the rootstock, as in last sketch.

Cleft graft is another method for propagation of cacti. Upper row, from left: Slice top from rootstock. Cut away a V-shaped wedge. Cut scion from its branch (black bar), and remove a wedge from each side, exposing its interior. Last sketch shows scion inserted into V cut rootstock. It may be held in place with a rubber band until rooted.

seedling related to the tree you wish to propagate. Cut a 4- to 6-inch scion from a shoot which is of the preceding year's wood. Make a long sloping cut (using a sharp knife) on both scion and understock. Make tongues in both by vertical cuts starting near the point of the diagonal. Then fit stock and scion together with the tongue of one pushed into the slit of the other. They should then be tied with thin cotton twine, buried in a moist sand and peat-moss mixture and treated the same way as hardwood cuttings.

The saddle graft is made simply by cutting the understock to a wedge shape, splitting the scion about 1 inch up the middle and then slipping it over the wedge. This graft is favored when lilac is put on rooted cuttings of privet during the winter. The idea in this case is to use privet (which roots faster than lilac) merely as a nurse plant, in the expectation that in a short time the lilac will form its own roots and the privet can be dispensed with. Naturally, then, there is no danger of "graft blight," which is attributed to incompatibility between the lilac and privet. A wedge graft is just the opposite of a saddle graft. The scion is cut to a wedge, and the understock is split to receive it.

Side and veneer grafting are done in the winter. A greenhouse is needed. These are used chiefly in propagation of Japanese maples and evergreens, both broad-leaved (rhododendron) and narrow-leaved such as spruce, fir and pine. The understocks are seedlings of related plants potted the preceding spring. Keep them in a cold greenhouse until about the first of February; then put them in a temperature of 60° to 65° to start root action. When new roots start, in about three or four weeks, they are ready to be grafted. For side grafting, near the base of the understock make a cut extending downward almost to the center of the stem. Cut the scion to a long wedge shape, put it down into the slit and tie it in place. Keep the completed grafts in an enclosed propagating case in the greenhouse, plunged almost horizontally in moist peat moss, with the graft uppermost. Gradually cut back the tops of the understocks until they are entirely removed.

The veneer graft is similar to this except that the flap made by the cut in the understock is removed with a second, horizontal cut. Prepare the scion by making a long cut on one side and a shorter one almost straight across the stem on the other so that it fits into the cut made on the understock. Tie the scions rather tightly with thin cotton twine. In about four weeks the stock and scion should be united, and about one-third of the stock is then cut off and the humidity is reduced. In another four or five weeks, the remainder of the understock is removed, and the final grafted plants are then ready to be lined out in the nursery.

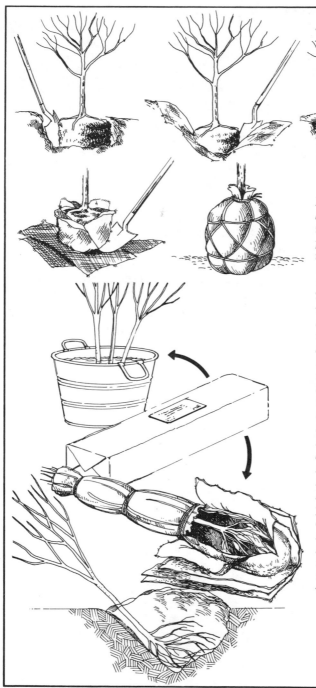

Five steps in balling and burlapping a tree for safe transplanting: First, soil is removed outside the main concentration of roots. Second, burlap is worked down, under and around the rootball. Third, an additional piece of burlap likely will be needed for complete coverage. Fourth, the tree is lifted out of the hole to allow easy access for tying securely, the fifth and final step. Plants shipped bareroot, as sketched, should be soaked 24 hours before planting. If you can't plant them for several days, after soaking, heel in— that is, set in a trench, and cover with mounded earth.

4. Keys to Successful Planting

Planting and transplanting are two of the gardener's greatest pleasures. To plant or transplant properly is not always easy, either. There are a thousand variables, not the least of which is the tricky element of timing. In this chapter you will find the basic guidelines for planting trees, shrubs and lawns. Seeds are discussed in Chapter 3, bulbs and herbaceous flowers in Chapter 6. For planting information pertaining specifically to vegetables, see Chapter 8; for herbs, Chapter 9.

Planting Trees and Shrubs

For outdoors, early spring and fall are the times to plant trees and shrubs, although more fall planting for spring bloom is done in the South. The plants should be dormant. In the spring, plant about a week before the buds begin to break. In fall, plant just after the leaves drop— or, if you're in a hurry or live in a very cold climate, when they begin to turn. If you simply must set out plants after they have leafed out, make sure they are balled and burlapped or container-grown. It will also help if the leaves have been coated with an antidesiccant spray to help slow the loss of moisture.

Trees and shrubs shipped bareroot—that is, without earth surrounding the root system—should be soaked 24 hours before planting. Mound the earth at the bottom of the planting hole, and set the roots over the mound and down around the mound into the hole. It is particularly important that bareroot subjects be well watered at planting time and throughout their early weeks.

Large plants from a nursery usually will come to you balled and burlapped. This protects the roots, helps to alleviate the shock of planting and makes handling easier. If you are moving specimens from one spot to another in your own garden, it is not necessary to ball and burlap them, although it helps. If you don't, follow this procedure: Soak the soil around the roots thoroughly. With a very sharp spade, cut straight down through the soil all the way around the plant. (The size of the ball you take depends on the spread of the roots.) Then dig out behind the cut and cut horizontally under the roots as far as possible. Pry up the root ball carefully with a couple of planks reinforced by a crowbar. Then lift out and take as much of the soil as you can.

One of the cardinal rules of all planting is: Get the plant into the ground quickly. The longer you wait, the harder it is for it to start growing again and survive the shock of planting.

If a balled-and-burlapped plant should arrive from a nursery several days before you can plant it, set it in a shady place and keep the ball damp and covered with porous material such as straw. If bareroot nursery stock, such as privet and tree whips, arrives before you're ready for it, it must be heeled in. Just dig a trench in the shade, and lay in the roots so that the plant is resting at a 45° angle. Cover the roots with soil and keep them damp.

The permanent hole for the plant should be about twice as wide and somewhat deeper than the root ball. As you dig out the soil, separate it into three piles: (1) topsoil, (2) good subsoil, (3) poor subsoil. Put the topsoil into the bottom of the hole and add to it all the additional topsoil and humus you can find. If possible, use nothing but topsoil and humus to fill in around the plant. Otherwise, use the good subsoil on top of the topsoil, and use the poor subsoil only at the very top of the hole.

Before setting the plant into the hole, examine the roots and cut off any broken or injured parts with a clean, diagonal snip of your pruning shears. It's also a good idea to trim back all large roots a little, whether injured or not.

Set the plant into the hole at the same depth that it formerly grew. (A few plants, such as privet and box, are set a little deeper.) If you were not successful in bringing a good ball of earth with the plant, make sure that the bare roots are spread out in a natural position.

Fill in around the roots, as previously noted, with topsoil, then good subsoil and the poor subsoil last. Fill in a few inches at a time and tamp down to eliminate air pockets.

When the hole is filled and tamped, make a 6-in.-high wall of earth—like a dike—all the way around the perimeter of the hole. Inside, place a good mulch of rotted manure (for broadleaf evergreens, use oak leaves or pine needles, preferably partially rotted). Then fill the reservoir with water. Refill it three days later; then every week for a month.

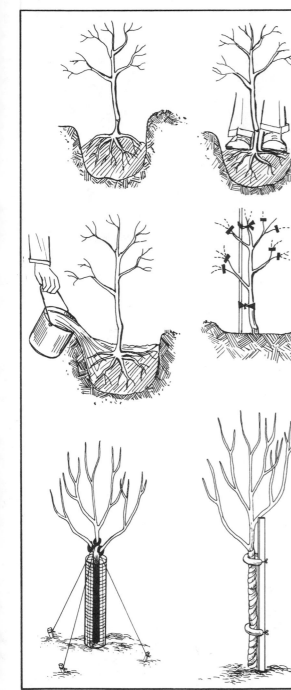

For bareroot tree, dig hole twice as wide and deeper than roots. Soak roots 24 hours. Set on mounded soil, TOP LEFT, at depth it grew before. Fill hole ⅔ full; tamp every few inches, TOP RIGHT. Slowly add one or two buckets of water, BOTTOM LEFT, in depression for water retention. Stake, prune, as BOTTOM RIGHT.

Adequate water, trunk protection and staking help young trees prosper. Plant below soil line for watering ease. Support large trees as at LEFT, small ones as at RIGHT. Wire mesh protects trunk from gnawing animals; special paper wrapping protects it from sun, and also preserves moisture.

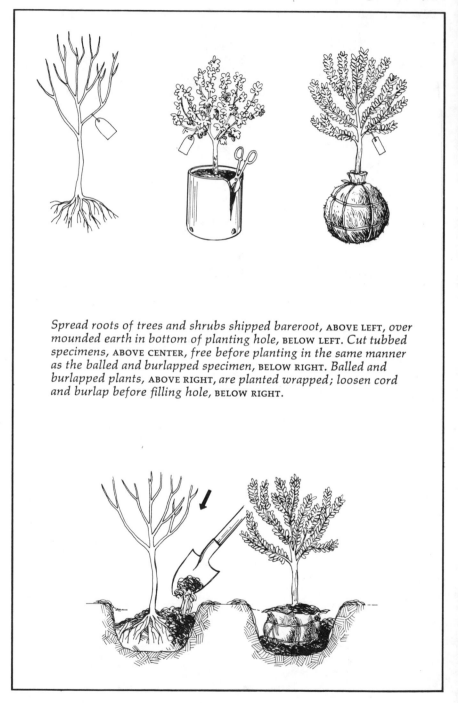

Spread roots of trees and shrubs shipped bareroot, ABOVE LEFT, over mounded earth in bottom of planting hole, BELOW LEFT. Cut tubbed specimens, ABOVE CENTER, free before planting in the same manner as the balled and burlapped specimen, BELOW RIGHT. Balled and burlapped plants, ABOVE RIGHT, are planted wrapped; loosen cord and burlap before filling hole, BELOW RIGHT.

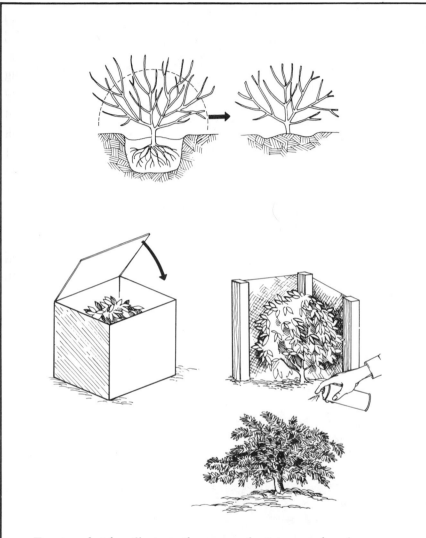

Two top sketches illustrate the proper planting procedure for shrubs. Note size of the planting hole, left sketch, and depression created to improve watering, right sketch. Semicircle indicates way to prune back, reducing shrub to size in sketch, right. Center sketches show two methods of winter protection. Lower sketch shows spraying of newly set shrub with antidesiccant, to prevent loss of moisture. This latter technique is worthwhile following when transplanting at any season.

After the plant is in the ground (or before, if you wish), cut the top back one-fourth. This is a necessity with all deciduous species, but should not be done with evergreens. The purpose is to reduce the plant's water requirements during its first year of growth.

If the plant is large, it should be supported against winds and heavy snow. Single-stemmed plants, such as young fruits, can be wired to a stout stake driven deep into the ground about 4 in. from the trunk. (Be careful not to injure the roots; put the stake in before the planting hole is completely filled.) Somewhat larger single-stemmed plants may require two stakes. Conifers and very large deciduous plants are best held by three guy wires, which should extend from well up on the trunk to strong stakes driven into the ground in an equilateral triangle 6 or more ft. from the trunk. In all cases, the wire around the stem should be covered with a short length of hose to prevent it from cutting into the wood. Don't remove the supports for about two years.

How to Plant a Hedge

In planting a hedge of privet (or other deciduous hedges which are sold with bare roots), dig a trench and set in the plants at 9- to 12-in. intervals. Use two- or three-year-old plants, and plant them about 2 in. deeper than they formerly grew. Cut the branches back to 4-in. stubs. If the hedge is started in the spring, you may cut it each time new growth is 4 to 6 in. long during the summer (up to Labor Day). Let the new shoots make three to six nodes (joints) and then cut them back to half. This forces branching. Prune so sides slope inward toward the top of the hedge.

Evergreens for hedges should be balled and burlapped. Although they, too, can be set into a trench, it is easier to dig individual holes—12 to 24 in. apart if you intend to keep the hedge low; up to 36 in. apart if you let the hedge go to 6 ft. or thereabouts. Evergreens should be set at the depth they previously grew. Do not clip them until they are making strong growth.

No matter which plants are used in a hedge, they should always be trimmed so they are wider at the bottom than at the top. This assures that the lower branches receive enough light to leaf out and grow. If a hedge is allowed to become wider at the top than at the bottom, growth at the base soon becomes sparse and then usually dies out altogether.

Mulching for Better Growth

After you do all the right spadework in planting or transplanting, one final step in the right direction is to apply a mulch. This means a layer of loose material applied to the soil surface in the vicinity of growing plants. In summer, it stabilizes soil temperature, conserves soil moisture

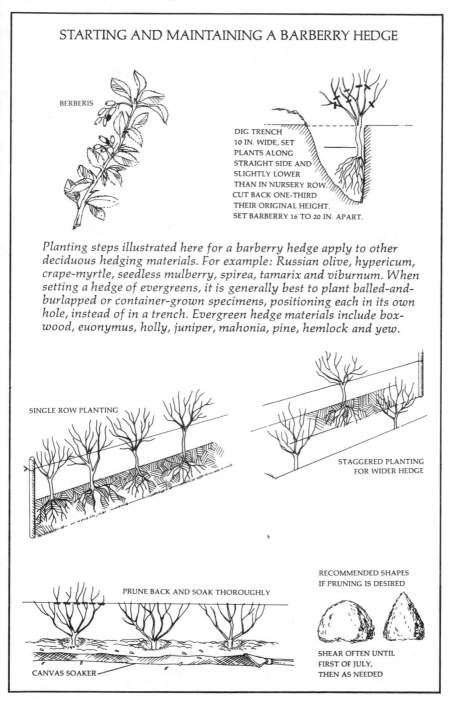

STARTING AND MAINTAINING A BARBERRY HEDGE

BERBERIS

DIG TRENCH 10 IN. WIDE, SET PLANTS ALONG STRAIGHT SIDE AND SLIGHTLY LOWER THAN IN NURSERY ROW. CUT BACK ONE-THIRD THEIR ORIGINAL HEIGHT. SET BARBERRY 16 TO 20 IN. APART.

Planting steps illustrated here for a barberry hedge apply to other deciduous hedging materials. For example: Russian olive, hypericum, crape-myrtle, seedless mulberry, spirea, tamarix and viburnum. When setting a hedge of evergreens, it is generally best to plant balled-and-burlapped or container-grown specimens, positioning each in its own hole, instead of in a trench. Evergreen hedge materials include boxwood, euonymus, holly, juniper, mahonia, pine, hemlock and yew.

SINGLE ROW PLANTING

STAGGERED PLANTING FOR WIDER HEDGE

PRUNE BACK AND SOAK THOROUGHLY

CANVAS SOAKER

RECOMMENDED SHAPES IF PRUNING IS DESIRED

SHEAR OFTEN UNTIL FIRST OF JULY, THEN AS NEEDED

ABOVE: *Roses mulched with buckwheat hulls. Readily available at garden-supply centers, the hulls are light, but resistant to wind. Color is close to that of soil, and this makes them an attractive mulch for use in borders.*

RIGHT: *Black plastic mulch, laid a few yards at a time, has holes punched in it to allow air to circulate beneath and water to penetrate. Weeds rarely come through holes. Plastic is covered with grass clippings, to give a more natural look.*

and keeps down weeds. In winter and spring, it prevents heaving of the soil from alternate freezing and thawing; through the year it increases the humus content of the soil. Not all mulches accomplish all these things with the same degree of success. Some are better for one purpose; some for others.

The following materials are among those most frequently used as surface mulches.

Dust. The top 1 to 2 in. of the garden are kept pulverized by regular cultivation to prevent the escape of moisture.

Leaves. Primarily used for holding in moisture and frost. Oak leaves are also used for increasing soil acidity beneath ericaceous plants. Leaves are a good mulching agent because they eventually decay and add humus to the soil. However, they may need to be weighted down with branches to prevent their blowing away. Also, leaves should not be allowed to remain indefinitely around herbaceous plants; if the mulch stays frozen late into the spring, it may cause plant crowns to rot. Shredded leaves permit better penetration of moisture and do not blow away so easily.

Pine boughs. These are a useful winter mulch to keep beds of perennial bulbs from heaving or to protect the roots of shrubs and young trees.

Straw. Primarily used for mulching strawberry beds in order to control weeds, retain moisture and keep the berries on the ground from being spattered with mud during rains.

Salt-marsh hay. A very good mulch for the conservation of moisture. Widely used on pansy beds in winter. It's cleaner than leaves, won't blow around so much or pack so tightly around plants, is weed-free and slow to decompose.

Chopped alfalfa hay. In addition to mulching qualities similar to other hay, this one decomposes quite rapidly, adding humus to the soil.

Pine needles. An excellent, airy mulch for any use. It also increases soil acidity when left to decompose around rhododendrons, laurel and similar plants.

Grass cuttings. Dry too rapidly in the sun to be of use for very long, but are the most readily available material in many home gardens. When freshly cut and applied too thickly, they may heat up and cause burning.

Cornstalks. Be sure these are free of borers before using them. Used whole, crisscrossed, they make a fine nonpacking winter mulch; chopped, they're a year-round garden mulch.

Ground corncobs. These have many uses but are said to be especially beneficial to roses. There is a theory that they help prevent black spot on roses.

Bagasse (chopped sugarcane). The high water-retaining capacity of this material makes it an especially desirable summer mulch. It also breaks down satisfactorily to form humus.

Buckwheat hulls. One of the neatest and best summer mulching materials—loose, inert, slow to rot. Apply a 1- to 2-in. layer. As a winter mulch, it needs to be much deeper to be useful.

Peanut shells. Besides being an effective mulch, these are especially rich in nitrogen. They make an excellent fertilizer as they decompose.

Cocoa-bean hulls. An attractive dark brown mulch that does not blow in the wind and is easy to handle. When fresh, they smell of chocolate. Like all organic substances, they become a fertilizer as they disintegrate. They retain more than twice their weight in water. As a mulch the cocoa-bean hulls should be about 2 in. deep. A deeper application may injure some plants, such as rhododendron and tomatoes.

Rotted manure. Thoroughly composted cow and horse manure not only make an excellent mulch for almost every need, but serve the dual purpose of feeding the plants they mulch.

Wood chips and sawdust. These form a useful if not especially decorative mulch. They are particularly suitable as a mulch around rhododendrons, hollies and other broadleaf evergreens, although it is necessary to add supplementary nitrogen.

Shredded bark. Composed of conifer, redwood or mixed hardwood bark, several proprietary bark materials are widely distributed for general mulching use. Those consisting mainly of fir bark are least likely to harbor pests or diseases and break down more slowly than the others.

Stones and pebbles. These have the advantage of being a nearly permanent mulch. There is, however, some disintegration of the stones on the underside, enriching the soil. Excellent for both moisture retention and temperature control.

Tobacco stems. These provide a good source of potash as well as nitrogen and phosphorus when used as a mulch.

Spent hops. As a mulch, these have the disadvantage of having a brewery smell at first; however, it is quickly dissipated. They do not blow away and do retain moisture satisfactorily.

Shredded newspaper. This is a cheap and effective mulch, though not a handsome one. It is useful in keeping down weeds and conserving moisture, especially between rows in the vegetable garden. Its easy availability is a plus in its favor.

Synthetics. Special mulching paper, aluminum foil, fiber-glass mats and flexible plastics, such as black polyethylene film, are often used to conserve moisture and control weeds between vegetable rows. They can also be used to comparable advantage in home gardens. They may be cut to any shape to fit the planting layout.

When To Start a Lawn

In the best of all possible worlds, cool-climate grasses would be planted in the fall, so they would be well rooted by winter and ready to rise in good health when called forth by the lengthening days of spring.

Since soils are generally more workable in the autumn (not as sticky and soggy as in spring), it is a good idea to sow the bluegrasses even if temperatures have become too low for sprouting. The seed will remain unharmed through winter, ready to go with the first suitable weather of spring. If some of the seed should wash away, it is reasonably easy to repair damaged spots by an inexpensive overseeding.

In warm climates, the grass ideally would be set out in early spring or, later, at the beginning of the summer rainy season. But from a practical point of view, lawns are usually planted when they are needed. Few people are willing to live through a season of dirt and dust around a new house, waiting for the perfect season to plant the grass. If you are willing to take the extra care, primarily in watering, you can start a lawn almost any time during the growing season.

The easiest way to start an off-season lawn, in any climate, is to use sod instead of seed, sprigs or stolons. Strips or squares of rooted grass, weed-free and fresh from the growing fields, are brought in and laid like a carpet on the prepared ground. On earth that is bare in the morning, there can be a perfect lawn in the afternoon.

How To Grade the Land

Grading is an integral part of the overall planning of walks, drives, walls and terraces. In grading the land, think of how the water will move across the surface. There should be no low places where it will accumulate in puddles. The slopes should be gentle, so it will penetrate the root area before it runs off.

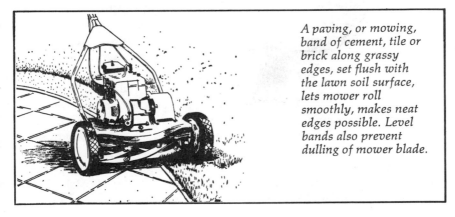

A paving, or mowing, band of cement, tile or brick along grassy edges, set flush with the lawn soil surface, lets mower roll smoothly, makes neat edges possible. Level bands also prevent dulling of mower blade.

A mowing band eliminates time-consuming hand-trimming and protects tree bark from mower damage. Here, stones inside the band keep weeds from growing around the trunk and preserve soil moisture.

The lawn should always slope away from the house. The grass should be level with drives and walks, to make the edges easier to trim. If existing trees are too high above the level of the lawn-to-be, retaining walls can be built and the lawn lowered. If the trees are too low, a tree-well can be built and the surrounding lawn raised to a grade that will drain properly.

It may be necessary to use underground drainage tile to divert roof water to storm drains or dry wells. Unavoidable low spots can also be drained into lower dry wells.

If a sprinkler system is to be installed—and this is indeed a labor saver—it should be done in conjunction with the basic grading.

Soils for Healthy Turf

In building a lawn we think first of the soil and seedbed, then of the kind of grass we are to plant and aids to its early establishment. Even a poor soil, properly fertilized and watered, can support a good growth of grass. And this grass in turn improves the soil as its myriad small roots permeate anything from tight clay to loose sand.

This is not to gainsay the desirability of a rich topsoil of good structure. And preparing a deep seedbed is your last chance for doing something "down under." Actually structure is more important than richness, since by use of plant foods the fertility level can be improved readily. But if the soil is such that water will not penetrate, or if the soil is so sandy that it will not hold much moisture, added effort to supply fertilizer and water will be necessary. Thus one would prefer friable soil, containing at least moderate percentages of organic matter and clay, but loose enough to accept sprinkling at the rate of at least an inch or so of water per hour.

The ground in which a lawn is to be planted should be cultivated thoroughly to a depth of six to ten inches.

Heavy (clay) soil and light (sandy) soil can be improved by mixing in two to four bales of peat moss per 1,000 square feet of area. Vermiculite, sawdust, composted leaves, peat humus or other organic matter may also be used. This humus-forming material gives body to the sandy soil, and will lighten soil that has too much clay.

Other materials needed to improve the soil can be applied and worked in at the same time. In this way, topsoil can be practically made to order, and it will probably be better and less expensive than any you buy. Following are two of the ingredients that may be needed to improve the soil.

Lime. In much the same way as peat moss, lime can improve the structure of soils that are too light or too heavy. It is also used to regulate the acid-alkaline balance, which is so important in the growing of grass. This balance is indicated by the symbol pH. On a graded scale from 0 to 14, 7 is neutral. Numbers above 7 indicate alkalinity. Lawn grasses will grow in a wider range than is usually realized, but a slightly acid condition—from pH 6.0 to 6.9—is best for most of them. To determine the pH of your soil, use a home-testing kit, or send a sample to your State Experiment Station. Unless the soil is definitely alkaline, an application of about 70 pounds of ground limestone to 1,000 square feet would be helpful.

Phosphorus. Most soils are deficient in phosphorus, which, along with nitrogen and potassium, is required for the growth of plants. Because it moves very slowly through the ground and is available to roots only in its immediate area, it should be mixed in thoroughly before planting. A standard recommendation is 50 pounds of superphosphate per 1,000 square feet.

Changes of lawn level in the garden or storage areas should have ramps instead of steps or rocky paths, so machine's power can take it anywhere. Paths and gates through which mower will pass should be sized to fit.

Soil Compaction

Sandy light soils generally need little preparation. They can be worked wet or dry, don't compact under the compression from delivery trucks or tillage. Clays and heavier soils should be worked only at favorable moisture content—this usually is when slightly dry, several days after rain or sprinkling. Unfortunately the exigencies of a building program put heavy equipment on the lawn-to-be wet or dry, packing the soil.

In the latter instance the first step is to loosen compacted soil to a depth of several inches. In a mechanical age this is usually handled on a contract basis, by tractor and agricultural disk. If the homeowner wants to do it himself it can be done with a rotary tiller or by hand-spading.

Tilling for Best Soil Preparation

The soil tillage will mix the layers that result from sand left by the builder or soil bulldozed from a different area. This mixing is important, for layers of differing texture will forever cause trouble by interfering with solution movement and root penetration. So be certain that the soil and bulk additions (such as peat) are evenly mixed.

There is a mistaken idea that the more the soil is pulverized in seedbed preparation, the better. Actually this is not the case. A pebbled surface, with soil chunks ranging from pea to golf-ball size, is usually preferable to a dust-fine one. The reason is that seeds can lodge among these soil chunks, chinks and crevices, finding humid protected niches in which to get a fast start. Dusty surfaces will wash, or pack, upon first watering, most certainly not accept water well, maybe crust so hard that air cannot get to the seed or the seedling break through the crust to daylight. Save yourself some expense by not refining the seedbed surface excessively. Rain or watering will soon enough level the soil to a reasonably smooth surface.

Though we will have a good bit to say about seeding later, let's presume for a moment now that the lawn has been seeded. The immediate need then is for humidity but no soil wash. A sensible solution is to mulch the seedbed.

Mulching To Encourage Sprouting

Many different materials can be used as mulch. Probably the most common are straw and sphagnum peat moss. Of course, grass clippings, wood chips, even pebbles or ground corncobs may find service as a seedbed cover. A mulch should not be so thick as to smother the grass—three or four straws deep with straw, or about a quarter of an inch of peat moss. Such mulches may be left in place to decay, for they will soon be obscured by the thriving young grass seedlings.

Mulches, by holding humidity, hasten grass sprouting. They also prevent soil wash and loss of seed. The combination of mulch and moderate warmth (among autumn's blessings in the northern part of the country) is ideal for starting seed. With mulch, sprinkling need not be so frequent as might be required for unprotected soil. With or without mulch, for a quick grass cover, the soil surface must not be allowed to dry out completely. Of course, seed not started can remain indefinitely in the seedbed.

The First Mowing

If the lawn has enough food, water and sunlight, it should show a welcome tinge of green in about a week. When the grass is 2 to 2½ inches high, it should be cut back to about 1½ inches. Mow with a *sharp* blade, and only when perfectly dry. Cut as often as necessary to maintain the right height, and water at least once a week if there is no rain.

Apply the water slowly so it will not run off the surface. To encourage deep rooting, the water should penetrate to 6 inches or so. If the clippings are long, remove them so they will not mat down and keep air and water from reaching the root area.

The First Feeding

Spring-planted lawns will need added fertilizer in early fall. Fall-planted lawns will need it in the spring.

The first feeding of a newly planted bluegrass lawn (with one of the many balanced lawn foods) is best applied in two light applications about two weeks apart. This will reduce the chance of "burning" the grass by overfeeding.

Some of the best lawn foods contain urea-form nitrogen, which is released slowly over a long period of time. This is especially helpful in establishing new lawns.

Should you decide to turn your lawn-making over to a nurseryman or landscape contractor, ask to see the work they have done, and talk to the owners before signing a contract.

The price quoted usually includes a complete job. Such details as grading, tilling, seeding, fertilizing, and the kind and amount of seed to be used should all be specified in writing.

Guarantees for seeded lawns usually provide for a minimum of 80 per cent coverage of grass two to three weeks after sowing. Guarantees for sodded or sprigged lawns call for continuous growth until the first or second cutting.

Let's review the kinds of lawn grasses generally used. There is a confusing array of new selections and varieties, but these are representatives of only a few proved species. For Northern areas, started from seed, they are generally varieties of Kentucky bluegrass, red fescue or one of the bentgrasses. For Southern locations they are likely to be Bermuda, centipede or carpetgrass from seed; or St. Augustine, zoysia or special strains of Bermuda if hand-planted.

A Good Seed Mixture

It is possible to generalize about where desirable Northern lawn species are adapted. A good seed mixture for this section would ordinarily predominate in Kentucky bluegrass (including perhaps named strains if of proved local value), backed primarily by the red fescue group. Nurse grasses are best left out, since they compete rather strongly in the seedling stages with the more desirable grasses that one hopes to establish as quickly and efficiently as possible. Thus a quality seed mixture will contain little or no ryegrass, no Alta fescue or other hay grasses. Redtop is perhaps the most acceptable of temporary nurse grasses if any is to be used. But with the trend toward mulching, nurse grasses are finding a place less and less often.

Sowing Grass Seed

If the seedbed is well prepared, as detailed in a previous section, little seed is needed. There are, for example, over 2 million blueglass seeds to the pound—8 thousand potential plants per square foot when uniformly distributed at the 4-pound/M recommended rate (M signifies 1,000 square feet). Ordinarily none of the appliances available to the homeowner can spread less than two pounds of seed uniformly. Since seed cost is inconsequential compared to labor costs in making the lawn, two or three pounds of seed to insure good coverage are not amiss. Best means of application is with a spreader cart adjusted to distribute just the right amount of seed as one pushes it over the lawn area. Spreading half the seed in one direction, the other half at right angles, insures against missed areas.

Cyclone seeders, the wheeled type or with shoulder strap, will do a good job—although not with the exactness of a spreader. Hand-seeding is also possible, although the potential for uneven distribution is greater this way. Diluting the seed with an equal volume of cornmeal, dried soil or sand can help provide greater bulk for hand-seeding so that more uniform distribution is obtained. Distribute half the seed walking back and forth in one direction, the other half at right angles to this.

After seed has been sown distribute a mulch (as previously described) if at all possible. Wait for a good rain to start seeds off, but from then on sprinkle as necessary to keep soil surface moist (perhaps daily or twice daily, lightly, in the beginning) until grass is tall enough for mowing, and with enough root system to reach deep for its water.

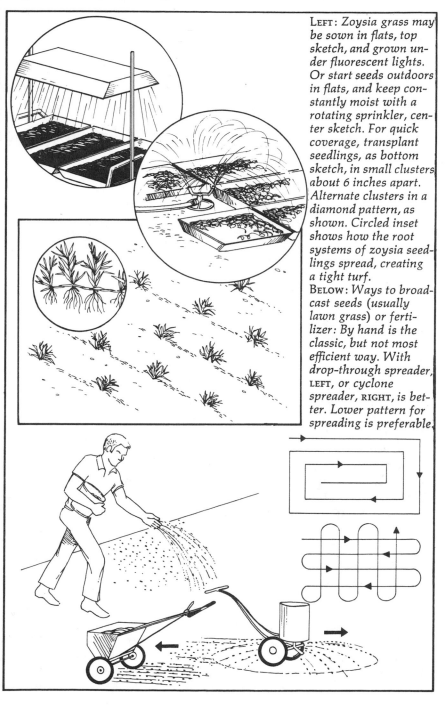

LEFT: *Zoysia grass may be sown in flats, top sketch, and grown under fluorescent lights. Or start seeds outdoors in flats, and keep constantly moist with a rotating sprinkler, center sketch. For quick coverage, transplant seedlings, as bottom sketch, in small clusters about 6 inches apart. Alternate clusters in a diamond pattern, as shown. Circled inset shows how the root systems of zoysia seedlings spread, creating a tight turf.*

BELOW: *Ways to broadcast seeds (usually lawn grass) or fertilizer: By hand is the classic, but not most efficient way. With drop-through spreader,* LEFT, *or cyclone spreader,* RIGHT, *is better. Lower pattern for spreading is preferable.*

5. How To Prune Almost Everything

When you take a piece of stem or root from a plant, you are pruning it. The whole point of pruning is to get more from the plant. The goal may be to make the plant bloom better, and, possibly, to set more and better fruit; or it may be to improve the shape of the plant or to make it more dense. If a plant is in poor health it may be cut back, first to remove diseased or infested portions and, second, to encourage fresh, healthy, new growth. Except for hedges and sheared specimens in truly formal gardens, there is no excuse at all for pruning to restrict the development of a plant. If a plant grows too large for its location, pruning will only reduce it to a formless leafy blob. Remove it and plant a new specimen that, when mature, will be suited to the site.

Generally I mean selective cutting of individual branches when I say "pruning," but shearing the hedge is a form of pruning. So are disbudding and pinching out. Also, when you cut flowers for the house or to remove spent blossoms from woody plants or herbaceous sorts, you are pruning, and you should make your cuts in such a way that the plant will quickly make more flowers and not be misshapen.

Pruning is a simple operation; many people make it difficult because they do not understand how plants grow. All growth comes from buds; buds at the tips of stems or buds along the sides of stems. Included in the latter class are buds at the base of the plant. True roots have no buds, but grow only from the tip outward. To shorten a branch (for any reason: health, to shorten for appearance, to gather a flower) follow down to a side (lateral) bud that points in the direction a new shoot should develop to make a properly shaped plant. The bud probably will be tucked in the crotch (axil) of a leaf. Make a clean, diagonal cut with a sharp tool directly above the bud. The face of the cut should slope away from the bud; the stub above the bud should be as short as possible without injuring the bud itself. Winter pruning takes the same technique; prune over the tree or shrub to remove too dense, interfering (rubbing or crowding) or injured twigs and branches. When you are through, the plant ought to have exactly the same general shape as before, but be more open, and possibly somewhat shorter. To achieve this as you prune, step back occasionally to look at the effect you have achieved so far. Are you maintaining a natural form for the specimen? If so, proceed. If you are overcutting, go easier on the remainder of the plant.

Never resort to butchery. Just because people with pruning equipment and trucks stop around the neighborhood and cut the tops from shade trees (often called "dehorning," a fair term for a horrible practice), chop flowering bushes to the ground and "prune" needle evergreens with a hedge shears, is no reason to adopt such poor practices. When a high tree needs top work (they seldom do, except to repair storm damage or to lighten the crown of overgrowth) call in a trained specialist. He will drop-prune the tree. That means he will selectively remove branches, dropping back on each limb to a crotch to make his cut. When he is through he may have removed as much as one-third of the crown of the tree, but you will see no difference in the shape of the tree (it will be considerably less dense, though) and you will see no stubs, only a number of painted cuts almost paralleling remaining branches. When you need to do something about overgrown lilacs, mock-orange or other flowering bushes, do it over a period of two or three years. The plants will suffer less and will maintain a reasonably good appearance during the job.

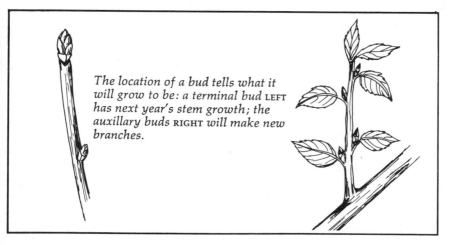

The location of a bud tells what it will grow to be: a terminal bud LEFT has next year's stem growth; the auxillary buds RIGHT will make new branches.

Keep several generalities in mind as you prune; they guide your thinking, and, accordingly, your pruning tool.

1. Pruning during the dormant season results in a vigorous burst of growth (often, overgrowth) the following spring. Pruning during early summer tends to inhibit much replacement growth and it encourages the development of flower buds.

2. Use the proper tool for the job. If the branch is smaller than your middle finger, a hand pruner (properly, secateurs) is right; from finger-sized to garden-hose-size branches you ought to reach for the lopping shears; very hard wood, or branches larger than the hose, ought to be sawed with a pruning saw. You will need one small, curved and tapered pruning saw—ideal for slipping into the center of a crowded forsythia to take out a few of the oldest canes at the ground line—and a curved, or straight, larger saw for removing tree limbs.

3. Make all cuts clean, as close to the main stem or supporting branch as possible, and, always, just above a bud. Leave no stubs.

4. When the face of a cut is larger than a penny, coat it with tree-wound dressing. There are two sorts: One is a thick, sticky paste and you apply it with a wooden plant label or a very stiff brush. The other is a thinner preparation that comes in an aerosol can. Avoid modern household paints, as they may contain solvents that would injure plant tissues and discourage healing.

5. When removing limbs of any size, do it piecemeal. Well away from the crotch make an undercut (saw from the bottom upward) a fourth of the way through the limb; then overcut to drop the branch. Now you have to remove the stub; follow the same procedure, taking care to match up your cuts. If the surface of the cut is not quite smooth (rough wood often harbors decay organisms, even when painted) use a draw knife to smooth it. Then paint. I insist on this technique because it is so easy to achieve a tear-down if a branch is just cut off any old way. A tear-down is a wound made when a strip of bark is torn away with the falling branch.

6. Prune so bleeding is kept to a minimum. Almost all woody plants will bleed if pruned in late winter or early spring. Prune in early summer when growth has almost stopped, or early in winter. Maple, walnut, yellowwood, beech, birch and a few other species are notorious "bleeders" and are safest pruned in the dead of summer.

7. If a plant that you are pruning is diseased, dip your pruning tool in denatured alcohol after every cut you make.

Hedges. Sheared hedges need to be clipped with a sharp hedge shears or electric tool every time the new growth reaches 2 or 3 inches; otherwise, the hedge soon looks ragged. Do the job correctly; stretch a guiding cord

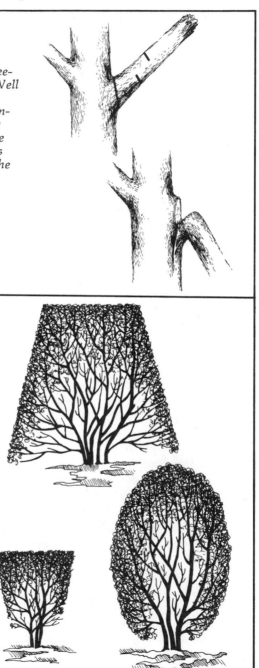

Right, top, and wrong, bottom, way to remove a tree limb. Top sketch shows three-cut system recommended. Well away from the crotch, saw from the bottom upward (undercut) a quarter of the way through the limb or until the saw binds. The second cut is made two inches out from the first. Cut until the limb falls. Bark and wood that splinter and tear will tear back only as far as first cut, the undercut. Remove stub, as long bar shows. Bottom sketch, tear-down caused by one-cut pruning.

Sketch, top, shows right way to prune a hedge. Bevel hedge so bottom is half again as wide as the top. This allows light to reach clear to the base of the hedge on both sides; thus leaves will be produced all the way down. Sketch, bottom left, shows hedge pruned so top is wider than bottom; this keeps light from reaching hedge bottom and usually results, as here, in spindly bottom growth with few leaves. Sketch, bottom right, of shrub in "natural" shape. To keep trim, clip when new growth reaches 2 to 3 inches.

along both upper edges of the hedge so the surface is absolutely level and the edges square. Move the cords to the bottom and level the sides. A well-sited hedge of vigorous leafy plants such as privet or barberry can be trimmed with vertical sides and hold its foliage right to the bottom. But it is far better to bevel the hedge so the bottom is half again as wide as the top. This allows light to reach clear to the base of the hedge on both sides, and leaves will go all the way down. If all the plants in a deciduous hedge are alive but perhaps weak and bare at the base, the hedge can be saved. For one season cultivate along the sides and fertilize in late winter and mid-spring. The following spring before buds begin to break, cut the hedge to the ground, or at least to very short stubs. As new growth develops, let the shoots reach 10 inches or so, then cut them back to half. Keep this up all summer, gradually building the hedge back to a dense barrier. It will take a few years to get it up to waist height. Needle and broadleaf evergreen hedges that have deteriorated should be replaced.

Flowering bushes. Prune over your shrubberies throughout the year and you never will be faced with a massive overhaul job. In late winter bring in branches of forsythia, Japanese quince, bridal-wreath spirea and others to force for blossoms; take these branches where the plant is out of shape or crowded. In summer bring in flowering sprays the same way. When the spring rush is past, with a sharp, narrow spade remove almost all of the underground sprouts that come up around the base of older shrubs. At the same time, watch for those long, unbranched, whippy shoots that spring from the base or low in the older branches. These still will be tender and soft; cut them back to one or two leaves (or pairs of leaves, if the foliage is opposite). Come back in a month and pinch again. In the dead of winter, with your narrow little pruning saw take out one-fourth or less of the oldest canes in bushes that are more than five years old. This keeps new wood coming on. If you have time, nip off spent flower heads as flowering shrubs go out of bloom—a nice idea with valuable rhododendrons and the newest lilacs, but impossible in most gardens save with a few specimen plants.

Broadleaf evergreens. Hollies, *Euonymus* species and cultivars, mahonias, aucuba and the cherry-laurels (to name a few) are vigorous broadleaf evergreens that may be trimmed freely. Theoretically, these should be pruned as necessary to keep them dense and in good health, just as the spring growth hardens. And it is a good idea to do a fair amount of pruning and pinching at that time. But think of the value of the cut-away branches for home decorating. So long as the temperature is above freezing, you can go out quite safely in late November or early

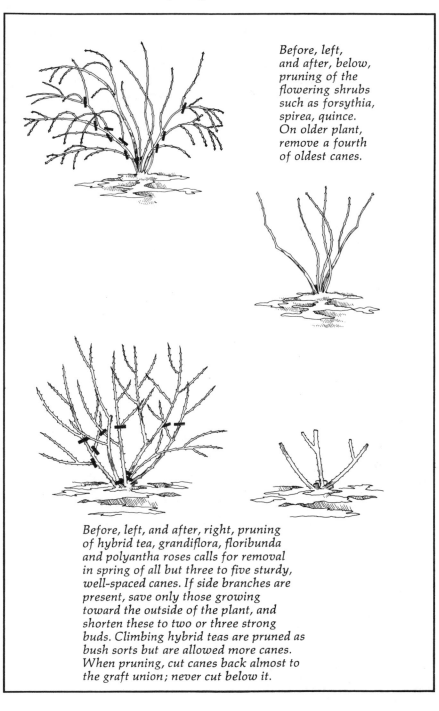

Before, left,
and after, below,
pruning of the
flowering shrubs
such as forsythia,
spirea, quince.
On older plant,
remove a fourth
of oldest canes.

Before, left, and after, right, pruning
of hybrid tea, grandiflora, floribunda
and polyantha roses calls for removal
in spring of all but three to five sturdy,
well-spaced canes. If side branches are
present, save only those growing
toward the outside of the plant, and
shorten these to two or three strong
buds. Climbing hybrid teas are pruned as
bush sorts but are allowed more canes.
When pruning, cut canes back almost to
the graft union; never cut below it.

December and do a pruning job aimed at properly shaping the plants, but with an eye toward handsome sprays for holiday decor. Try to make all cuts face inward, so the garden is not marred for the rest of winter by exposed, white patches of bare wood. Less vigorous broadleaf evergreens are best pinched, not pruned at all, or rarely. As rhododendrons and semi-evergreen azaleas go out of flower and the new shoots break beneath the spent blossom cluster, nip out this old flower head and pinch the new shoots below where they have made three or four leaves. This will prevent leggy overgrowth, and it limits pruning to a once-a-year proposition. Experts at the Arnold Arboretum have shown that it is quite possible to renew old rhododendrons by bringing the plants into strong growth by cultivating, mulching and feeding; then large branches may be sawed out at the base of the plant, and soon new growth appears. Ideally, such an overhaul should be spread over two or three years and carried out in spring as the plants normally would begin to blossom. Azaleas may be pruned almost any time, as they are well furnished with latent buds on all old stems. But for the sake of next year's bloom, prune in late spring or early summer. Very old bushes should be brought into prime condition by fertilizing and mulching prior to heavy pruning intended for renewal.

Some broadleaf evergreens, particularly more primitive ones such as the magnolias, require careful pruning of newly developed shoots while plants are young. Older wood does not heal well when cut. Citrus species also are included in this category. Pinching and light pruning of

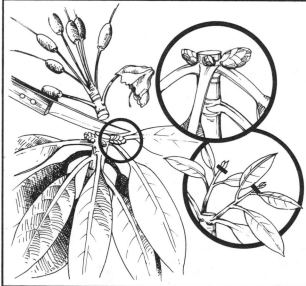

Prune spent flower heads to force development of new buds for heavier bloom next year (left, top right). Pinching spring growth increases flowers, too (lower right).

Prune needle evergreens, such as Abies, *back far enough to prevent unsightly stubs from showing after trimming.*

half-ripe new growth in early summer are most successful. If you have to saw off a branch, do it in midsummer and come back to repaint the scar two or three times over the next 18 months.

Needle evergreens. Junipers, arborvitae and yews may be pruned any time and at almost any place. With upright junipers, follow along the branch that needs to be shortened until you come to a side shoot lying on top of it, or inside of it. Select a side shoot that exactly parallels the unwanted branch. Slip your clippers under this little branch and make a clean cut. On a spreading juniper, place the cut so that it will face downward and no one will know that a cut has been made. The tiny wisp of greenery left soon will stiffen up and begin to replace the branch you have removed. On upright plants, the cut will show, but only briefly, as new growth soon will hide it. *Never* prune junipers and yews with hedge shears unless the plants are part of a formal hedge. To preserve those graceful, natural lines, remove part of the growth at random over the plant. As yews and arborvitae tend to replace branches quickly, and as both have latent buds buried in the bark, you can make your cuts almost anywhere. Just take care to maintain the natural form of the plant.

Specimen hemlocks, firs, spruces and Douglas firs should be left untouched if possible. City gardeners delight in the beautiful forms and color of these when they see knee- to waist-high plants in the nursery and they carry them home. Soon the plant begins to grow vigorously and it must be butchered or cut down. Avoid this problem by searching out the specialty nursery companies that sell the many miniature forms of these evergreens. As they grow extremely slowly and are tricky to propagate, the cost is high; but then you have a specimen that will probably outlive your house and still be in proportion to the garden.

Pines may be pruned so long as you have a high enough ladder to be able to work over the entire tree. In spring the new growth, called a "candle," grows at the ends of all branches. Generally there is a central candle surrounded by several slightly smaller ones. You must preserve this size relationship. If you cut the central candle back half, cut the side ones surrounding it to one-third. If you wish to almost halt the growth of the tree, you may cut all central candles to two or three needle clusters, and the side candles to one or two needle clusters. Do this pruning when the candles are developed enough so that the needles are beginning to break from their papery sheaths, but before they are fully expanded. A sharp knife is the best tool. Avoid clipping new needles, as the tree will look bobtailed for the next two or three years if new growth is injured. Needless to say, you must work over the entire tree from top to bottom.

Fruit trees. Look at commercial plantings of fruit trees in your area to determine the form used successfully by commercial people. Apple trees may be pruned to a modified leader system, where a strongly controlled central trunk surrounded by almost equally strong lateral branches makes the scaffold. The other system used for apples is the open-center system, where there is no leader at all but several strong branches at almost the same point, low on the trunk, to form a sort of bowl-shaped scaffold. These same systems are used for peach, apricot and nectarine,

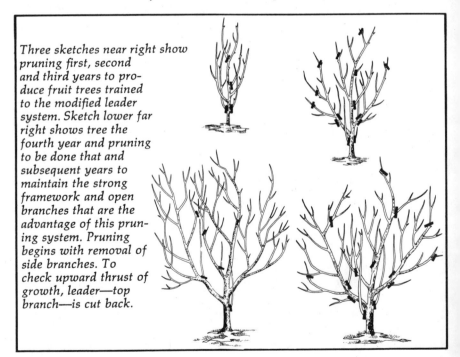

Three sketches near right show pruning first, second and third years to produce fruit trees trained to the modified leader system. Sketch lower far right shows tree the fourth year and pruning to be done that and subsequent years to maintain the strong framework and open branches that are the advantage of this pruning system. Pruning begins with removal of side branches. To check upward thrust of growth, leader—top branch—is cut back.

though the open-center form is far more common and produces better-colored fruit. Plum trees receive a minimum of pruning, just enough to keep them relatively open in the center, and with well-spaced main branches insuring good ventilation throughout the tree and a well-balanced crown. Sour cherries are pruned similarly, and sweet cherries are pruned scarcely at all. All of the cherries and plums are likely to bleed or ooze gum where branches over a year old are removed, so corrective pruning is almost impossible.

The trick in creating first-class fruit trees is to start with a scarcely branched or unbranched (maiden) switch. Determine the pattern it is to take and prune accordingly. Your County Extension Agent will supply pamphlets on proper pruning for fruit trees in your area. While fruit trees are young, do as much pruning as possible in midsummer. When they have come into bearing, you will be able to remove excess leafy growth in summer but major shaping and balancing will have to be done during the winter months after a few hard freezes.

Pears are a sort of law unto themselves. If you wish to prune and pinch frequently throughout the growing season, you can shape them as open-centered or as modified-leader trees. Otherwise, let them have a leader but prune sufficiently often to prevent too much growth in any season and shorten all side branches frequently.

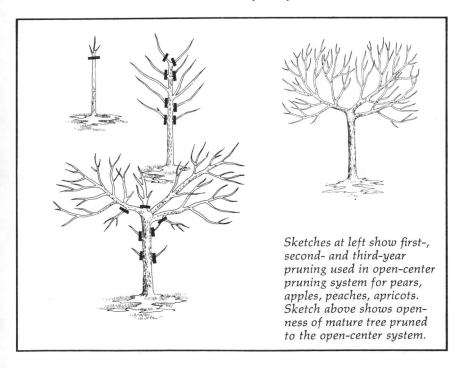

Sketches at left show first-, second- and third-year pruning used in open-center pruning system for pears, apples, peaches, apricots. Sketch above shows openness of mature tree pruned to the open-center system.

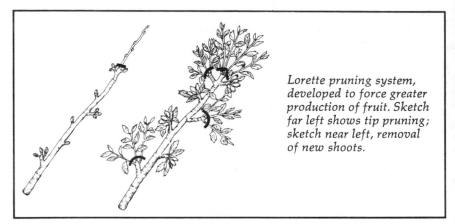

Lorette pruning system, developed to force greater production of fruit. Sketch far left shows tip pruning; sketch near left, removal of new shoots.

Lorette pruning. A pruning system used by professional growers to improve production of orchard fruits, in particular apples and pears, is the Lorette pruning system. Most espaliers are pruned according to this method.

The Lorette system is designed to encourage "fruiting spurs." Some varieties make natural fruiting spurs freely, but pruning encourages (or creates) more spurs and therefore improves fruit production. Spurs are short, stubby branchlets each of which usually carries one or more clusters of fruit buds.

The Lorette system is based on summer pruning though the leaders are cut back in the spring. All lateral shoots more than 12 inches long are removed toward the end of June, cut back cleanly to a basal cluster of leaves, where the dormant and invisible "eyes" that will form fruiting spurs are situated. During the rest of the summer, the remaining lateral shoots, whether they come from the branch itself or from these spurs, are cut back to the first cluster of leaves as they grow out to 12 inches. Those shoots that don't grow to 12 inches by fall can be cut back then unless they carry fat little buds at the ends. Shoots 6 inches or so long often bear fruit at the tips.

Bark-ringing fruit trees. An age-old technique used by orchardists to discourage too much leafy growth at the expense of fruit production. Largely limited to apples and pears, in mid-spring an inch-wide strip of bark is removed from the trunk of the tree halfway around. This girdling effect decreases the flow of photosynthetic nutrients from the leaves to the roots; the starved roots take in less water and minerals, and reduced leafy growth—usually with increased flower production—results. To achieve the same result in bark-sensitive stone fruits, resort to root pruning.

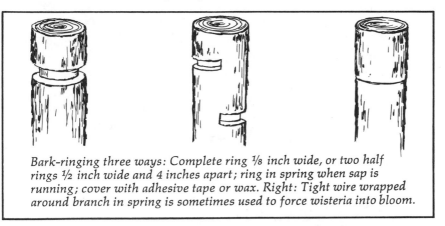

Bark-ringing three ways: Complete ring ⅛ inch wide, or two half rings ½ inch wide and 4 inches apart; ring in spring when sap is running; cover with adhesive tape or wax. Right: Tight wire wrapped around branch in spring is sometimes used to force wisteria into bloom.

Bramble fruits. Blackberries, raspberries, dewberries and all their relatives bear the best fruit on year-old shoots. Determine if your plants are spring-bearing or everbearing. If spring-bearing, remove the spent canes as the crop finishes in early summer. At this same time a good crop of new canes should be growing from below. Use a cane hook or a heavy knife to remove all but three to five of the strongest, best-placed ones by making a clean cut at the stump. It is a good idea to spray these cuts, if possible, with tree-wound dressing. If the new growth is overly vigorous, top it at a convenient picking height. If not, tie to prevent wind whipping over winter. Early next spring as buds begin to swell, cut back to picking height; strong side shoots will break, and these will bear fruit.

If your plants are everbearing, you should leave the fruit-bearing canes until the end of summer to encourage that choice early-fall crop of berries. This makes tending the brambles over summer somewhat difficult, because you have to work around the old canes while developing the new ones.

Blueberries, gooseberries and currants. Prune these so there is about the same amount of well-spaced one-, two- and three-year-old wood. Nothing older. This year's growth bears no fruit. Second-year branches bear the main crop, third-year branches also bear very well, but are becoming too woody. Older wood will fruit, but when old wood is present, not much vigorous new growth breaks and the plants tend to deteriorate. Prune currants and gooseberries in late winter; prune blueberries in midsummer or later.

Grapes. Consult your County Extension Agent for specialized instructions that match local conditions. Generally speaking, the standard

Before, left, and after, right, pruning of blueberries and huckleberries. After harvest, shorten some current-season canes to induce branching, and thin out laterals that have borne the season's crop. Remove surplus low branches and all weak wood. One third of these brambles should be removed each year.

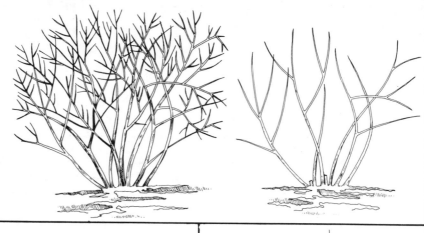

Pruning red raspberries. Black canes are old wood, white ones new wood. Leave three to five new canes. Bars show removal of old wood after harvest and where to prune new growth.

Pruning system for gooseberries and red and white currants is to cut to the ground all three-year-old wood before harvest and to pick from the cut canes. Berries from one- and two-year-old wood are then harvested on the bush and all but three canes of each are cut to the ground. Prune away all but three or four of the sturdiest of current year's growth. Bars show where to remove older canes and newest shoots of these bramble fruits.

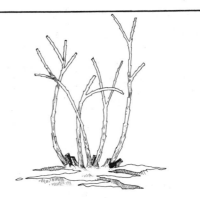

Before, LEFT, and after, RIGHT, pruning black and purple raspberries, blackberries, dewberries, youngberries, boysenberries. After harvest, remove canes that fruited, all but three to five new ones.

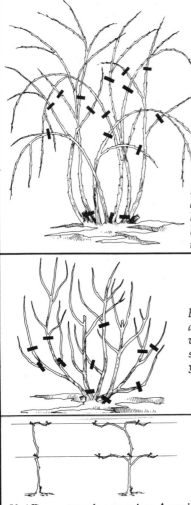

Black-currant bush is pruned to retain equal amounts of one-, two- and three-year-old wood. This year's growth bears no fruit; second-year canes bear main crop; three-year-old wood also bears well.

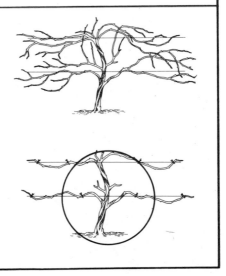

Kniffin system for pruning American grapevines, which fruit on previous year's wood. Sketches, above left, show training young vine to wire and pruning during first winter's dormant period. Sketch, upper right, shows mature vine's summer growth. To prepare for pruning, tag four of strongest shoots and four more close by. In winter, cut these back so vine has four short and four long canes, as lower sketch.

grapevines are trellis-grown with a main trunk and two or four permanent lateral arms that produce carefully spaced and limited year-old
fruiting branches. The Southern-type grapes, muscadines and scupper-
nongs, grow rangier. They have a lot more vine and longer year-old
fruiting canes. Vinifera (European wine grapes) vines are pruned to a
stump, from which come several fruiting canes in the spring—possible
as these fruit on the current year's wood. All grapes are pruned in late
winter when the plants are at maximum dormancy. Avoid summer
pruning as much as possible. A spring-pruned grape may bleed to death.

Roses. In spring cut hybrid teas, grandifloras, floribundas and poly-
anthas back to healthy, undiscolored wood with sound pith. This may
mean cutting almost to the graft union (be careful not to cut below it)
but keep as much healthy wood as possible. Retain three to five sturdy
well-spaced canes and remove spindly, crowded or injured ones. If side
branches are present, save only those growing toward the outside of the
plant, and shorten these to two or three strong buds. Until midsummer,
pick your roses with short stems, and when you cut a spent flower or
take blooms for the house, cut to the uppermost leaf with five leaflets
that points toward the outside of the bush. This retains the maximum
number of blossom-producing buds and keeps the plant open in the
center. In the fall, before putting the roses to bed for the winter, pull the
canes loosely together and tie them with a piece of soft cord; if you live
in a very windy area, reduce the canes to about 30 inches after the leaves
are dried by repeated frosts. Fall pruning is touchy, as it may stimulate
growth during winter.

Climbing hybrid teas and their relatives are pruned exactly like
bush sorts except that you make extra effort to maintain as much
healthy cane as possible. The true climbers bred from *Rosa wichuraiana*
bloom on last year's canes; treat them like raspberries. In spring clip out
winter-injured wood as lightly as possible. As canes finish flowering,
remove them at the base and encourage the strong new shoots that
break from low on the plant. Most of this group of roses will make some
flowers on older wood but too much old wood reduces production of
vigorous new shoots.

The ramblers are a major trial if properly maintained. As the
blooms fade, remove all the canes from the trellis and lay them out
across the lawn. Cut each back to a strong basal bud; this bud will grow
to make a replacement cane during the summer. If too many canes
appear, remove a suitable number of the crowded and weak ones while
they are small.

Treat shrub roses as you would any flowering bush. Each winter
consider the removal of one or two of the oldest, woodiest canes in the

center of the clump and with a sharp spade remove crowded or weak new shoots. During summer reach in with the clippers to nip back new basal shoots to two or three leaves.

Garden climbers and creepers. Honeysuckle, wisteria, trumpet vine and the like all need attention from time to time. Do not wait until the plant is a hopeless tangle. While it is young, train into a neat, well-spaced pattern. Then, every year or two, during the plant's dormant period, prune out twiggy growth, overcrowded shoots and dead wood. During the growing season immediately clip off any tendril that pulls away from the support or hangs downward.

Clematis are a special case. Some bloom best on new wood, some on older wood and some on both. Lists of clematis cultivars indicating how they flower and including instructions relating to the pruning of that group are all very well for the clematis expert, but the average gardener will do well to leave his clematis as much to itself as possible. In late winter it is advisable to prune out some of the tangle to achieve a neat appearing plant. After new growth is well along in early spring, prune out any dead or weak wood. As flowers fade during summer, nip off overly vigorous or badly placed tendrils. You may not have the largest flowers possible using this method but you have a large, vigorously blooming specimen.

How To Pinch Off and Pinch Out

When you remove, with thumb and forefinger, a flower or leaf bud to encourage better-shaped plants, larger or later blooms, you are "pinch-

Sketch at top shows where to pinch out tips of young seedlings to encourage bushiness. Black bars in lower sketch indicate where to cut back bloomed-out petunias in late summer, to produce fresh, sturdy growth that will give end-of-season bloom.

ing" in the gardener's terms. Pinching is most often done to plants in the seedling stage to encourage branching or development of side shoots. Examples: snapdragons, impatiens. Plants that grow from a single crown, at ground level, such as African violets, should not be pinched, as growth develops from a central basal point. A few plants, especially annuals, have been developed for self-branching habit, as in the newer asters.

Pinching off flower buds is also recommended when a plant develops clusters of buds, as the peony. Side buds are removed to encourage the greater development of the larger or terminal buds to produce one large central flower. This disbudding, as it is called, is also used by commercial greenhouse growers to achieve the large-flowered chrysanthemums, often referred to as "disbuds."

Although the term "pinching off" is not strictly applied to the removal of stems, the general idea can be utilized to encourage proper development in a plant that puts out too many side stems. Pruning of axil shoots in tomato plants is a good example. Removal of these axil stems encourages growth in a plant, with more fruit-bearing branches. This is also true with some flowering plants, such as dahlias.

The term "disbud" is closely related to pinching. Disbud means to remove certain buds on a plant in order to produce better flowers from remaining buds; to induce stronger growth or a more symmetrical shape. On many flowering plants, such as the chrysanthemum, dahlia, peony and rose, and especially when grown for exhibition, it is advisable to remove or "pinch" all but the terminal bud on each stem. This forces the plant to put extra nourishment into the remaining bud, thus producing a larger bloom. The buds that are to be removed should be cut or pinched just above the first leaf or leaf cluster below them. Flower seedlings will often develop into stronger, larger plants if the first terminal bud that appears is removed. This forces the plant to develop side stems and more flowers.

On herbaceous plants, it is often desirable to remove leaf buds that would ultimately develop into branches, and thus help concentrate growth in the main branches, and to develop a more shapely plant.

The Benefits of Root Pruning

There is no foundation for the common fear that the welfare of trees, shrubs and other woody plants is necessarily threatened when one or more of their roots—even very large roots—are severed. On the contrary, the process may invigorate the plant by forcing it to develop the fibrous roots that take in most of the water and minerals needed for growth.

That root pruning may be beneficial is best shown by the fact that

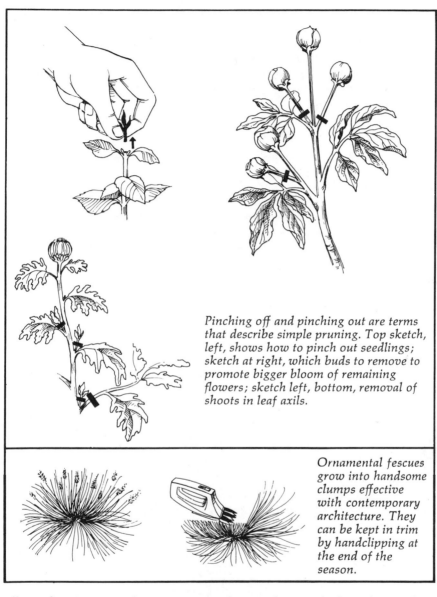

Pinching off and pinching out are terms that describe simple pruning. Top sketch, left, shows how to pinch out seedlings; sketch at right, which buds to remove to promote bigger bloom of remaining flowers; sketch left, bottom, removal of shoots in leaf axils.

Ornamental fescues grow into handsome clumps effective with contemporary architecture. They can be kept in trim by handclipping at the end of the season.

all good nursery stock is root-pruned several times before the stock is sold, and that such stock is much more likely to survive transplanting than wild plants or those whose roots have not been pruned prior to digging.

Root pruning, however, is not a common gardening practice except under the following circumstances:

If you maintain a home nursery, root-prune the stock every two or three years.

If you plan to move a large or long established plant, cut through the roots 1 to 3 ft. from the stem (depending on whether the plant is small or large) a year prior to digging it. Then when the plant is moved, it will have developed good fibrous roots within the limits of the soil to be dug with the plant.

If you plan to move a wild plant, prune the roots as above. If you must dig and move at once, take as much of the root system with the plant as you can. Trim off ends that are torn or broken.

If you are trying to restore the vigor of an old fruit tree, trench around it in a wide circle and cut off large roots, but not small, fibrous roots. Then fill in the trench with fertile soil.

If a large tree's roots are encroaching on the lawn or garden, cut the roots where they begin to invade but never all of them at once and not less than 6 ft. from the trunk. Cut both large and small roots.

Remember that a broken, split or torn root is an invitation to trouble; cut it off cleanly. When moving small plants, if you prune the roots you should also prune the top of the plant to lessen the burden on the reduced root system.

Top sketch shows amount of roots to be pruned in proportion to size of plant. Lifting and pruning roots of young plants toughens them. Vigor is restored to older plants by root pruning, as shown in bottom sketches. Circle of bold bars shows amount of roots to remove; at right, cross-section of trench and roots pruned.

Sensible, artistic pruning of roots and branches is a vital part of bonsai culture. This rock formation holds a dwarfed balsam fir (left) and a zelkova (elmlike tree, upper) along with sedum and mosses. A planter similar to this one could be made of Featherrock or you might find a suitably shaped piece of driftwood.

Plants forced into early bloom are likely to be unusually
tender. To transport a gift plant like these paperwhite
narcissus, enclose in cellophane or plastic wrappings.

6. Forcing Plants Out of Season

Forcing is the technique used by gardeners to make plants bloom or fruit out of season—usually in winter or very early spring. Thus you can have paper-white narcissus for Christmas, tulips for Valentine's Day, Belgian endive for winter salads.

Forcing is practiced to some extent by all florists, many amateur greenhouse operators—and, for that matter, by indoor gardeners generally. The rules of procedure include the following: 1. Use top-grade plants and bulbs. Plants should have strong root systems. 2. Start plants at normally low temperatures, then increase warmth every week several degrees to the permissible maximum. 3. Keep plants well watered, but not overwatered, at all times. 4. In the greenhouse, keep walks, areas under benches and foliage sprayed with water to keep humidity up to favorable levels for the temperatures prevailing. 5. Ventilate greenhouse normally, but prevent strong drafts. 6. Keep plants insect- and disease-free.

Azaleas and hydrangeas should be planted in good soil in pots and stored at a temperature of not over 50 degrees until flower buds develop. Thereafter, gradually increase temperature to not more than 65 degrees for azaleas, 60 degrees for hydrangeas. Water regularly. Spray azalea foliage once or twice daily. Feed hydrangeas liquid manure.

Forcing is a relative matter. In a sense it is the normal condition of greenhouse plants in winter and, to some degree, a part of all greenhouse practice. In addition to ornamental plants, extra-early crops of vegetables, such as carrots, cucumbers, lettuce and radishes, can be raised from seeds in the greenhouse or on a less accelerated scale in a hotbed.

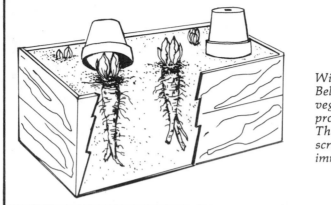

Witloof chicory or Belgian endive is a vegetable that is produced by forcing. The process is described in the text immediately below.

Witloof chicory (Belgian endive) is produced by forcing the roots. In fall they are trimmed at the bottom to 8 or 9 inches, placed upright in a box of sand, soil or humus, and kept in near-darkness at a temperature of 60 degrees. In two to four weeks heads of witloof are formed and ready for eating as salad or as a boiling or braising vegetable. Growth is encouraged if several inches of well-rotted manure are placed over the roots before forcing.

Cut branches of forsythia, apple, cherry and mimosa can be forced into early bloom if they are cut in January or February (not before) and kept in fresh water in a warm room. The procedure for forcing mimosa, as practiced in the orchards of southern France, involves fairly elaborate steaming and cooling rooms, but most flowering trees and many flowering shrubs can be forced into bloom by the home gardener. Toward the end of winter when the weather begins to afford slightly warmer days, cut branches 2 to 3 feet long, bearing in mind that this is a form of pruning and you don't want to ruin the shape of the plant. In Scandinavia, the practice is to plunge branches into a pail filled with loosely packed snow, and after two or three days in a cool, dark room indoors, they are placed in a vase in cool water and set in a sunny window in a warm room. In New England, the custom is to place the branches in a vase of cold water in a sunny window as soon as they are cut. Many gardeners crush the bottom inch or so of branch stems before placing them in water, a trick which helps the plant take up water more easily. Branches will generally bloom within two weeks.

How To Force Bulbs

The bulb is nature's well-wrapped marvel, a perfect holiday package. Late October or early November is the time to start the growth cycle that first sends down roots into moist soil or pebbles, then sends up fresh greening leaves, buds furling jewel colors and, finally, flowers as fragant as spring. The best kinds to plant for flowering gifts and decorating the house in December are the tender narcissus (paper-white, golden Soleil d'Or and Chinese sacred lily), amaryllis, hyacinths and precooled early tulips.

To grow narcissus, all you need is water, pebbles, the bulbs and a bowl or flowerpot at least 2 inches deep and large enough to hold three to twelve of them. Fill the container half full of pebbles. Set the bulbs on

ABOVE, LEFT: *Any attractive waterproof container may be used for forcing paper-white narcissus. Half-fill the bowl with pebbles. Brightly-colored fish-tank pebbles are suitable, as are smooth, polished stones.*
ABOVE, RIGHT: *Press the bulbs into the pebbles so they almost touch; add water to cover stones.*
LEFT: *Keep the bowl in a moderately cool (60–70 degrees), dark closet for two weeks, until strong roots form. Then move it to a sunny window, or into a fluorescent-lighted garden for blooms. Avoid drafts of hot, dry air. As soon as the buds begin to open, keep out of hot, direct sun as it will shorten the life of the fragile petals. Golden Soleil d'Or narcissus force the same way.*

this surface, allowing about a half-inch of space between. Pour in more pebbles until a third of each bulb is in the gravel. Add water until it touches the bulbs and place the planting in a dark, cool place (60 to 70°) for about two weeks to encourage root growth. After this time bring the planter to a sunny, warm place. Keep moist at all times and avoid hot, dry drafts.

Hybrid amaryllis in white, pink, rose and red, or patterned reds and whites, send up splendid scapes of flowers two to eight weeks after planting. Plant in commercially prepared potting soil (or in a mixture of equal parts garden loam, peat moss and sand), allowing about an inch of space between bulb and pot, and leaving at least one-third of the bulb above the surface. Keep evenly moist at all times, but water more freely when growth becomes active. Amaryllis need a well-lighted, warm place until buds begin to open; then they may be moved to a cooler, shaded interior where the blooms will last longer.

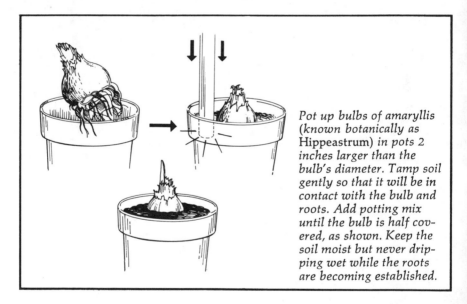

Pot up bulbs of amaryllis (known botanically as Hippeastrum) in pots 2 inches larger than the bulb's diameter. Tamp soil gently so that it will be in contact with the bulb and roots. Add potting mix until the bulb is half covered, as shown. Keep the soil moist but never dripping wet while the roots are becoming established.

Fragrant Dutch and French Roman hyacinths force into bloom easily in eight to ten weeks. Colors range from palest yellow to orange, from red to rose and pink, and through all the blues to delicate lavender. Plant the bulbs in the same kind of soil recommended for amaryllis, positioning them so that the tips are near the surface, even protruding slightly. Moisten well. Keep cool (less than 60°, if possible), moist and dark for two weeks, then move to a warmer place (about 70°), but continue to keep in the dark until leaves are 4 or 5 inches tall. After this period, provide abundant light.

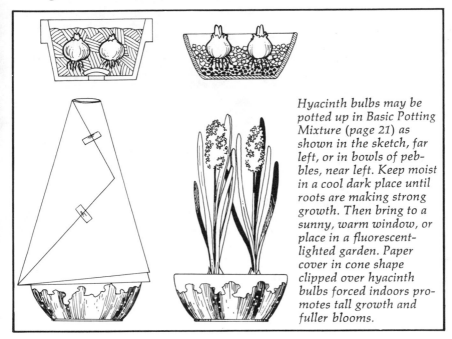

Hyacinth bulbs may be potted up in Basic Potting Mixture (page 21) as shown in the sketch, far left, or in bowls of pebbles, near left. Keep moist in a cool dark place until roots are making strong growth. Then bring to a sunny, warm window, or place in a fluorescent-lighted garden. Paper cover in cone shape clipped over hyacinth bulbs forced indoors promotes tall growth and fuller blooms.

Precooled early tulips can also be forced to bloom by Christmas. Plant and care for as hyacinths, but keep tulips cool, moist and dark for three weeks, then move to a sunny, warm place to finish the growth cycle.

Other bulbs that may be planted and treated as tulips for flowers in late December and January include ixia, ornithogalum, sparaxis, freesia, ranunculus, *Iris reticulata* and *I. danfordiae*. While lily-of-the-valley is not considered a bulb, its sweet-smelling flowers may be enjoyed any time after Thanksgiving by planting pips that have been specially prepared for forcing into bloom in 21 days.

In choosing other bulbs for forcing, first be careful to pick adaptable varieties. Check with your dealer if you are not sure, for there is a vast difference in the behavior of the different varieties. For instance, 'King Alfred' daffodil is an excellent forcer; 'Emperor' is not. Darwin tulip 'William Pitt' is an excellent forcer; 'Pride of Haarlem' is not.

Most hardy bulbs such as tulips and daffodils need a rooting period before being placed in a light, moderately warm spot to make top growth. If you pot up tulips and daffodils, for instance, it is best to prepare an outdoor pit with drainage where the potted bulbs can be stored while rooting. Make this by digging to a depth of 18 inches and laying down 6 inches of sand or ashes in the bottom for drainage. Set pots on the sand or ashes and cover with soil to ground level. Hay is

ABOVE LEFT: *To force tulips, daffodils and hyacinths, pot up bulbs in autumn in Basic Potting Mixture (page 21); water.*
ABOVE RIGHT: *Label each pot. Place in cold frame or in box on garage floor. Invert pot over each. Cover with peat.*
LEFT: *Add a mulch of salt hay or leaves.*
LOWER LEFT: *Check frequently to be sure the soil is moist. When leaf growth is obvious, a healthy growth of roots has probably also occurred (sketch) and forcing can begin in a warm, sunny place.*

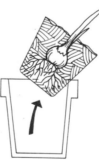

BELOW: *Hyacinths may be forced in pots of soil, in glasses of water especially shaped to hold the bulbs, or in pebbles (see page 123). Paper cones may be needed to encourage proper elongation of leaves and flowers.*

Corms of Anemone coronaria *arrive from the grower in an apparently lifeless state—hard, dry and shriveled. (The one shown is actual size.) Soak overnight in room-temperature water before planting about 1 inch deep and 2 inches apart in an 8-inch bulb pan. Keep moist in a cool, dark place until leaf growth begins.*

Caladium tubers are so eager to grow they'll oblige even if you plant them upside down. They'll have smaller leaves but more of them. Start tubers in flats of peat moss in February or March. When roots show, move them to 4-inch pots. Frequent misting helps develop strong roots. Pot them next in 6-inch pots. They'll grow in sun or even full shade.

Miniature daffodils, all species of Narcissus, *may be forced into winter bloom in a sunny, moderately warm window.*

NARCISSUS JUNCIFOLIUS

Freesias are usually grown in pots, even outdoors. Plant six corms to a 6-inch pot, with the top of each an inch below the soil surface. Stake with bamboo and soft ties.

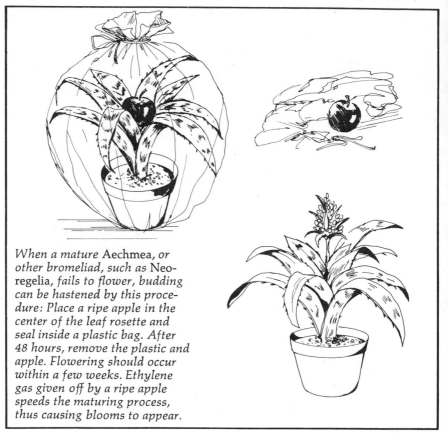

When a mature Aechmea, or other bromeliad, such as Neoregelia, fails to flower, budding can be hastened by this procedure: Place a ripe apple in the center of the leaf rosette and seal inside a plastic bag. After 48 hours, remove the plastic and apple. Flowering should occur within a few weeks. Ethylene gas given off by a ripe apple speeds the maturing process, thus causing blooms to appear.

then mounded on top to a depth of 18 inches. Be sure the bulbs are well moistened before placing them in storage. It is also a good idea to enclose all excepting daffodils in some kind of improvised wire-mesh cage to prevent mice and other rodents from having a feast.

It is also possible to force hardy bulbs by using part of a household refrigerator in which to store them for the rooting period, or you can set the pots in a dark cabinet in the garage or other room where temperatures stay above freezing but below 60 degrees. Most bulbs need at least six weeks in which to form a root system of sufficient strength to produce leaves and flowers out of season. Besides tulips and daffodils, try crocus, grape-hyacinths, Dutch and Roman hyacinths, Dutch iris and scillas.

Forcing Earlier, Larger Flowers

When otherwise healthy, mature plants fail to bloom, there are ways to force them. Wisteria is a good example. Midsummer pruning of lateral shoots back to five leaves or fewer helps the formation of flower spurs. When a mature bromeliad—an aechmea or neoregelia, for example— fails to flower, budding can be hastened by placing a ripe apple in the center of the leaf rosette and sealing the entire plant with the apple inside a plastic bag. After 48 hours, remove the plastic and apple. Flowering should occur within a few weeks. (Ethylene gas given off by a ripe apple speeds the maturing process, thus causing earlier flowering.) When flowering house plants such as geraniums and African violets are fed with a fertilizer high in nitrogen content, all leaf growth may be produced at the expense of flowers; change to a fertilizer with a relatively high phosphorus content—4-12-4 or 5-10-5, for example.

Disbudding, described in Chapter 5, is another form of forcing. By removing all buds on a stem except one, a larger single flower is produced instead of a "bouquet" of smaller ones. Camellia growers practice a highly specialized kind of forcing. Camellia buds treated with gibberellic acid, a process known as "gibbing," produce exceptionally large specimen flowers. Here is the procedure: Remove the leaf bud that is nearest the largest flower bud and drop gibberellic acid into the calyx that remains after the leaf bud has been taken out.

Camellia buds treated with gibberellic acid, a process known as "gibbing," produce exceptionally large specimen flowers. Remove leaf bud that is nearest the largest flower bud (upper sketch) and drop gibberellic acid into the calyx that remains after the bud has been taken out.

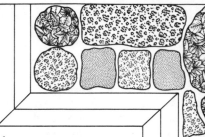

RIGHT: *This plan for a corner area, measuring approximately 28 feet across the top, suggests a raised retaining wall about 18 inches high along the front. Select low- to medium-growing annuals for the front of the border and around the flowering tree, which might be an ornamental crab apple, dogwood or redbud. Use taller flowers at the back of the border. To develop this plan as an all white and yellow summer border, select varieties of sweet-alyssum, wax begonia, baby's-breath, candytuft, celosia, cleome, marigold, nicotiana, snapdragon, thymophylla and zinnia. In autumn interplant bulbs of tulip, daffodil and hyacinth.*

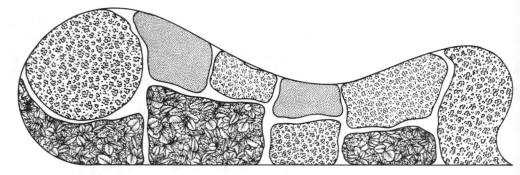

ABOVE: *A border plan like this one can be laid out easily with a length of garden hose to help establish the curves. Depending on space and personal preference this could be developed with fragrant annuals, kinds for cutting or in a color scheme.* RIGHT: *For a partly shaded nook that receives only early morning or late afternoon sun, try begonia, browallia, clarkia, impatiens, nicotiana and salvia. Scented flowers for shady positions include lunaria, mimulus, the viola species, myosotis and Monopsis campanulata.*

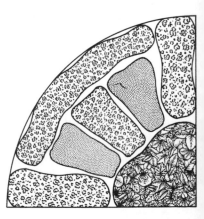

7. How To Grow Flowers

A real flower! What could be nicer than an honest-to-goodness flower with velvety petals and God-made fragrance? Maybe a bouquet or a whole garden of flowers. And that is what this chapter is about—annuals, biennials, perennials, roses and bulbs. Among these are flowers of all colors suited to every climate, light exposure, soil and moisture condition. There are kinds for showy garden display, for cutting and for drying to bring indoors.

Annuals: Flowers for a Season

An annual plant completes its life cycle from germination to seed formation within a single year. Following seed formation, the plant, exhausted of energy reserves, dies. Some annual plants complete their life cycles in a remarkably short time; desert species, stimulated by a brief rainy season, germinate, flower and make seed in a few weeks. Horticulturists have, by selection and breeding, extended the blooming period of flowering annuals and, likewise, extended the useful period of annual vegetable crops.

Not every plant that we set in the annual bed is truly an annual. Tender perennial plants are used as annuals for display bedding, for window boxes and in many other ways. Geraniums, lantanas, marguerites, fuchsias, periwinkles, wax begonias—these and more all live for several years in their frost-free native habitats. But, as they bloom quickly from seed or from cutting, we use them as single-season plants and group them with the annuals.

Some plants that grow from bulbs, corms and tubers also have come to be used as annuals. By its very nature, no "bulbous" plant is a single-season grower. But many of the inexpensive, frost-sensitive sorts sometimes are handled as annuals. Dahlias from seed and from tubers, inexpensive gladioli, tuberoses, montbretias, acidantheras, tigridias and the like make a grand summer show. If you are dollar-conscious, dig and store these over winter; however, it is a great saving in time and trouble to let the winter take them, and buy more next spring.

Annuals thrive during the summer months, or complete their life cycles from fall to early spring. Lobelias, petunias, marigolds, cosmos and most other ornamental garden annuals grow through the summer months. Hardy annuals stand frost; you may enjoy an early burst of color from bachelor's buttons, larkspur, Shirley poppies and other winter (hardy) annuals if you sow seed of these in the fall.

Uses of Annual Flowers

The greatest use of annual flowers is for summer bedding. Apparently it all started during the eighteenth century when palace owners wanted something brighter than colored stones in their scrollwork-hedged gardens. By Victorian days public parks were filled with extremely complicated geometric flower beds. Annual flowers quickly became the backbone of the cottage garden because packets of seeds were cheap. "Penny packets" sell for twenty-five cents or more today, but still they are a bargain. A hundred and fifty seeds for a quarter, yielding at least one hundred blooming plants—that's a real buy in any age. Cottagers and mansion dwellers alike use annuals.

We use many annuals and it is not just a matter of price. Annual flowers tolerate a wide range of soil conditions; properly handled, they bloom for week after week, and they do not require the degree of year-round care and attention essential for longer-lived species. You draw open a furrow and sow seed, or you buy plants in the spring, you cultivate and water only a few weeks before the first blossoms come, you enjoy bright flowers throughout summer, and you clean off the bed after the first frost in the fall.

Annuals fit into modern gardens in several ways. We plant bright drifts of them at the doorway and around the terrace. We fill our window boxes and hanging baskets with them. They look fine and grow well in various sorts of planters and containers. Apartment dwellers, gardening on a balcony or on the roof, depend almost entirely on annuals for color. Even the twentieth-century nomad brightens the front step of his mobile home with annuals when he settles down for a few weeks, and that burgeoning breed, the summer cottager, stops increasingly at the roadside stand for annuals as he heads for his hideaway.

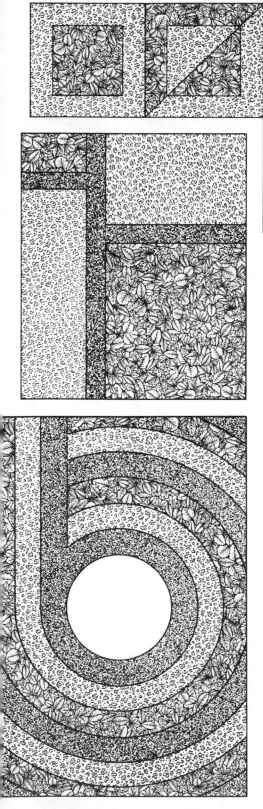

Gardens have always inspired artists, but here we have gardens inspired by art. The modules above suggest the geometrics of Victor Vasarely. These might be worked out as squares 2 by 2 feet or up to 6 by 6 feet. Depending on the individual landscape, they could be detailed in low-growing annual or perennial flowers, spring bulbs or no-maintenance evergreen shrubs. The best flowers for this kind of landscape "painting" are those that naturally grow low and bushy and cover themselves with tightly spaced flowers over a long season. Shrubs should grow low, neatly and slowly.

UPPER LEFT: The paintings of Piet Mondrian inspired this garden, a pleasure to view at ground level, but even more from a second-story balcony or other elevated vantage point. Translated to a real garden, this design works well in a space 10 by 12 feet. With black stones used for the narrow divisions, this garden in spring might be worked out with red and yellow tulips and blue hyacinths (be sure to select varieties that bloom at the same time). For summer, red petunias, yellow marigolds and blue ageratum could be used.

LOWER LEFT: Enter the supergraphic as the basis for a contemporary garden. The design shown needs a space about 13 by 17 feet, so that each band is 12 inches wide. A birdbath or sundial might be placed in the center.

ABOVE: *A Victorian-inspired garden might be created today in a space as small as 6 x 8 feet, or as large as desired. For the dark areas a low-growing evergreen that clips well is suggested; perennial candytuft* (Iberis sempervirens), *teucrium, dwarf boxwood or dwarf Japanese holly.*

BELOW: *Formal beds detailed by clipped boxwood hedges and featuring stylish topiaries may be planted in season with spring bulbs, summer annuals or fall chrysanthemums and hardy asters.*

BELOW: *Small sketches show contemporary geometric (left) and more traditional design (right) for borders of bedding plants. When planning, keep in mind color, texture, bloomtime and height of each variety you are considering.*

Early Sowing, Indoors

Most annuals can be sown directly in the garden where they are to bloom. Many of us, however, like to start seedlings early, indoors. Seeds of annuals usually germinate quickly, and the seedlings tolerate a wide range of conditions. Use sieved sphagnum moss, vermiculite or a germinating medium of your own concocting. Shallow clay pots (bulb pans), compressed paper plant trays, three-inch-deep wooden flats or almost any other shallow container with drain holes holds the germinating medium. Fill to within half an inch of the rim; the medium should be only slightly compacted. Sprinkle seeds sparsely over the surface of the germinating medium. Fine seeds (petunia, forget-me-not, lobelia, snapdragon, for example) are pressed gently into the medium; cover larger seeds with an eighth-inch of the germinating medium or with crumbly, damp, sieved sphagnum or peat, or with clean sand. Set the container in a tray of tepid water for two or three hours (water droplets should glisten on the surface of the germinating mix), then stretch a piece of clear plastic over the face of the container and secure it with a rubber band. Place in dim light, at moderate room temperature. My choice is to lay slats on the tops of the reflectors of my fluorescent plant light units and set the seeded flats on these. The mild bottom heat brings the seedlings right out.

New germinating gadgets, such as Jiffy-Sevens, come in handy for certain seeds. I soak up a batch of them, poke two seeds each of morning glory, cardinal creeper, cypress vine or other ornamentals into every container. The seedlings grow in these, and container and all goes into the garden.

As quickly as germination begins, give the seedlings dim light for a day, then bright light—a south-facing window, fluorescent or greenhouse daylight. As seedlings develop the second set of true leaves, prick them off into flats, spacing them two inches apart. As growth resumes, apply half-strength liquid fertilizer.

Seeding in the Garden

In the garden work up the soil in a well-drained bed; dress prior to turning with one-fourth cup of 5-10-5 fertilizer and two cups of dehydrated manure per square yard (this is a general rule of thumb, and may be modified to meet local conditions), then spade deeply. Rake down the soil, working it to crumble the clods and to develop a reasonably well-settled, even surface.

Plan your annual bed with low-growing sorts in front, intermediate heights in the center and higher varieties at the rear if the bed backs up to shrubbery or a building. A freestanding bed is high in the center and

FLOWER SEEDLINGS IDENTIFIED

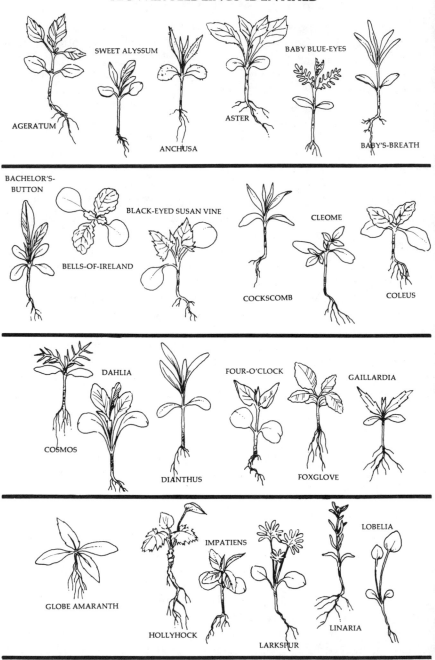

AGERATUM

SWEET ALYSSUM

ANCHUSA

ASTER

BABY BLUE-EYES

BABY'S-BREATH

BACHELOR'S-BUTTON

BELLS-OF-IRELAND

BLACK-EYED SUSAN VINE

CLEOME

COCKSCOMB

COLEUS

DAHLIA

COSMOS

DIANTHUS

FOUR-O'CLOCK

FOXGLOVE

GAILLARDIA

GLOBE AMARANTH

HOLLYHOCK

IMPATIENS

LARKSPUR

LINARIA

LOBELIA

It is important to know a flower-seedling from a weed-seedling. Note that the first leaves to appear—cotyledons—are usually different from the true leaves.

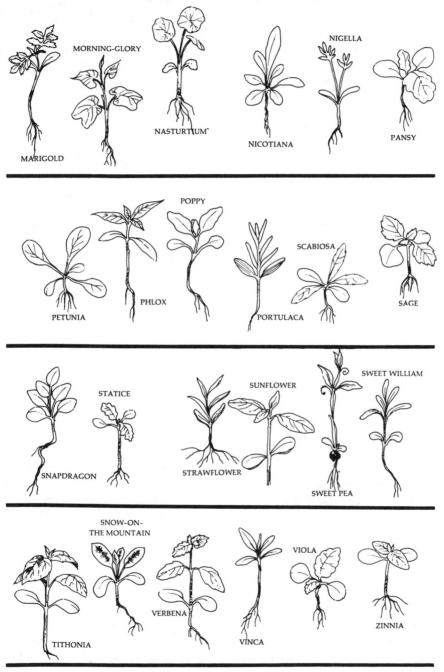

MORNING-GLORY

NIGELLA

MARIGOLD

NASTURTIUM

NICOTIANA

PANSY

POPPY

SCABIOSA

PETUNIA

PHLOX

PORTULACA

SAGE

STATICE

SUNFLOWER

SWEET WILLIAM

SNAPDRAGON

STRAWFLOWER

SWEET PEA

SNOW-ON-
THE MOUNTAIN

VIOLA

TITHONIA

VERBENA

VINCA

ZINNIA

low at the edges or low all the way across. With a hoe handle, scratch out roughly rectangular, trapizoidal or triangular "patches" for each sort of seed. Then, with a fine-pointed cultivating tool or with a small Warren hoe, mark out shallow drills. At the front of the bed the drills ought to run at acute angles to the face of the bed. Drills in a given patch are parallel, but those in adjacent patches are not parallel.

For a modest-sized bed, say one 10 feet by 25 feet for the home garden, plan on three or four low-growing annuals for the front, four or five annuals of intermediate height, and, perhaps, three tall-growing kinds for the rear of the bed.

In all cases, make the drills roughly 6 inches apart (closer for very fine sorts such as Dahlberg daisy or 'Twinkle' phlox, wider for large kinds such as tithonia, castor-bean or annual hollyhock). Sow seed generously in the drills and plan to thin later; the excess plants may be discarded or transplanted. Cover all seed two to three times its diameter with finely crumbled soil.

As seedlings appear, keep the bed in clean cultivation and, when of a size to be well established but before they begin to crowd badly, thin them.

Plants you have grown yourself or purchased from the garden shop may be planted in the same carefully organized, informal manner. Push young annuals with biweekly feeding of balanced, low-nitrogen liquid fertilizer, keep the soil loose and free of weeds. Most annuals require one or two pinchings to make them branch well. Water often enough so the soil never dries completely throughout the top inch. When buds begin to show color, discontinue fertilizing.

Maintaining the Annual Flower Bed

Cultivate annuals frequently; use a scuffle hoe or just rake the soil; avoid deep cultivation as it may injure roots. Stake larger kinds when half-grown. An easy way is to use brushy, leafless, dry branches. Stick these among the growing plants, butts downward, shoving them firmly into the soil. As buds show color, with a pruning tool clip off twigs that show. Stems and branches supported throughout by a mesh of twigs are much more secure than those tied to single stakes.

Remove spent blossoms when it is practical. For example, when most snapdragons are fairly bloomed out, step into the bed and clip back the flower stalks just above a leaf. Probably new secondary shoots will develop shortly, particularly if the plants get a light feeding. On the other hand, you should nip off zinnia heads, spent petunia blossoms and spent cosmos once or twice each week, so the plants bloom continuously. Shear back sweet alyssum after each flush of flowering, and it will renew itself.

ANNUALS FOR WINDOW BOXES

ABRONIA	GRAMMANTHES	PETUNIA
AGERATUM	IPOMOEA	PHLOX (dwarf)
ANTIRRHINUM (dwarf)	LINARIA	RESEDA
ASTER (dwarf)	LOBELIA	SALVIA
BEGONIA	MATTHIOLA	STATICE (dwarf)
CELOSIA	MESEMBRYANTHEMUM	TROPAEOLUM (dwarf)
COLEUS	NEMESIA	URSINIA
ESCHSCHOLTZIA	NIEREMBERGIA	VERBENA

SOW WHERE THEY ARE TO FLOWER

ADONIS	DOWNINGIA	LINARIA
ALYSSUM	ECHIUM	LINUM
ANCHUSA	EMILIA	LUPINUS
BORAGO	ERYSIMUM	MALCOMIA
CALENDULA	ESCHSCHOLTZIA	MALOPE
CALLIOPSIS	EUPHORBIA	MATTHIOLA
CAMPANULA	GILIA	NEMOPHILA
CENTAUREA	GLAUCIUM	NICOTIANA
CHRYSANTHEMUM	GODETIA	NIGELLA
CLARKIA	GYPSOPHILA	PAPAVER
CLEOME	HELIANTHUS	PHACELIA
COLLINSIA	IBERIS	RESEDA
COLLOMIA	IPOMOEA	RUDBECKIA
CONVOLVULUS	LATHYRUS	TAGETES
CYNOGLOSSUM	LAVATERA	TROPAEOLUM
DELPHINIUM	LEPTOSYNE	VISCARIA
DIMORPHOTHECA	LIMNANTHES	ZINNIA

BEDDING ANNUALS FOR PARTLY SHADED PLACES

ANCHUSA	ESCHSCHOLTZIA	NICOTIANA
ANTIRRHINUM	GODETIA	OENOTHERA
BEGONIA	IMPATIENS	OXALIS
BELLIS	LINARIA	PAPAVER
CALLISTEPHUS	LOBULARIA	PETUNIA
CAMPANULA	MATRICARIA	SALVIA
CLARKIA	MIMULUS	VIOLA
CYNOGLOSSUM	MYOSOTIS	
DELPHINIUM	NEMOPHILA	

ANNUALS WITH SCENTED FLOWERS

ABRONIA UMBELLATA
ASPERULA ORIENTALIS
BRACHYCOME IBERIDIFOLIA
CENTAUREA MOSCHATA
CLEOME SPINOSA
DIANTHUS BARBATUS
ERYSIMUM ASPERUM
HEDYSARUM CORONARIUM
HELIOTROPIUM ARBORESCENS
HESPERIS FRAGRANS
HESPERIS MATRONALIS
IBERIS AMARA
LIMNANTHES DOUGLASII

LOBULARIA MARITIMA
LUNARIA ANNUA
LUPINUS MUTABILIS
MATTHIOLA INCANA
MENTZELIA LINDLEYI
MYOSOTIS SYLVATICA
NICOTIANA ALATA
RESEDA ODORATA
TAGETES LUCIDA
VIOLA CORNUTA
VIOLA HYBRIDA
VIOLA TRICOLOR

Shady Positions

ANDROSACE ARMENIACA
COLLINSIA GRANDIFLORA
IONOPSIDIUM ACAULE
LUNARIA ANNUA
MIMULUS SPP.

MONOPSIS CAMPANULATA
MYOSOTIS SPP.
NEMOPHILA SPP.
TORENIA FOURNIERI
VIOLA SPP.

ANNUALS FOR CUT FLOWERS

ACROCLINIUM
ANTIRRHINUM
CALENDULA
CALLIOPSIS
CALLISTEPHUS
CENTAUREA
CHEIRANTHUS
CHRYSANTHEMUM
CLARKIA
COSMOS
CYANUS
DAHLIA
DELPHINIUM

DIANTHUS
ESCHSCHOLTZIA
GAILLARDIA
GODETIA
GYPSOPHILA
HELICHRYSUM
HELIPTERUM
LATHYRUS
LEPTOSYNE
LINARIA
LUPINUS
LYCHNIS
MATRICARIA

MATTHIOLA
NIEREMBERGIA
NIGELLA
PENSTEMON
RESEDA
RHODANTHE
RUDBECKIA
SALPIGLOSSIS
SCABIOSA
STATICE
TROPAEOLUM
VERBENA
ZINNIA

Plants that bloom throughout the season, as cosmos, bachelor's-buttons, calendulas and marigolds, will be pretty well bloomed out after the hot weather. Many will have a second season of bloom however, if dead seed heads are removed. The best tool for the job is kitchen or garden shears, but seed heads can be nipped off by hand as well.

Wallflowers and snapdragons become much bushier plants if the leader, or first flowering stem, is cut out when the flowers are beginning to fade. Keep dying blossoms picked, to encourage continued production. Almost all annuals and perennials will go on producing flowers for a much longer period if the fading blossoms are removed. Some will bloom all summer. Toward the end of the season, plants that have bloomed all summer long may begin to have a straggly look and seem to be ending their blooming season. This is true of the garden standbys alyssum and petunias. In August, use pruning shears to remove flower tips of alyssum hedges and petunia plantings. In a few weeks, they'll produce a whole new set of blossoms.

Top: *Plant sweet-peas singly or staggered in rows.*
Center: *Pinching sweet-peas. Remove tip when four leaves have grown; pinch as black bars indicate, leaving a single main stem; pinch secondary stems as they develop above leaf axils as plant begins to climb stake.*
Below: *Sweet-peas trained to wires of a container. Peas staked by twiggy branches set in soil at planting.*

5 INCHES

Right, bottom: *The prime do's and don'ts of cultivation are shown here. Plants roots grow close to the surface. Proper cultivation is shallow, and leaves these roots untouched. Surface soil is only loosened enough to break surface and uproot weeds. At far right, deep cultivation close to the plant cuts off roots to the right and to the left, leaving the plant short of substance and in a state of severe shock.*

Biennials: Flowers from a Two-Season Cycle

A biennial plant, in nature, makes vegetative growth (usually a leafy rosette) the first season after seed germinates, and the following season the plant blooms, sets seed and dies. We gardeners have learned to manipulate these plants to our advantage; often, quick-blooming biennials are seeded in the greenhouse or hotbed in late winter, and the plants flower during the following summer. Or, where weather is severe in winter, we sow biennials in late summer in frames, and overwinter the rather small plants inside the cold frames where they are somewhat protected. These small plants then are set out early the following spring to make more growth and then blossom.

Most biennials are somewhat troublesome unless environmental conditions are ideal. Biennials grow well consistently in, for example, Zone 6 maritime gardens (usually not colder than 10° below zero). With the tempering effect of the sea and a generally mild year-round condition, foxgloves, Canterbury bells, honesty and other biennials self-seed freely. These same species, in harsher climates or in the central part of the country, away from the modifying effect of the ocean, often succumb over winter, and volunteer plants are virtually unknown.

Many of our finest border plants are biennial. Garden favorites of a biennial nature include: Canterbury bells, English daisies, some forget-me-nots, some foxgloves, most hollyhocks, sweet rocket (*Hesperis*), sweet William, some mulleins, English wallflowers and Siberian wallflowers. You will notice that recurring word "some." With garden varieties (cultivars), exposure, particularly the severity of winter and the intensity of summer, determine the longevity of a given sort. Some fairly tender annuals in the mild Pacific Northwest shed seed during summer. The resulting late-summer seedlings overwinter as rosettes and bloom the following spring. This makes that cultivar a biennial. Or perennials, especially those originating in cool, oceanic climates or mild mountainous environments, when grown in the garden, make vegetative growth the first year and so strain themselves blooming in a foreign environment the following season that they die after having flowered. The hybridized English daisies, Iceland poppies and many strains of pansies and violas fall into this category.

Cultural Directions for Biennial Flowers

Where July-to-September temperatures seldom exceed 85°, most biennial flowers should be sown in July. But where summer heat is extreme and constant, it is better to wait until late August or even into September. Then sow the seed in a cold frame that will be closed after cold weather settles in to stay for the winter season.

I prefer to sow seed of most biennials in a bulb pan (squatty clay flowerpot) filled with a mixture of equal parts vermiculite, sphagnum peat moss and good garden loam. It is also possible to produce fine plants by sowing seed in carefully blended cold-frame soil which may or may not have been sterilized by heat or by chemicals. Most biennials, like annuals, germinate quickly. Thin or transplant all when they begin their second set of true leaves. In my garden I transplant the seedlings from bulb pans into the well-loosened, carefully blended cold-frame soil, setting them on two-inch centers. Later I transplant every other one, or, if space requires, two out of three, so plants are not crowded. In a more congenial climate these young plants would go directly to the garden, to be set where they are to bloom. In the open garden, mulch young biennials after the soil is thoroughly chilled to keep winter heaving to a minimum and to keep the plants dormant through freak warm spells in late winter and early spring.

Perennials: Flowers for Several Seasons

Perennial plants grow on, year after year, as compared to annuals, which bloom and die in a single season, and biennials, which complete their life cycle in two seasons. Woody plants are perennial; but when we gardeners say "perennial" we refer to flowering plants, usually those that die to the ground each year, that brighten our beds and borders from spring until fall. A perennial plant that freezes back each fall is called a herbaceous perennial. Examples are garden peonies, Michaelmas daisies, balloon-flowers and Japanese anemones. Not all herbaceous perennials stay green until frost; some die back soon after flowering, as Oriental poppies and Virginia bluebells. Other nonwoody perennials may be evergreen, at least in certain climates; the hellebores, Shasta daisies, certain daylilies and statice often maintain at least a rosette of green foliage through most of the winter. This matter of location, climate-wise, is significant. A given cultivar of the daylily is quite evergreen in Mobile; it holds its foliage until midwinter, then browns off at Little Rock; it is quite deciduous at St. Louis; and it will not survive the winter at Des Moines. Often, we fail to realize that many of our favorite garden plants may be quite persistent—truly perennial—in a milder climate. Begonias, pelargoniums (garden geraniums), shrimp plant and several other "annual" bedding plants are quite perennial, perhaps even semi-woody, in their tropical, native habitats. Snapdragons and petunias frequently go on for two or more years in the Pacific Northwest. We have to think of perennial plants in two ways: how they behave in *our* gardens and how they behave in the place where they grow natively.

Perennials are the backbone of the garden. In a rock garden, almost every plant is a perennial. In the border, many, often most, plants are

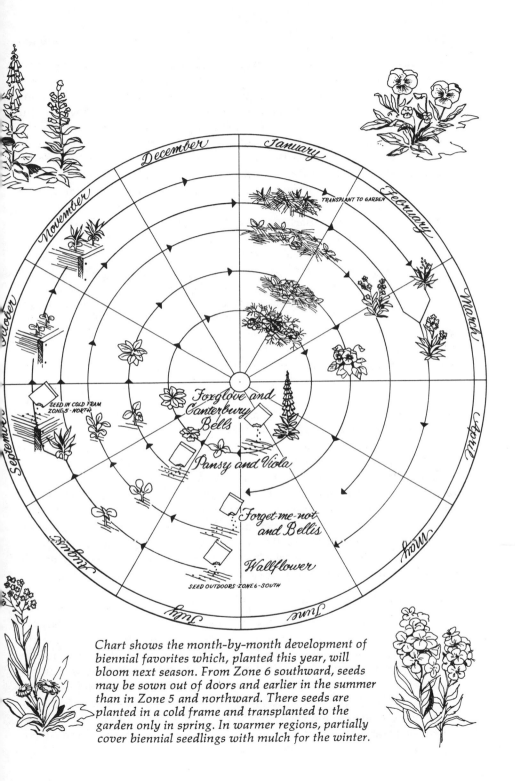

Chart shows the month-by-month development of biennial favorites which, planted this year, will bloom next season. From Zone 6 southward, seeds may be sown out of doors and earlier in the summer than in Zone 5 and northward. There seeds are planted in a cold frame and transplanted to the garden only in spring. In warmer regions, partially cover biennial seedlings with mulch for the winter.

perennial. An English garden lover would think it heresy to plant anything but perennials in his border. We are more flexible in America, and I believe our borders are the better for being fortified with flowering masses of annuals and biennials throughout summer. Most of the flowers in the wild garden are perennial. Our lilies, daffodils, hyacinths, tulips, crocuses and similar dependable bulbs, corms and tubers, are, of course, perennials. So are the more tender sorts, as dahlias, gladiolus, acidanthera, cannas and crocosmia; obviously, these go on year after year. But they cannot stand frost. It is hard to think of a home garden without perennial flowers; beds of nothing but annuals conjure up thoughts of Victorian park plantings or masses of petunias at a shopping center. Perennials mean home gardening.

A careful selection of perennials provides flowers month after month. Very early in the spring the low-growing perennials begin to bloom. Hellebores often bloom in the snow; in the rock garden arabis species, the earliest dianthuses, some primroses and candytufts come out in March or early April. At the same time, marsh-marigold and skunk-cabbage blossom in the bog garden and a few miniature irises bloom in the border. In most climates the greatest showing of perennials comes through May, June and July. Autumn is climaxed by displays of chrysanthemums, Michaelmas daisies, the artemisias and Japanese anemones.

When working up a landscape plan, contrive various habitats. The perennial border gets full sun and requires a well-drained site. Two or three closely planted shade trees, closed in toward the east, south and west by low-growing, understory trees such as dogwood, redbud or black-haw, provide a site for the woodland and woods wild-flower garden. If you are lucky enough to have a low place where the ground is soggy throughout the year, you may make a bog garden, with or without a pond for aquatic perennials. A rock garden is a wonderful thing provided you have the time to maintain it; quite a few rock-garden perennials thrive in a properly laid-up dry wall and the maintenance is very light. By all means, contrive growing sites for perennials.

Structure of Perennial Plants

Perennial plants have strong root systems. Going on, year after year, the roots of perennials grow outward toward moisture and nutrients. Some perennial plants develop at the ground line a mass of stem-root tissue, more or less well defined, called a crown. Delphinium crowns, for example, are somewhat woody, producing thick, very tender shoots above and rather weak but longish roots below. Summer phlox and hardy aster crowns become extremely woody with age; so woody, in fact, that movement of water and minerals from roots to shoots is retarded, and bloom

Delphiniums require lots of feeding in order to prosper. Set started seedlings at the levels at which they grew before in holes fed with bone meal. Water well and when seedlings have started to grow, dig a half-handful of rich organic fertilizer in around each plant (below, left). Stake plants when 12 inches tall and tie with soft cord or raffia. Set a tall stake to begin with and continue tying as the stem lengthens (sketch at right).

When delphinium flowers begin to fade, cut off the stem as indicated by the black bar (sketch, left). Side-dress with a handful of fertilizer (above). Water well. Secondary flower spikes will develop. Start seeds of delphiniums in early spring or late summer in a place where temperatures do not exceed 70 degrees, if possible. Transplant to peat pots.

DIVIDING AND PLANTING PEONY ROOTS

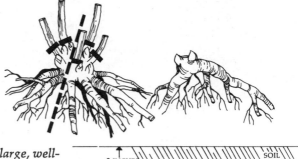

If you wish to divide a large, well-established clump of peonies, late summer or early fall is the time. Be sure each division has a growth bud or "eye." Peonies hardly ever need transplanting or division. Prepare the soil well, plant properly and then you can forget about them year after year. Sketch at right indicates adequate soil preparation. Be sure bud is not more than two inches deep.

becomes poor. The crowns of primulas and forget-me-nots remain soft. Other perennials do not have well-organized crowns, but thickened, fairly woody main roots. Garden peonies, old-fashioned bleeding-heart and false indigo roots are intertwined and tangled, thick, becoming woody with age; these produce strong buds (eyes) near the soil surface that grow into flowering shoots. Smaller, fibrous roots extend outward from the thickened roots, and these absorb water and nutrients.

Some perennials produce more or less thickened, fleshy stems that creep horizontally just at the ground line. Iris rhizomes are typical. When a creeping rootstock is soft and fleshy, it is subject to decay. Plants with fleshy rhizomes need very well-drained soil. Rootstocks and rhizomes of aquatic plants usually are tough, sometimes woody. Cattails, sweet flag, water-willow, pickerelweed and the aquatic irises all have these ropy or woody creeping stems, with a mass of fibrous roots beneath. Border perennial stems usually rise straight up from the crown or from the roots. Sturdy, well-spaced stems produce masses of large-sized, long-lasting flowers. On older clumps, when the leafy shoots are half-developed, clip out (at the base) all weak stems; it usually pays to remove half of the remaining stems on perennial clumps older than three years. For strong bloom and healthy plants lift and divide border perennials every fourth or fifth year. Some perennials resent disturbance, however; peonies, hostas, the gasplant and bleeding-heart make little or no bloom for two or three years after being lifted. Woodland and aquatic perennial stems usually are not thinned.

Perennials bloom in many ways; delphiniums, lupines and hollyhocks produce flowers on a strong vertical stem. While most of the perennials with flowers in spikes bloom from the bottom upward, a few, notably the *Liatris* species (Kansas gayfeather, blazing star), bloom from the top downward. Other perennials bloom with flowers in close-set panicles or clusters, as summer phlox; still others bear flowers in looser clusters, as coral-bells, or in very open sprays, as columbine. A few perennials bloom on unbranched stems, or with branching limited to second-crop flowers that originate low on the stem of the primary flower, as Shasta daisy. Remove flower heads of perennials as quickly as blooms fade, to prevent seed formation, which saps the strength of the plant.

The Perennial Border

The major use of perennials is in the perennial border. Ideally, this is a flower bed designed to be approached from the end, with the length of the bed stretching away from the viewer. The bed appears to advantage when backed with a screen; trimmed or natural hedges, garden walls and solid fences all make good backgrounds for a perennial border. Traditionally, the foreground is fine turf; the green grass provides a wonderful foil for the display of bright flowers.

Lay out the perennial border in full sun, where drainage is good. As plants will grow in place for several years, prepare the soil deeply so roots will reach far down, supporting strong, heavily flowering stems. Where soil is shallow or of poor quality, it should be removed to a depth of 2 to 4 feet, to be replaced with a fertile loam. I recommend trenching the perennial bed, that is, digging in such a fashion that the soil is turned to a depth of several feet, with ample well-decayed manure, humus-yielding products such as peat and compost and various chemical fertilizers (particularly root-producing phosphates) turned deeply into the bed. It is difficult to overemphasize the importance of deep soil preparation for a perennial border.

If trees or shrubs grow close to the border, with a sharpshooter spade a trench between the bed and the woody plants each spring. This cuts roots that invade the border and compete with the flowering plants.

Perennial borders usually are laid out with almost prostrate plants at the front, with higher and higher plants planted in drifts toward the back of the bed, and with very high-growing sorts—plume-poppy, meadow-rue, white mugwort, hollyhocks, tall delphinium cultivars and the like—clumped at the back. Dozens of designs of perennial borders have been published, giving lists of flowers for each area of the bed.

20 FEET WIDE

38 FEET LONG

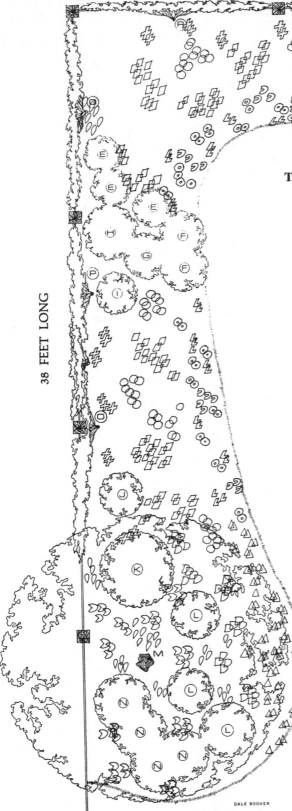

TREES, SHRUBS AND PERENNIALS TO PLANT IN FALL OR SPRING

- Ⓐ SPURIA IRIS
- Ⓑ GYPSOPHILA
- Ⓒ HEUCHERA
- Ⓓ DICTAMNUS
- Ⓔ CONNECTICUT YANKEE DELPH
- Ⓕ BERGENIA CORDIFOLIA
- Ⓖ SHASTA DAISY
- Ⓗ PLUME POPPY
- Ⓘ JAPANESE ANEMONE
- Ⓙ ACONITE
- Ⓚ HOSTA
- Ⓛ HELLEBORUS
- Ⓜ FLOWERING DOGWOOD
- Ⓝ MAIDENHAIR FERN
- Ⓞ INSPIRATION ROSE
- Ⓟ JACKMANI CLEMATIS
- Ⓠ BITTERSWEET VINE
- Ⓡ SILVERLACE VINE
- Ⓢ SPARRIESHOOP ROSE

BULBS TO PLANT IN FALL

- HYACINTH
- TULIP
- CYCLAMEN
- COLCHICUM
- ERANTHIS
- WINTER CROCUS
- GALANTHUS
- IRIS RETICULATA
- DAFFODIL
- LILY

DALE BOOHER

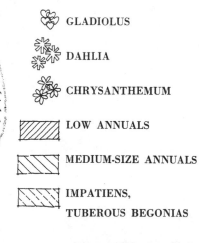

TREES, SHRUBS AND PERENNIALS TO PLANT IN THE SPRING OR FALL

Ⓐ SPURIA IRIS
Ⓑ GYPSOPHILA
Ⓒ HEUCHERA
Ⓓ DICTAMNUS
Ⓔ CONNECTICUT YANKEES DELPHINIUM
Ⓕ BERGENIA CORDIFOLIA
Ⓖ SHASTA DAISY
Ⓗ PLUME POPPY
Ⓘ JAPANESE ANEMONE
Ⓙ ACONITE
Ⓚ HOSTA
Ⓛ HELLEBORUS
Ⓜ FLOWERING DOGWOOD
Ⓝ MAIDENHAIR FERN
Ⓞ INSPIRATION ROSE
Ⓟ JACKMANI CLEMATIS
Ⓠ BITTERSWEET VINE
Ⓡ SILVERLACE VINE
Ⓢ SPARRIESHOOP ROSE

SEEDS AND BULBS TO PLANT IN SPRING

GLADIOLUS

DAHLIA

CHRYSANTHEMUM

LOW ANNUALS

MEDIUM-SIZE ANNUALS

IMPATIENS, TUBEROUS BEGONIAS

DALE BOOHER

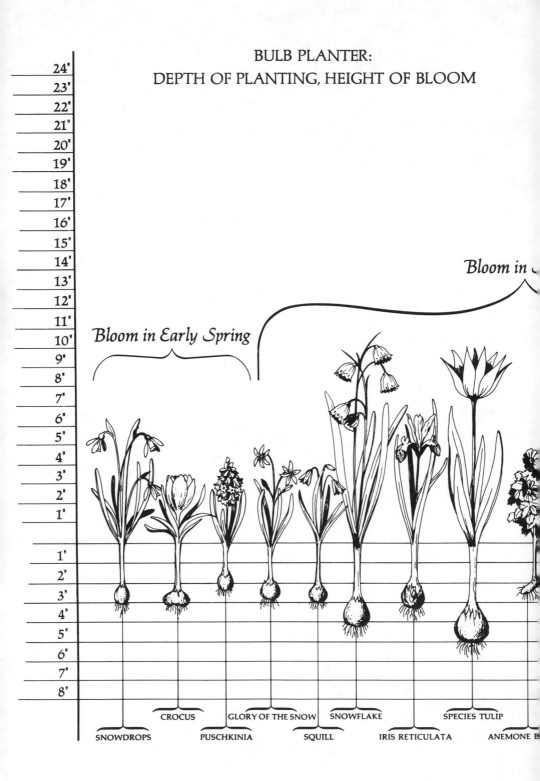

BULB PLANTER:
DEPTH OF PLANTING, HEIGHT OF BLOOM

Bloom in Early Spring

Bloom in

| 24" |
| 23" |
| 22" |
| 21" |
| 20" |
| 19" |
| 18" |
| 17" |
| 16" |
| 15" |
| 14" |
| 13" |
| 12" |
| 11" |
| 10" |
| 9" |
| 8" |
| 7" |
| 6" |
| 5" |
| 4" |
| 3" |
| 2" |
| 1" |

| 1" |
| 2" |
| 3" |
| 4" |
| 5" |
| 6" |
| 7" |
| 8" |

CROCUS   GLORY OF THE SNOW   SNOWFLAKE   SPECIES TULIP

SNOWDROPS   PUSCHKINIA   SQUILL   IRIS RETICULATA   ANEMONE B

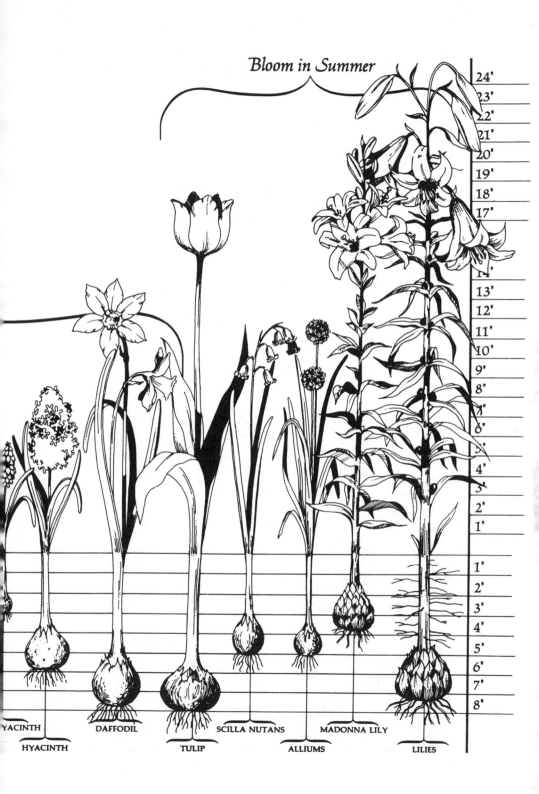

Bloom in Summer

24'
23'
22'
21'
20'
19'
18'
17'

13'
12'
11'
10'
9'
8'

6'

4'
3'
2'
1'

1'
2'
3'
4'
5'
6'
7'
8'

YACINTH   DAFFODIL   SCILLA NUTANS   MADONNA LILY

HYACINTH   TULIP   ALLIUMS   LILIES

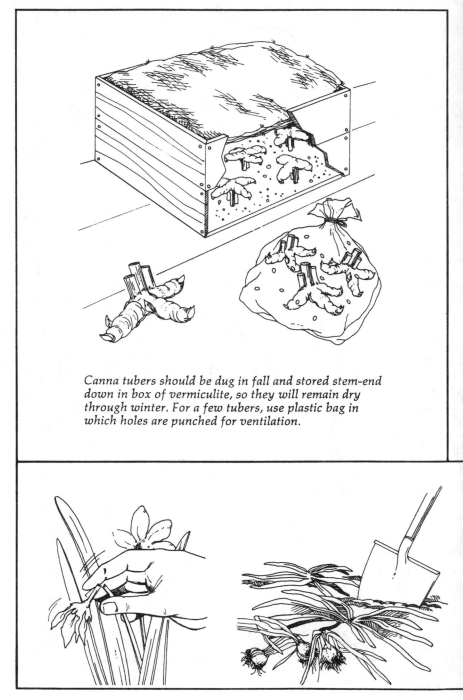

Canna tubers should be dug in fall and stored stem-end
down in box of vermiculite, so they will remain dry
through winter. For a few tubers, use plastic bag in
which holes are punched for ventilation.

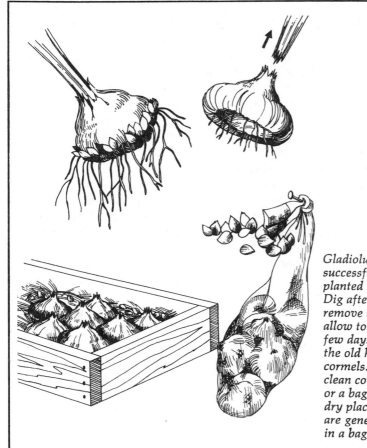

Gladiolus are most successful when re-planted annually. Dig after a frost, remove tops and allow to dry for a few days. Slip off the old husk and the cormels. Store the clean corms in a box or a bag in a cool, dry place. Cormels are generally stored in a bag.

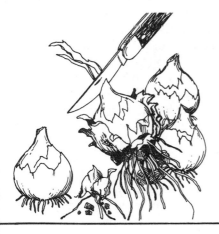

FAR LEFT: To encourage production of large flowers in narcissus and many other bulbs, it is important to break off flower heads once they have faded to prevent the ripening of seeds.
CENTER LEFT: Allow foliage to yellow and die down before digging bulbs for storage or for transplanting.
NEAR LEFT: Cut foliage back to the bulb before storing or transplanting so that the bulbs can thoroughly dry out.

While this sort of diagram has some value as a possible example, too often it is taken literally. The best perennials for a Midwestern border would not necessarily be the best ones for New England, the Deep South or the Southwest. Principles of design are important, however.

A perennial border may be very long and narrow or relatively short and not so narrow. But the concept of a border calls for a bed that is an elongated rectangle. I think that no perennial border should be less than 30 feet long (I would make one of this length 6 to 8 feet from front to back) and longer is better. While a 100-yard-long border might be 20 feet deep, usually a perennial border is less than 12 feet in depth. My 85-foot border is just about 10 feet deep.

The size of the "patches" of plants varies with the size of the border and with the massive quality of the various plants. The best borders feature long, narrow strips of "front" row, low-growing plants, and moderate rectangular clumps of flowers behind this. The clumps of intermediate and background perennials change with the boldness of foliage and flowers. Three or four clumps (growing together) of soup-bowl-sized Oriental poppy flowers easily balance a 5-foot-across patch of misty baby's-breath.

When making up your list of plants for the perennial border, note, first, all kinds that are reliable in your immediate area. Separate these into kinds that bloom April-May, May-June, June-July, July-August, August-September. Next, subdivide each of these lists into plants by height. Finally, list the color of each plant. With this information at hand, you are set to fill in names in your border design. Stick to those kinds that bloom longest and are best suited to growing in the soil and under the weather conditions you have to offer. Blend colors to suit your taste. A perennial border should not be a wishy-washy collection of faded pastels; the best ones are filled with bright colors—just enough white, pale yellow and cool colors to keep the bright flowers from clashing. You may choose to feature a midsummer border because your bulb garden is the great event of early spring and your dahlias and chrysanthemums demand full attention in the fall. You may want to do the border largely in shades of pink and blue, or some other color combination. These are matters of personal choice, and you have to do your own deciding. While true perennials make up the main planting, use showy biennials and hardy bulbs in your perennial border for more color and texture.

Maintenance of the Perennial Border

Well in advance, schedule the seasonal chores required to keep your perennial border in good shape. The border that is worked in leftover time looks it. In early spring, when danger of frost is past, remove the

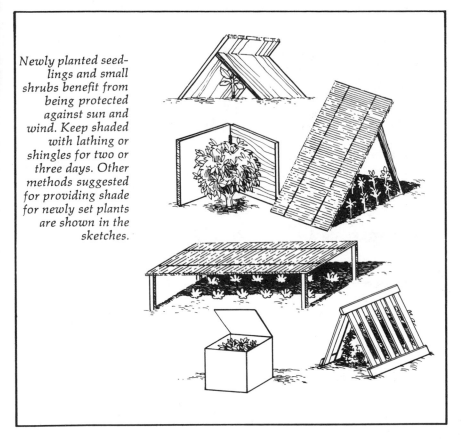

Newly planted seedlings and small shrubs benefit from being protected against sun and wind. Keep shaded with lathing or shingles for two or three days. Other methods suggested for providing shade for newly set plants are shown in the sketches.

mulch; partial removal at each work period, spread over ten days, is better than lifting all the mulch at once. As the ground is cleared, apply a light dressing of an all-purpose balanced fertilizer. Five pounds of a 5–10–5 fertilizer dressed over 100 square feet of bed suffices. I use a mixture of 25 pounds dehydrated cattle manure, 10 pounds 5–10–5 fertilizer, 10 pounds each cottonseed meal, hoof meal, blood meal and bone meal, and a pound of copperas (iron sulfate) *or* one-fourth pound chelated iron such as Sequestrene. I scatter 2 cups of this mixture over each square yard of the bed, keeping it off the crowns of the plants. After the fertilizer is spread, cultivate shallowly with a three- or four-pronged cultivator. As you work around each clump, remove moldy, decayed and discolored leaves. If slime trails indicate the presence of slugs and snails, apply a drench of Sluggit or use slug bait. Keep the bed in clean cultivation throughout the summer, or, when all plants are up and new growth is hardened off, apply a summer mulch of old sawdust, coarse compost or chopped straw. Perennial beds look best when cultivated weekly.

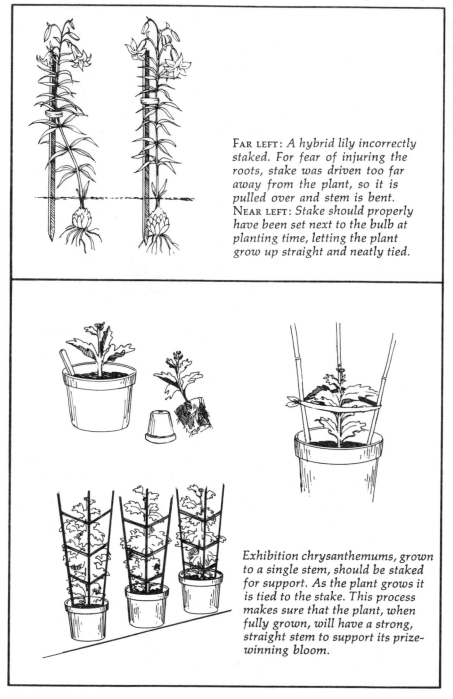

FAR LEFT: *A hybrid lily incorrectly staked. For fear of injuring the roots, stake was driven too far away from the plant, so it is pulled over and stem is bent.* NEAR LEFT: *Stake should properly have been set next to the bulb at planting time, letting the plant grow up straight and neatly tied.*

Exhibition chrysanthemums, grown to a single stem, should be staked for support. As the plant grows it is tied to the stake. This process makes sure that the plant, when fully grown, will have a strong, straight stem to support its prize-winning bloom.

Staking for Better Perennials

As taller-growing plants reach 6 to 8 inches, thin the crowded and weak shoots. Set stakes at this stage, so foliage will cover them by blooming time. There are three alternatives in staking: wire loops on wire supports, one or several garden stakes—such as bamboo stakes—per clump, and brush. Brush as support for plants came into English gardens during the labor shortage of World War II and proved so successful that it has continued. During fall and winter assemble twiggy brush, as pea-sticks. Upper branches of brushy sorts such as elm, beech, hornbeam and birch work very well. Each piece should be a finger-sized main stick with plenty of twiggy branches growing from it, broom fashion. These can be bundled, according to length, for storage. For staking, say, a clump of Michaelmas daisies, when the shoots are 15 inches high ring the clump closely with half a dozen or more of the brushy sticks, butts pushed firmly into the soil. The brush should make a loose, continuous ring around and among the daisy shoots. The daisy stems will grow upwards through the twigs; their soft branches, well furnished with leaves, grow outward through the brush and mask it. Brush twigs that show can be clipped away in a few weeks. I have never seen a well-brushed clump of perennials knocked crooked by even the strongest wind. Brush staking is a one-time job, while the use of clean stakes requires weekly visits to add more ties.

Water and Fertilizer for Perennials

Never let the perennial bed suffer for want of water. Usually spring and early summer rains provide enough (sometimes, too much) water. Occasionally, however, we encounter a dry season; then soak beds and borders once each week. I recommend watering with canvas soil soakers, or, with an underground watering system, bubbler heads, so foliage remains dry.

The pre-blossom regimen, then, is fertilization, continuous cultivation, staking and disease and insect control. As plants come into flower, feed again. In cool climates a light fertilizer application is spread over the bed. In my garden, I prefer to fertilize each clump individually, adjusting the application and the amount to the blooming time and the size of the plant. Midsummer care is limited largely to snipping off dead flowers and guarding against drought, insect pests and disease.

As a clump goes out of flower, cut back the flower stalks so the plant looks neat, but preserve as much foliage as possible. These green leaves make food that is stored in the roots for next year. In the fall, when frost blackens the foliage, cut back the plants immediately, and carry the debris to the compost pile or have it hauled away. Cultivate the bed one last time; probably not all plants will die back at the same time, so you will have to do a cleanup job two or three times a month through October and November. Do not fertilize in the fall. Do not mulch early. But carry on with clean cultivation as in summer.

Winter Mulching for Perennials

When the ground has frost in it, begin protecting sensitive species. Because slugs are a problem in my garden, I always scatter a few slug pellets near each plant and cover them with hand-sized pieces of broken flowerpot. Then I cover the crowns with an appropriate material. Most things are covered with pine or juniper branches; these are porous, and they do not compact, smother or cause decay. Moisture-sensitive sorts, the foxtail-lilies, delphiniums and hardy agapanthus, for example, are mounded. Years ago we used sifted cinders from the coal furnace for this, and I still think cinders cannot be replaced—though the furnace has been changed. Today I use coarse grit: granite grit meant for turkeys, screened sharp river pebbles or crushed brick. This material has to be scraped away and carried off in the spring. Over winter, the mound sheds excess moisture, deflecting it from the crown beneath, and the weight helps prevent frost heaving. After the Christmas holidays, when the ground is frozen hard, I like to pile more evergreen boughs over the entire border to keep the winter sun from thawing the soil on mild days. The point of winter mulch is to shade the ground and hold frost in the soil. Other materials that are suitable include straw, prairie hay, salt-marsh hay and shredded wood products.

Sources of Perennials

Grow your own from seed. Most perennials are as easy as annuals; sow seed in the cold frame in midsummer, overwinter the young plants in the frame and bed them in the spring. Or start seeds in early spring, indoors under the lights or in your home greenhouse. I do this often, and row out the young plants in the vegetable garden when danger of frost is past. There they are cultivated and cared for just like so many bean plants for an entire summer. In the fall they go into the border.

Perennial plants are available locally from specialists and from various mail-order nurseries. When plants are shipped, these days, they suffer. Usually they are packed semidormant, slightly damp. If the package is delayed (often in a warm place) the plants begin to grow and then decay. I recommend air mail, air parcel post or air freight (depending on the size of the shipment) every time. When the plants arrive, open the package immediately. Set the plants in a windless, bright place, out of direct sunlight. Those that appear to be dry, soak in a shallow pan of water. Hold the plants until late afternoon, then plant them, giving each a thorough watering. I use two wood shingles, stuck in at an angle over the plants, to protect them from direct sunlight for three or four days after transplanting.

Some perennials are shipped dormant, during the summer. Oriental poppy is a good example of this. Others are shipped semidormant, after flowering; bearded irises are an example.

Many perennials grow well from cuttings. Delphinium, chrysanthemums and coral-bell shoots, for example, root easily in perlite or other rooting medium. Root cuttings of others, such as Oriental poppy, bleeding-heart and globe thistle, are equally successful. Try a few cuttings each year. Friends with unusual plants will furnish the material for propagating.

PERENNIALS FOR CUT FLOWERS

Achillea filipendulina; millefolium; ptarmica; in varieties
Aconitum napellus
Alstroemeria aurantiaca and hybrids
Anemone elegans
Aquilegia hybrids
Artemisia lactiflora
Aruncus sylvester
Aster
Astilbe
Buphthalmum salicifolium
Campanula glomerata; latifolia; persicifolia; in varieties
Catananche

Centaurea dealbata; montana; in varieties
Cephalaria alpina
Chrysanthemum species and cultivars
Cimicifuga racemosa
Clematis recta
Coreopsis
Delphinium in varieties
Dianthus caryophyllus
Dicentra spectabilis
Dictamnus albus
Digitalis gloxinioides
Doronicum
Echinops
Erigeron hybrids
Eryngium

Filipendula hexapetala; ulmaria; in varieties
Gaillardia hybrids
Gentiana asclepiadea
Gypsophila
Helenium
Helianthus
Heliopsis scabra
Helleborus
Heuchera
Inula glandulosa
Iris
Kniphofia
Lupinus
Lychnis chalcedonica
Lysimachia clethroides
Lythrum salicaria
Monarda didyma

Oenothera fruticosa
Paeonia
Papaver orientale
Phlox paniculata
Physalis franchetii
Platycodon grandiflorum
Polygonum affine
Pyrethrum roseum hybridum
Ranunculus
Rudbeckia
Salvia superba
Scabiosa caucasica
Solidago
Thalictrum
Trollius
Veronica

PERENNIALS FOR DRY POSITIONS

*(Drought-resistant and will bloom with little trouble
if planted in dry soil)*

Achillea	Centaurea	Euphorbia	Nepeta
Anaphalis	dealbata	epithymoides	Oenothera spe-
Anthemis	Centranthus	Geranium	ciosa rosea
Aquilegia	ruber	Gypsophila	Potentilla
Artemisia	Cephalaria	Heliopsis	Sedum specta-
Asclepias	Dianthus—	Inula	bile
Asphodelus	some species	Iris germanica	Solidago
Bergenia	Dictamnus	Kniphofia	Veronica
Buphthalmum	albus	uvaria	spicata
Campanula	Doronicum	Limonium	Zauschneria
latifolia	Epimedium	Lupinus—	
Catananche	Eryngium	most sorts	

PERENNIALS FOR MOIST, SHADY POSITIONS

Aconitum	Cimicifuga	Lithospermum	Ranunculus
Actaea	Dicentra eximia	purpureo-	aconitifolius
Ajuga	Digitalis	caeruleum	Thalictrum
Anchusa myo-	Doronicum	Lysimachia	aquilegi-
sotidiflora	Filipendula	clethroides	folium
Anemone	Gentiana	Mertensia	Tolmiea
Anemonopsis	asclepiadea	Phlox	Tradescantia
Astilbe	Helleborus	Polygonatum	Trillium
Bergenia	Hemerocallis	Primula	Vinca
Campanula	Hosta	Pulmonaria	
persicifolia			

PERENNIALS WITH ATTRACTIVE FOLIAGE

Acanthus	Bergenia	Hosta
Achillea	Centaurea	Macleaya
clypeolata	Cimicifuga	Morina
Aconitum	Crambe	Paeonia
Anaphalis	Echinops	Sedum
Anemone	Epimedium	Senecio
elegans	Eryngium	Stachys olym-
Armeria	Filipendula	pica
Artemisia	Helleborus	Thalictrum
Astilbe	Heuchera	Veratrum

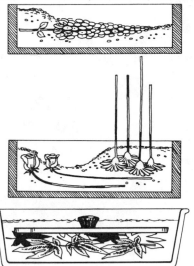

There are many ways to preserve flowers. ABOVE LEFT: *Air drying of flowers and leaves that contain little moisture is simple. Large subjects may be tied singly to a string suspended in a warm, dry, dark attic or storage room, while smaller subjects can be tied in bunches and hung.* LOWER LEFT: *Evergreens, such as holly and euonymus and tree foliage, are preserved differently: split branch ends and mash the lower ends of the branches. Prepare a solution of two parts drugstore glycerin to one part water and warm to 80 degrees. Immerse mashed stems in this solution and leave them there for two to three weeks.*
ABOVE, BOTTOM: *Trailing foliage of euonymus, ivy and individual leaves such as canna can be preserved by immersing for six days or more in a solution half glycerin and half water.* ABOVE: TOP *and* CENTER: *Fresh, garden-grown flowers are preserved by burying in a drying agent that removes their moisture so quickly they retain their color and form.*

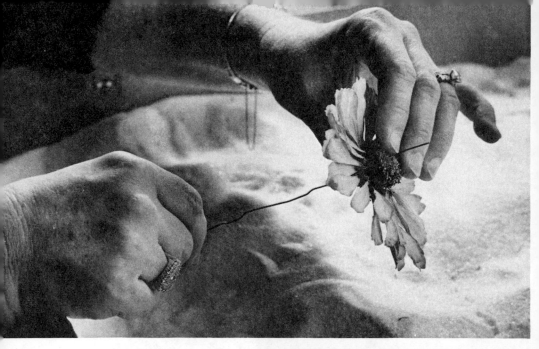

ABOVE: *Zinnia blossom gets wire "stem" before immersion in silica gel, a modern drying agent that resembles sand. Silica gel can be used over and over again. When blue grains in it turn white or pinkish, dry in a 300-degree oven until blue reappears.* RIGHT: *Silica gel is carefully poured over flower placed face up in box. Drying time, a matter of days, depends on flower's moisture content and thickness. Bury a test flower in a corner of the box and check regularly; overdried flowers fall apart. Some flowers to dry simply by hanging (page 161): baby's-breath, salvia, cockscomb, dock, globe amaranth, goldenrod, statice, yarrow, tansy, hydrangea, heather, globe thistle, strawflower, lavender and grasses. To dry in silica gel: most annuals and perennials, roses, dogwood, clematis.*

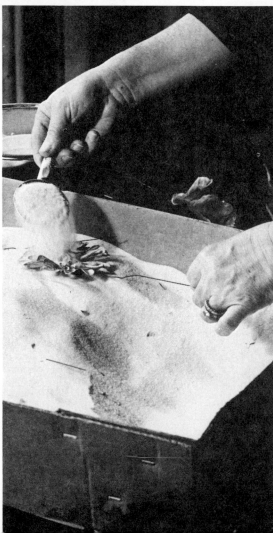

To enjoy flower arranging, it helps to have the necessary supplies and equipment. Sketches here suggest containers for conditioning cut flowers, shears, misting devices, pruning saws and knives, hammer and nails, needle and other types of holders for securing stems, florist foam, chickenwire, tape, wire and sharp pocket or paring knife. Your florist will be happy to sell you specialized supplies not found at a nursery or garden center. Organize your tools and supplies in a cabinet or on pegboard near a sink and countertop.

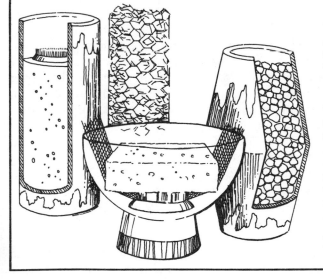

With suitable mechanics inside, almost any bowl or vase can be used for cut flowers. FAR LEFT: Sand with needle holder on top will support short-stemmed flowers in tall vase. Coil of chickenwire might also be used. CENTER: Secure florists foam in low bowl with tape or clay to hold flowers. NEAR LEFT: Clean pebbles hold stems.

Ten Rules for Success with Roses

1. Locate rose beds properly. Select a site with reasonably good drainage. Dig a hole 18 inches deep and fill with water. If the water does not seep away within a couple of hours, try another location. Full sun is good, afternoon shade is not bad, and sun for only five or six hours will do, but the roses *must* be away from the roots of trees and shrubs.

2. Prepare the soil thoroughly. It is no longer considered necessary, or even desirable, to dig out the soil 3 or 4 feet deep and put in a drainage layer. It *is* necessary to loosen the soil at least 18 inches deep and to incorporate a good amount of organic matter. Dig out, onto a square of canvas, the top spade's depth of soil and break up the next, removing all stones and boulders. Fork into this second spade's depth a lot of peat moss and dehydrated manure, or real manure and sifted leafmold, or some of everything, along with a little superphosphate. More organic matter and superphosphate should be mixed into the topsoil as it is replaced. Ideally, a bed should be made and allowed to settle six weeks before planting, but this is not always possible. Sometimes, for just a few bushes, it is necessary to dig separate holes, and do it at planting time, rather than six weeks before.

Although roses are not particularly fussy, they do best in a slightly acid soil. If the soil is alkaline (testing much above pH 7.0), work in 1 to 2 pounds of powdered sulfur per hundred square feet of bed area. If the soil is well below pH 6.0, add 3 to 5 pounds of ground limestone per hundred square feet.

3. Plant carefully at the right time for your locality. The right time to plant roses depends on where you live. In Florida, November and December are favored months; in California and other warm states, January and February are recommended. March is about right for the upper South, and in the far North, planting time is late April or early May. In New Jersey and other temperate states, you can plant dormant roses equally well in November or early spring, late March and early April. If you have to wait until late April or May, it is better to purchase potted roses, bushes already started in containers.

The roses will be shipped to you wrapped in polyethylene or sphagnum moss. If you cannot plant immediately, you can safely leave the package unopened in a cool place for a few days. If you must wait a week or two before final planting, remove the roses and bury them in a trench in the garden.

When you are ready to plant, open the package in the shade and examine each push very carefully before putting it in a pail of water. If

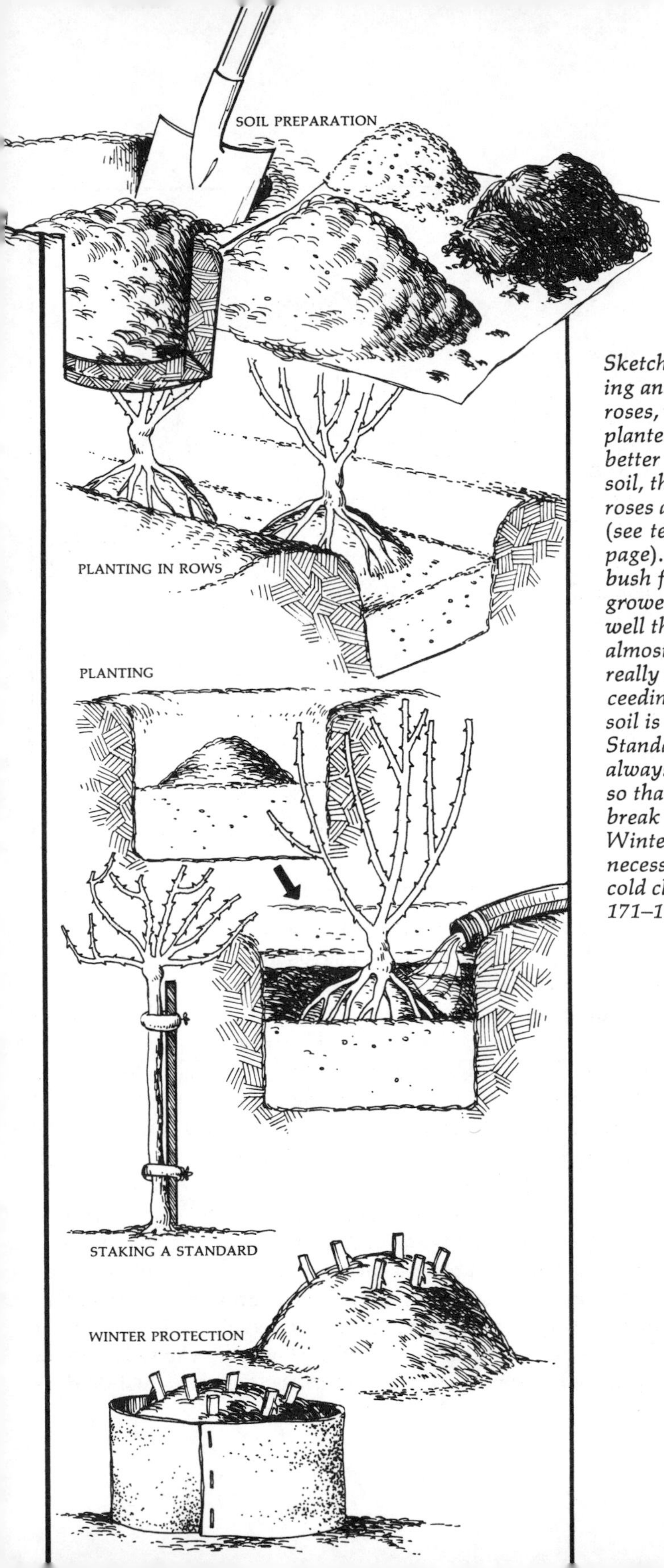

SOIL PREPARATION

PLANTING IN ROWS

PLANTING

STAKING A STANDARD

WINTER PROTECTION

Sketches show planting and winter care of roses, especially those planted in late fall. The better you prepare the soil, the better your roses are likely to grow (see text, opposite page). A first-rate rosebush from a good grower will do fairly well the first season in almost any soil, but to really thrive in succeeding years, good soil is a necessity. Standard or tree roses always need staking so that wind will not break or loosen roots. Winter protection is necessary only in very cold climates (see pages 171–173 for details).

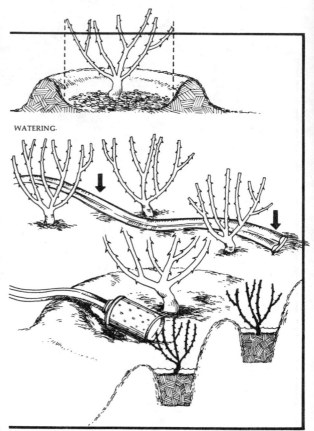

TOP: *Depression in soil at top of planting hole facilitates proper watering of newly planted rosebush (or other woody shrub or tree).* CENTER: *Two excellent watering methods for roses include the soil soaker hose for use in a bed and the soaker head or bubble for individual plantings. Both techniques keep moisture on the ground and away from the foliage where it might encourage disease.* BOTTOM: *To plant roses on a fairly steep bank or hillside, terrace as the sketch indicates with pockets created to catch water.*

WATERING.

there are rough roundish swellings near the crown (indicative of crown gall) or small swellings in the roots (these usually indicate root-knot nematodes), lay that plant aside to return to the nurseryman for replacement. Do not plant it; do not even put it in the water with the other roses.

Dig a large hole. The word "large" is relative, depending on the size of the root systems you receive and planting distances in the bed, but it might be 15 inches deep and 15 to 20 inches wide. Mound the soil in the center of the hole and spread the roots out and down over the mound, holding the bush so that the bump—the place where the desired variety was budded onto the understock—is at ground level or slightly below. In warm climates, this bud union is well kept an inch or so above the soil line, and in very cold regions, about 2 inches below it. Cut off the ends of the roots if they are too long; never coil them around the base. Cut off broken roots and damaged canes, then add friable soil, tamping it firmly when the hole is two-thirds full. Add water to fill the hole and let it drain entirely away before adding the rest of the soil, which should be left loose, not tamped in. Then add extra soil to make a mound 6 to 8 inches high around the canes. After fall planting, leave this mound undisturbed until spring; remove the mound in about two weeks after spring planting. This soil mound is very important in keeping the tops from drying out before the roots are established. Losses in new roses may often be attributed to ignoring this precaution.

Modern cold-storage methods keep roses dormant into late May, but such plants started after hot weather sets in seldom do well. Instead of succumbing to end-of-season bargains offered in advertisements, try potted roses. Many companies now specialize in roses grown in plastic containers. You buy them in full foliage, sometimes in flower, and they continue without interruption in your garden. Dig a hole, cut away or otherwise remove the plastic container without disturbing the roots, and carefully set the plant. Firm in soil around the root ball, keeping the bush at the same level it was growing in the container.

4. Prune with common sense. Leave all pruning until spring; never prune back in autumn except to remove damaged growth. Spring can mean December in Florida, January in California, late February or early March in North Carolina, late March and early April in New Jersey, late April in colder states. Wait until the buds swell and not much more freezing weather is expected. Be sure to remove all remnants of winter protection before pruning, because the cankers you want to eliminate are usually at the base of covered canes. With strong, recently sharpened pruning shears, preferably with a curved blade, cut out dead canes and those with discolored areas indicating cankers. Take out small, weak canes and those that crisscross in the center of the bush, then cut back remaining canes to sound wood. Make every cut *just above* a bud, slanting the cut upward in the direction the bud points. The cane always dies back to the bud, and such a dead stub affords entrance to canker fungi.

Sometimes a severe winter necessitates the cutting back of most canes nearly to the ground. Roses nearly always recover from such drastic treatment, but moderate pruning is now the rule wherever the winter permits it. Low pruning is no longer recommended, even for exhibition blooms. It is better to make cuts in last year's wood than to cut back in the old main canes, and to cut high enough so there will be plenty of leaves to manufacture food for continuous bloom.

Floribundas planted where they have room to develop to their natural height require little pruning in spring beyond cutting off dead tips. As new canes are produced in summer, some of the older canes die and these can be removed at any convenient time.

Cut out older canes of rambler roses in summer after flowering, but

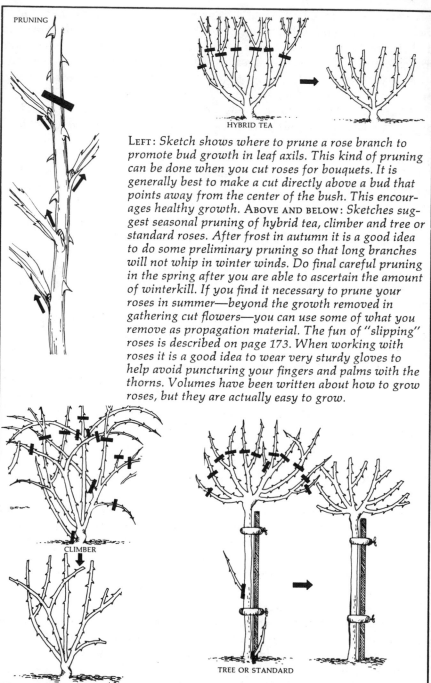

PRUNING

HYBRID TEA

Left: *Sketch shows where to prune a rose branch to promote bud growth in leaf axils. This kind of pruning can be done when you cut roses for bouquets. It is generally best to make a cut directly above a bud that points away from the center of the bush. This encourages healthy growth.* Above and below: *Sketches suggest seasonal pruning of hybrid tea, climber and tree or standard roses. After frost in autumn it is a good idea to do some preliminary pruning so that long branches will not whip in winter winds. Do final careful pruning in the spring after you are able to ascertain the amount of winterkill. If you find it necessary to prune your roses in summer—beyond the growth removed in gathering cut flowers—you can use some of what you remove as propagation material. The fun of "slipping" roses is described on page 173. When working with roses it is a good idea to wear very sturdy gloves to help avoid puncturing your fingers and palms with the thorns. Volumes have been written about how to grow roses, but they are actually easy to grow.*

CLIMBER

TREE OR STANDARD

UPPER: *The sketches suggest proper training and pruning of rambler roses—which may be planted on a fence (as shown), a wall, or it is possible to train them on a post or pillar. In the top sketch black bars at base suggest the removal of old, weak, dead or excessive growth. Third sketch from top shows desirable form at end of season.* LOWER: *Almost all cultivated roses have been budded onto a rootstock. Sometimes suckers sprout from the rootstock. If these are allowed to grow, they will weaken if not completely overshadow the more desirable budstock. Remove them immediately as indicated by the bars. A sucker usually comes up out of the ground (instead of above-ground from the main branchwork of the rose), and the leaves will have a different appearance.*

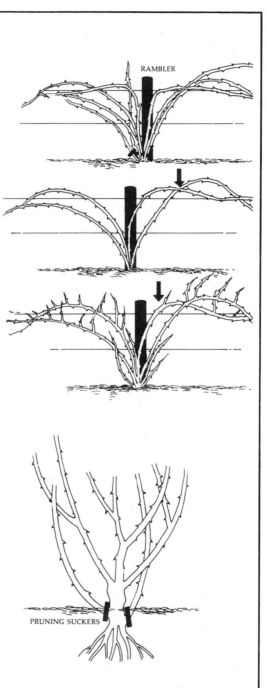

save most of the old wood of large-flowered climbers and cut back the laterals (the new canes growing out of old wood) to a foot or so from the main canes.

Every time you cut a rose for the house or cut off a dead bloom, consider it a pruning operation and *cut close to a bud,* that is, just above a leaf. On new roses, make that cut at the first leaf nearest the flower that has a good bud in the axil; on established roses you may, if you need a long stem, cut down to the second leaf from the base of a cane.

Removal of suckers as they appear through the season is vital in keeping the good rose alive, but don't cut out true basal breaks. The suckers always arise from below the bud union, and will always show a different type of foliage—gray-green if the rose is budded onto *R. multiflora* understock; reddish if on 'Dr. Huey.'

A dormant spray of liquid lime sulfur (use one part lime sulfur to nine parts water), applied immediately after pruning, will control rose scale (round, dirty white, shell-like scales that harbor insects on canes) and may help slightly in preventing disease. If this spray is applied too late, after the buds have broken to young leaves, it will burn the new foliage.

5. *Feed judiciously.* Do not feed newly planted roses at all. Established roses can have up to a trowelful of a complete fertilizer, such as 5–10–5, worked lightly around the bush right after pruning, again at the time of mass bloom, and perhaps in midsummer. Special rose foods may require monthly applications. Well-rotted cow manure applied as a mulch in early spring has some fertilizing value. Dehydrated manure can be used in addition to, but not as a substitute for, a complete chemical fertilizer.

Foliar feeding can replace or supplement some of the later ground feeding. I add water-soluble fertilizer to each gallon of my regular pesticide spray every other week from May 1 to the middle of August.

6. *Use a summer mulch.* A good mulch eliminates at least half the work in growing roses. Apply it as soon as convenient after the first feeding and after the ground has been lightly but thoroughly cultivated, to kill starting weeds. My personal preference is for buckwheat hulls applied 1 inch thick. They look good and allow water to penetrate freely. Cocoa shells have the same appearance and effect. Peat moss tends to absorb a lot of water before it gets to the roses and to cake on the surface so that water runs off, but it is satisfactory if rose beds can be watered regularly. Ground corncobs, sawdust and bagasse (sugarcane refuse) are useful if extra nitrogen is added to the soil to compensate for that used up by microorganisms breaking down the mulch. Pine needles and salt hay are possibilities.

A mulch reduces weeds, conserves moisture, keeps the soil friable and lowers soil temperature. In place early enough, it also provides a mechanical barrier between disease organisms on the ground and developing leaves overhead, and it reduces the splashing, which will spread black-spot spores from one rosebush to the next.

7. *Water adequately.* Roses usually survive periods of summer drought, but they stop growing and blooming. Their leaves may be burned by high temperatures, while those in adjoining gardens with artificial watering keep flowering and retain green leaves even though exposed to the same excessive temperatures. If water is unavailable, a good mulch will see your roses through the drought, but if you are allowed to use water, by all means apply it in generous quantities once a week.

The easiest, and probably the most wasteful, way to water is with a water fan that covers a large area at once. Such overhead sprinkling is best done early in the day so the roses can dry off before night, and should be omitted where black spot is a problem. The spores of black spot are spread by the water to nearby bushes and infect new leaves if the leaves are wet as long as six hours. A soil-soaker hose, a water wand or a water bubbler provides water without wetting foliage.

8. *Use pesticides regularly.* Roses will live for long periods even if you ignore their pests. I have one bed of scrawny roses that has not been sprayed or dusted for ten years. But if you want vigorous roses with abundant and continuous bloom on sturdy stems, with lustrous, unblemished foliage, then it is necessary to apply an all-purpose spray or dust, with the right chemicals for your area and problems, *every single week* from the time the bushes come into full foliage until frost.

There are a great many combinations of pesticides prepared especially for roses and marketed under trade names. All have advantages, all have some disadvantages. There is no one ideal combination for all rose varieties grown in all parts of the country under all climatic conditions for all pests. You select the one that is safe in your area and that takes care of the more important pests, and then you add an ingredient or apply a separate treatment as need arises.

9. *Use care in winter protection.* In many parts of the country, more roses are killed by coddling over the winter than by neglecting them. Over the years in New Jersey, I have gradually learned that established roses get along just as well completely unprotected (except for the summer mulch left in place to prevent some heaving) as they do when soil is brought in and hilled up around them. And they are more likely to be healthy the next spring than if their canes have been kept moist with

manure, peat moss or matted leaves, or if they were enclosed in soil so
that water could not drain away rapidly. I think salt hay is a good
summer mulch for roses but an abominable winter mulch for my section,
for the field mice have a heyday in it, completely girdling the canes with
their chewing.

The amount of winter protection is a local decision. In many cold
areas a simple soil mound, made by pouring a pail of friable soil into the
center of the bush to make a natural cone, is all that is necessary. In
other regions the soil mound may have to be covered with evergreen
boughs.

The safest way to winter a tree rose in a cold climate is to loosen
the roots on one side, dig a trench, and bury the rose completely. That is
a lot of trouble, and some winters you can get by with wrapping the rose
in place with straw or burlap. If the winter turns colder than anticipated,

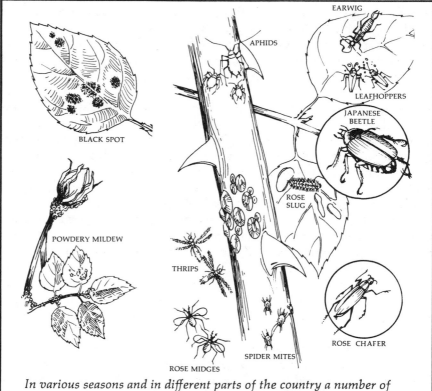

*In various seasons and in different parts of the country a number of
pests and diseases attack roses. Your best line of defense is a healthy
bush to begin with, properly planted and thoughtfully cared for. At
the first sign of trouble, seek advice from your local nurseryman, then
spray or dust.*

it may not be any more trouble to replace the tree than it would be to dig a trench out into the lawn and then have to fix it up again in spring.

10. *Enjoy your roses.* Take your roses casually or let them become a consuming hobby, but never let them be a burden. If you go off on an unexpected vacation and find not much foliage and few blooms on your return, don't worry too much. The roses will live to another year, when you can treat them better. But if you go away for two months every summer, forget about hybrid teas. Plant shrubs and climbers you can enjoy before leaving; plant 'The Fairy' and 'Betty Prior' to give you fall bloom without summer care.

Maybe you want roses in the house but lack the time for formal arrangements. Grow the colors that fit into your decorating scheme and cut the blooms at any convenient time, disregarding the usual rule of early in the morning or late afternoon. When you bring those roses into the house, hold each stem in 1 inch of almost boiling water while you count up to ten. Then place the stems in cool water and keep in a cool place, out of the wind, until you are ready to fix bouquets. Meanwhile, soak a block of Oasis (water-absorbing medium in which to arrange flowers, available from florists) for a couple of hours and cut it to fit your containers. The stems will hold in this at any angle.

Maybe you want the fun of "slipping" roses. Patented roses may not legally be propagated without permission and payment of royalty, but I know of no prosecutions of amateurs having fun in their own backyards. Take 6-inch cuttings in summer, just below the faded flowers of floribundas or hybrid teas. Cut off the top 2 inches, close to a leaf. From the 4-inch piece left, remove all except the top leaves, and stick it into a mixture of good soil, sand or vermiculite, and compost or peat moss, so that it protrudes only half an inch. Several such cuttings can go into a 6-inch pot, which is covered with a polyethylene bag and sunk in the garden. Or the cuttings can be put directly in the garden and covered with glass jars. Keep the soil around the pot or jar and leave the covering on for four months. Remove the jar or polyethylene and mound the slips with soil for winter.

For some, the supreme pleasure in growing roses comes from blue ribbons and silver trophies. All labor toward this end is fun. The true exhibitor does not mind disbudding (pinching out all side buds while very small), nor extra feeding with organic mixtures that may include fish, seaweed and dried blood, nor vast amounts of watering. He does not whimper when some of his roses have a short life with such a forced feeding regime, and he does not visibly shudder when, 4 days more or less before the show, he cuts back every flowering cane in the garden so that all will bloom at once.

8. Gardens for Eating

It is impossible to describe the difference between vegetables and fruits grown in your own garden and those you buy in the market. To experience home-grown food at its best, the eater must be brought close to the garden. "Run, don't walk, to the kitchen" might well become your motto. Delicacy of flavor and the ability to withstand shipping are mutually antagonistic. For finest flavor, a vegetable or fruit must be low in fiber and high in perishable sugars and esters. But the high fiber content and relatively dry, heavy-walled cellular structure, which give a vegetable or fruit the ability to withstand shipping, result in a poor-flavored product.

Planning the Vegetable Garden

How big the garden should be depends on the time and energy available. A big garden including the perennials supplies a family of six with fresh vegetables all season and provides plenty to pickle and preserve. A medium garden by today's standards is 40 by 60 feet and supplies a family of four or five with fresh vegetables and some to store and freeze. A garden 25 by 25 feet is small but keeps fresh salad makings and many vegetables available most of the season—and is a good way to begin.

The garden should be located in full sun, as hardly any of the vegetables succeed in shade. Timing for plants is discussed below and also in the tables that follow. Vegetables require good garden loam, well supplied with organic materials, with a pH between 6.0 and 6.8. It should be watered once weekly, and deeply. Mulched, watering needs will be less, and the necessity to weed almost nonexistent.

Opposite: *If you have an acreage in the country, and space for vegetables in an out-of-the-way corner, it is fine to have a simple "truck patch." However, in cramped quarters they can be cultivated more decoratively. Here strawberries grow in a terraced city space.*

Salad Greens. In the home garden you can grow a variety of salad greens that would cost fabulous prices at fine restaurants. You are not confined to lettuce, but can indulge in such luxury items as witloof chicory, forced dandelions, curly endive, escarole and forced white mustard.

Since variety is so important, here is a listing of quality lettuces for home-garden use. 'Matchless' and 'Bibb' top the list. 'Deer Tongue,' which in some past time was bred for 'Matchless,' is only a notch under them in quality. 'Oak Leaf' ranks below these three, but is worth growing because of its excellent resistance to heat. 'Mignonette,' a tiny, crisp-head variety with dark red staining on the outer leaves, is a delicious lettuce when well grown. It is the same general type, at least in theory, as 'Iceberg,' 'Great Lakes,' 'New York' and 'Wonderful,' but in quality it is far ahead of these rubbery shipping varieties.

For those who like a head lettuce with fully blanched leaves, 'California Cream Butter' is excellent in quality. It is a butterhead much like the older 'Big Boston.' The old 'Grand Rapids,' 'Prize Head' and 'Black Seeded Simpson' varieties of leaf lettuce lack the quality of the heading types already mentioned, except when cut very young. One of the most overrated lettuces is 'Salad Bowl,' a rubbery head which has all the faults of both leaf and crisp-head varieties.

Cos lettuce, often called romaine, can be good when grown in heavy peat or muck soil. When it is grown in ordinary garden soils, only the heart leaves are high in quality. Cos absorbs too much mineral matter; this produces leaves with hard ribs. When I serve cos in a salad mixed with 'Matchless' and 'Bibb,' the leaves are likely to go uneaten.

In theory, lettuce is a cool-weather crop. The seed will not sprout at high temperatures, nor will the plant grow. There is nothing worse than a crop of lettuce that has been allowed to stand all summer long and produce fibrous leaves. Two exceptions are 'Matchless' and 'Oak Leaf.' Both will produce satisfactory crops, even in the heat of summer.

All lettuce is best eaten when it is immature. The moment it shows signs of going to seed, the leaves turn bitter. For this reason, short rows, sown at three-week intervals during the growing season, should be the rule. The best soil is a sandy loam, with extra fertility added. Since lettuce is subject to root rot, drainage must be good.

In summer, when temperatures are high and the seed is not likely to germinate well, you can induce pre-sprouting by mixing the seed with damp sand and storing at the bottom of a refrigerator for a week. After this cold treatment, it should sprout at once. Or cover the row with aluminum foil until the seed germinates. The foil conserves moisture and repels the sun's heat. Allow 24 inches between rows, and thin the young plants to stand at least 6 inches apart in the row.

True endive or curly endive (mistakenly called chicory) is a plant with stiff, fringed leaves, dark green and bitter until they are blanched. When blanched, they have a delicious bittersweet flavor. For general planting, the variety called 'Green Curled Pancalier' or 'Rose Ribbed Curled' is best. This is the only one that does not turn so bitter in heat that it is unpalatable. Other curly endives can be sown very early in spring or seeded about August 1 for a late fall crop.

About August 1 (north of the Ohio River) to August 20 (south of the river) the plain-leaved variety of endive (called escarole), or one of its deep-hearted varieties such as 'Full Heart,' should be seeded. This is one vegetable that can stand considerable freezing. At the same time, a succession crop of 'Pancalier' can be sown. These two plantings will be at their best after frost and, with the protection of some loose hay, can be kept in good condition often until Thanksgiving Day. South of the Ohio, they usually survive without protection. Culture is about the same as for lettuce. The plants should be thinned to stand 10 inches apart.

Both escarole and 'Green Curled Pancalier' are likely to rot unless they are blanched carefully. To save trouble, grow a big crop and use only the lower parts of the leaves, which blanch naturally.

Witloof chicory is a relative of the plant used as a coffee substitute. The large root is dug in fall and used for forcing. The white shoots, sold as Belgian endive and grown under soil or sand, are perhaps the most luxurious and expensive of all salads. Forcing is not difficult. In fall, the mature roots of spring plants are dug and cut to a uniform length, usually about 6 to 7 inches long. They are placed upright in a box 12 inches or more deep, and sand poured over them to a depth of at least 5 inches. The box is then placed in a temperature of 60 degrees and watered well.

When the tips of the blanched leaves break through the sand, the grower should feel carefully along the shoot and cut it off about 1 inch above the crown. If this is done without injuring the bud, a second and sometimes a third crop can be taken from the same roots. Store the sand-filled boxes of surplus roots in a cold frame until the first forcing roots are exhausted.

Tomatoes. Perhaps no fruit or vegetable is more thoroughly abused when handled through commercial channels than the tomato. Shipped-in or greenhouse-grown fruits are picked green, without a trace of red or pink in the skin. Shipped to processors, they are placed in "ripening" rooms into which live steam is injected. This turns the fruit a dull pink, but has little or no effect in converting the starches into sugars.

A common impression is that in the temperate zone tomatoes can be grown only if they are started indoors or purchased as started seed-

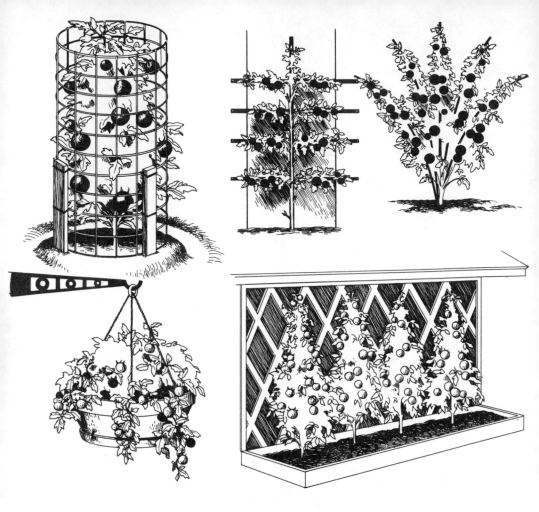

TOP ROW: *Three ways to handle tomatoes. At left, an easy method of staking is to surround plants with wire cylinder. Center, tomato espaliered against a building; severe pruning required by espalier produces large, handsome fruit. Right, tomato espaliered on stakes bent to fan shape.* CENTER ROW: *Left, hanging clay pot holds cherry tomatoes. Right, tomatoes pruned to tree shape against trellis.* BOTTOM ROW: *Three steps that improve tomato production: Left, remove suckers; center, pinch out tops on new shoots; right, sketch shows placing of stake at planting. Set seedlings so stems are 3 or 4 inches below original soil line.*

lings and transplanted into the open when danger from frost is over. This unnecessary labor deters many who might otherwise grow their own plants and produce fine crops. Actually most of the canning crops of the country are grown from plants sown directly in the open field. Although tomatoes are of tropical origin, the seeds can be sown as early in spring as the soil can be worked. About 10 pounds to 1,000 square feet of a 5–10–5 or 4–12–4 (or half that amount of a 10–8–6) should be applied before the seed is planted. The fertilizer can be worked into the soil when digging. If only nitrogen is used, the plants are likely to grow rank and produce few fruits.

The rows can be 4 feet apart for most varieties, although 3 feet is enough for small-vined sorts like 'Bounty,' 'Earliana' and 'Firesteel.' If the plants are to be staked (a device of doubtful value under most circumstances), they can be as close as 18 inches.

Sow several seeds in each spot where a vine is wanted. When these have formed four or five leaves, cut away all but one seedling. (Don't pull the extras—this may disturb the roots of the one left to grow.)

Sow indoors only if a sunny window (at least six hours of direct sun) that can be kept at 60 to 70 degrees is available. Start seedlings in 3-inch peat pots eight weeks before they are to be set out. Set the plants in the open garden about the time the tall bearded irises come into bloom.

All transplanted seedlings are helped by treating them with a high-nitrogen, high-potash starter solution. A cupful or so poured in the hole at transplanting time enables the new plants to quickly recover from the shock of being moved into a new environment. Tomatoes don't like deep cultivation. A heavy mulch of straw removes the need for stirring the soil and also forms a clean cushion to keep the fruits off the soil. When flower buds begin to appear and first fruits are seen as tiny green buttons, apply the same amount of plant food as you did at planting time, but spread it along the row, about 3 inches out from the main stem. The vines will be sprawling by this time, so be ready with the hose to quickly wash off any fertilizer that falls on the leaves.

Picking suckers off the stems of tomatoes is necessary only when tomatoes are pruned to single stems that are grown on stakes to produce extra-large fruit or because space is limited.

Plant only disease-resistant varieties. Two varieties especially recommended for the home garden are 'Wiltmaster' and 'Manalucie,' since they are resistant to many diseases and will usually produce a good crop. Blossom-end rot is sometimes a nuisance. It is not a disease but a physiological disturbance; its cause is not known. If the soil is kept constantly moist (not soaked), very little blossom-end rot develops. The soil should be well-supplied with calcium, but not overlimed. Use ground limestone rather than hydrated lime to supply any needed calcium.

VEGETABLES TO PLANT IN EARLY SPRING

VEGETABLES	SEEDS OR PLANTS 50-FT. ROW	YIELD 50-FT. ROW	SPACE BETWEEN ROWS	SPACE BETWEEN PLANTS	DEPTH TO PLANT	APPROXIMATE DAYS TO MATURITY
Asparagus (perennial)	35 plants	25 lbs.	4 ft.	18 in.	5–6 in.	second season
Beets	½ oz.	1 bushel	12–18 in.	2–3 in.	½ in.	early, 45 days; late, 65 days
Broccoli	25 plants (1 pk. seed)	25–40 heads	20–24 in.	18 in.	¼–½ in.	plants, 50–60 days seed, 80–100 days
Brussels sprouts	25 plants (1 pk. seed)	1–2 bushels	20–24 in.	18 in.	½ in.	plants, 60–70 days seed, 95 days
Cabbage	25 plants	25 heads	20–30 in.	18 in.	½ in.	early, 40–50 days; late, 70–90 days
Carrots	¼ oz.	1 bushel	20 in.	1–2 in.	¼ in.	75–80 days
Cauliflower	25 plants (1 pk. seed)	25 heads	20–30 in.	18 in.	½ in.	plants, 65–75 days seed, 80–100 days
Chard, Swiss	½ oz.	2 bushels	18 in.	4–6 in.	¼ in.	55 days
Cress, garden	1 pkt.	20 lbs.	24 in.	12 in.	¼ in.	20 days
Endive and escarole	½ pkt.	50 lbs.	12 in.	4 in.	¼ in.	65–90 days
Garlic (cloves)	½ lb.	¾ bushel	8 in.	3 in.	1¼ in.	125 days
Horseradish (perennial)	25 roots	¾ bushel	24 in.	15 in.	12 in.	120 days
Jerusalem-artichoke (perennial)	2–3 lbs.	2 bushels	3–4 ft.	18 in.	2 in.	second season
Kale	½ pkt.	125 lbs.	12–18 in.	10 in.	½ in.	56–75 days
Leeks	2 pkt.	100 plants	10–12 in.	2–3 in. later 6 in.	¼ in.	130 days
Lettuce	1 pkt.	50 lbs.	12 in.	2–3 in.	¼ in.	40–90 days
Onion sets	½ lb.	1 bushel	12 in.	8 in.	1 in.	110 days
Parsnips	2 pkt.	1½ bushels	12 in.	3–4 in.	½–1¼ in.	95–150 days
Peas	½ lb.	1 bushel	20–30 in.	3 in.	1–2 in.	early, 58 days; late, 80 days
Potatoes, Irish	2–3 lbs.	2 bushels	2–3 ft.	18 in.	trench 4–6 in. cover 2 in.	80–100 days
Radishes	2 pkt.	50 bunches	12 in.	1–2 in.	¼ in.	early, 20 days; late, 60 days
Rhubarb (perennial)	17 roots	too much	3 ft.	3 ft.	10 in.	second season
Spinach	½ oz.	1 bushel	12 in.	4 in.	¼–½ in.	40–50 days
Strawberries (perennial)	35 plants	½–1 quart	4 ft.	18 in.	1½ in.	second season
Turnips	1 pkt.	1 bushel	18 in.	6 in.	½ in.	early, 35 days; late, 60 days

VEGETABLES TO PLANT IN MID-SPRING

VEGETABLES	SEEDS OR PLANTS 50-FT. ROW	YIELD 50-FT. ROW	SPACE BETWEEN ROWS	SPACE BETWEEN PLANTS	DEPTH TO PLANT	APPROXIMATE DAYS TO MATURITY
Artichokes (perennial)	17 plants	2 bushels	36 in.	36 in.	5–6 in.	second season
Beans						
bush, snap	¼ lb.	25 quarts	20–30 in.	3–5 in.	1–1½ in.	55–65 days
limas, bush	¼ lb.	7 quarts	30–36 in.	4 in.	1–1½ in.	75 days
limas, pole	½ lb.	10 quarts	30–36 in.	4–6/pole	1 in.	12–14 weeks
pole	¼ lb.	2 bushels	30–36 in.	4–6/pole	1 in.	65 days
Celeriac	¼ pkt.	100 roots	20 in.	6 in.	¼ in.	120 days
Celery	¼ pkt.	100 bunches	20–24 in.	6 in.	¼ in.	120 days
Corn						
Indian	¼ lb.	75 ears	24–36 in.	10–12 in.	½–1 in.	105 days
popcorn	¼ lb.	12–15 lbs.	24–36 in.	10–12 in.	½–1 in.	90–105 days
sweet	¼ lb.	75 ears	36 in.	8 in.	½–1 in.	75 days
Cucumbers	½ pkt.	75 lbs.	48 in.	4–6 in.	½ in. in peat pot	50 days
Gourds	½ pkt.	too much	36 in.	5 ft.	1 in. in peat pot	100 days
Kohlrabi	¼ oz.	30 lbs.	18 in.	6–8 in.	½–1 in.	48–60 days
Parsley (biennial)	½ pkt.	25 lbs.	18 in.	6–8 in.	¼ in.	120 days
Peppers	35 plants	2 bushels	20–24 in.	18 in.	¼ in.	60–80 days
Pumpkins	½ pkt.	150 lbs.	5 ft.	5 ft.	1 in.	100–120 days
Rutabaga	1 pkt.	1 bushel	18 in.	8 in.	½ in.	85–90 days
Salsify	2 pkt.	1 bushel	12 in.	3–4 in.	¼–½ in.	120 days
Shallots	½ lb.	½ bushel	12 in.	3 in.	1 in.	80–100 days
Spinach, New Zealand	½ oz.	1 bushel	18 in.	6 in.	¼–½ in.	70 days
Squash						
summer	½ pkt.	60–70 lbs.	24–36 in.	6 in.	1 in.	45–50 days
winter	½ pkt.	150 lbs.	6 ft.	5 ft.	1 in.	90–110 days
Tomatoes	17 plants	75 lbs.	3–4 ft.	2–3 ft.	¼–½ in.	70–80 days

VEGETABLES TO PLANT IN LATE SPRING

Eggplant	½ pkt.	150 fruit	20–30 in.	18 in.	½ in.	60–75 days
Melons						
cantaloupe	½ pkt.	40–60 fruit	4 ft.	8–10 in.	1 in. in peat pot	70 days
watermelon	1 pkt.	150 lbs.	6 ft.	3 ft.	1 in.	70–85 days
Okra	2 pkt.	30 quarts	36 in.	15–24 in.	½ in.	56 days
Sweet potatoes	2–3 lbs.	2 bushels	24–36 in.	18 in.	5 in.	120–150 days

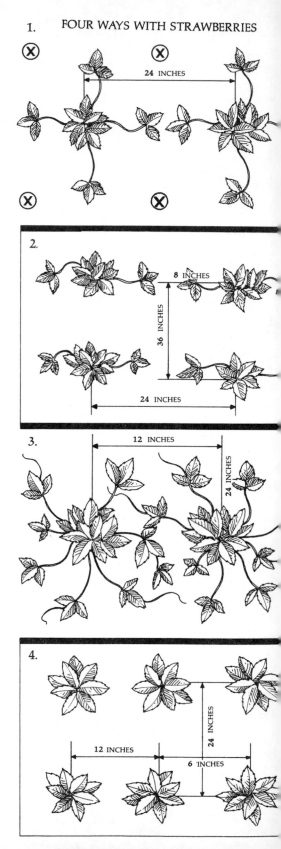

1. FOUR WAYS WITH STRAWBERRIES

Small Fruit Plants for the Home Garden

From home-grown fruit plants come harvests which can best be appreciated by someone who has actually eaten them. One's first taste of a truly
fine strawberry like the famous 'Royal Sovereign' (usually catalogued as
'British Sovereign' in this country) will soon point up the tremendous
gap which exists between such a fruit and the run-of-the-field stuff sold
at the supermarket.

The Strawberry. The most important of all garden fruits is the strawberry—*Fragaria.* It more nearly resembles a vegetable in its culture than
does any other fruit. It is not surprising that in many truck-gardening
areas growers switch from vegetables to strawberries and back again
almost at will.

Although the strawberry plant is a perennial and beds can be made
to last for more than one year, best commercial practice calls for a new
planting each year. The plants are grown in rows and for the first season
need the same cultivation as vegetable crops. The next season they
produce their best fruit. They can be left for four more years, but true
connoisseurs usually plow them under. The possible exceptions are
where everbearers are grown on the hill system, or where runnerless
Alpine strawberries are grown from seed. The latter are at their best
when grown as true perennials.

In the so-called hill system of growing, the mother plant is kept
pruned of all runners. This is the method by which the home gardener
can produce the largest and best-flavored berries. The plants are usually
set 12 inches by 24 inches apart in the bed and kept free of weeds.
Usually, a rather heavy mulch is maintained on the bed. The plants are
watched constantly to prevent runners from rooting.

While very large berries are produced, production per square foot is
probably lower than when other methods are used. As can be imagined,
the labor required is considerable. About 100 plants are as many as most
home gardeners care to cultivate when the hill system is used.

The variety used is important, since not all strawberries do well
when grown in this way. The Alpine variety 'Baron Solemacher' grown
from seed will produce perhaps the finest-flavored berries of all. These
have the aroma which makes wild strawberries such a delectable treat.
Where it will grow, the English 'Royal Sovereign' produces superb
berries by this system. These are of enormous size, deliciously rich and
sweet. In the South, 'Aroma' does well in hills.

OPPOSITE: *Besides growing strawberries in pots, boxes and barrels, they can be
cultivated by these systems: (1) hedge row (extra runners transplanted); (2)
row system (only two runners allowed to root); (3) matted row (after fruiting,
all runners rooted); and (4) hill system (all runners prevented from rooting).*

The matted-row system is exactly the opposite of the hill method. The mother plants are set 24 inches apart in rows 36 inches apart. After fruiting, the mother plants are encouraged to produce all the runners possible for twelve inches on either side of the row. Any forming outside these limits are cut off. This produces a matted row about 24 inches wide, with a twelve-inch lane between the rows of plants.

One advantage of the matted row is that it provides plenty of plants for setting new beds. The best way to produce these is to use one of the new peat-and-fiber pots in which to root them. These pots come in three-inch round or three-inch square sizes, just right to produce a husky plant. The pot is filled with a rich composted soil and plunged under a likely-looking runner. By late August the rooted plant can be cut from the parent plant and used to plant a new row. Although fall-planted rows require protection for one additional winter, they are usually more productive than spring-planted rows. They can even be allowed to bear a light crop the first spring.

It is a well-accepted rule, however, that all spring flowers should be removed the first season following planting. This keeps the plant from fruiting. Once the spring bloom is over, the June bearers (which produce only one set of flower buds a year) will not bloom again. The ever-bearers will produce additional flowers. Some of these can be allowed to produce a light crop the first fall after planting.

The row system of planting is a compromise between the matted row and the hill system. Here, plants are set 24 inches apart in rows 36 inches apart. One runner is allowed to set in the row on either side of the mother plant. In theory, each runner is about eight inches long, so the finished row is made up of plants spaced eight inches apart.

Sometimes a second set of runners is allowed to root at right angles to the row. This leaves the mother plant with four runners surrounding it. This is called the hedge-row system, since the bed resembles a series of triple hedges. An extra runner is allowed to root and is then transplanted to the spots marked X in the accompanying drawing, to complete the two outside rows.

Setting the Strawberry Bed. As previously mentioned, strawberries can be planted in fall if pot-grown plants are available. These are easy to plant, since they are set just as deep as they grew in the pot. Plants in clay pots will have to be knocked out (removed from the pot), but if in peat-and-fiber pots, they are planted pot and all.

Bareroot plants can also be set in fall, but few nurserymen have them available at that time. Plants available in spring are usually sold bareroot. They come tied in bundles. Before untying, cut the roots to a uniform length, about four inches below the soil line.

Cut off any dead or weak leaves, leaving only three or four of the new, healthy, young leaves to form the new top. Now the plant is ready to be set.

In the average garden there is not much choice of location. The strawberry does not like heavy soils, and if only a clay loam is available, it should be treated as mentioned under *soil*. A gardener's loam as mentioned in that entry is the ideal toward which to strive, although strawberries will do well in lighter sandy loams.

One of the most important steps in planting is to set the plant so the dividing line between the roots and the top or crown comes exactly at the surface of the soil. The crown should never be buried nor should roots show above the ground. Firm the soil around the roots so the crown will not be pulled below the surface when the plants are watered. If dirt works into the crown, it may rot.

Regular weeding is important, as strawberry plants make poor competitors for vigorous weeds. Do not cultivate deeply close to the plants and rooted runners, as these are shallow-rooted.

In regions where the thermometer can be expected to drop as low as 12 above zero regularly, a mulch is necessary. This is not, as many suppose, to keep the plants from freezing. On the contrary, it is to keep them frozen in early spring and prevent alternate thawing and freezing, which tend to pull the plants out of the ground. Being shallow-rooted, strawberries cannot resist the heaving action of frost.

In the South, a straw mulch is still desirable, largely to keep down weeds. It is of little value, however, if straw full of grain or marsh hay full of weed seeds is used. Clean, grain-free straw is the ideal material, if it can be had. An excellent substitute, much more readily available in most city and suburban areas, is excelsior. Most retail stores will be glad to give the home strawberry grower all he can use.

The mulching material is dumped right over the plants. By the time it settles, there should still be about three inches of it over the leaves in the North. In the South, the tips of the leaves should be showing.

In spring, when the daffodils are just showing yellow in their buds, pull away the mulch from the tips of the leaves so they show through. The new leaves will grow right through the mulch, which later will keep the berries clear of the soil.

The Bush Fruits. Although raspberries, blackberries and dewberries are borne on bushes, these are usually considered to be brambles. The true bush fruits, lumped under the general term *groseilles* by the French, include currants and gooseberries, both of the genus *Ribes*.

Both of the latter are now so hedged in by legal restrictions on their planting that at first they hardly seem worth the trouble. One's first taste of a vine-ripened gooseberry or of homemade currant jelly will, however, make the trouble they involve seem of little importance. The flavor of these should not be judged by commercial grass-green gooseberries, too sour and flat to be worth eating.

Culturally, gooseberries and currants are alike. Both are distinctly cool-climate plants and of little value in the South and in Southern California. South of the Ohio River they are best grown in light shade, such as is found under oak trees trimmed high. Even in the North they do well in such a spot and are considered the one fruit that can be grown by the owner of a shaded lot.

Both prefer heavier soils. If there is any choice, pick a clay loam. They can be grown on lighter soils, but only if plenty of organic matter is worked in to hold water. Bush fruits need plenty of moisture, but will not grow where the roots stand in water.

Because they like moist, cool soil, mulching is good practice. Sawdust (with a handful of ammonium sulfate added to every peck of sawdust) is excellent. Peat moss, leafmold, rice and buckwheat hulls are all good. The mulch can be two to three inches deep. Fall planting is best, since the bushes leaf out too early in spring to move them in time. Some nurserymen carry them in storage for spring planting, but even such stock should be set out as early as the soil can be worked.

On the Great Plains, where winters are likely to be dry and without snow, spring planting may be necessary. To conserve moisture, the bushes should be watered heavily and mulched at once.

Plants should be set about four feet by six feet apart. This allows ample room for working between them and permits the gardener to detect runners and to pull them before they spread too far. One reason for mulching rather than cultivating *groseilles* is that each time a root is cut, it sends up a runner. If a mulch is not used, the surface of the soil should be barely stirred when cultivating, to avoid cutting roots.

Fruit is borne on one-, two- and three-year-old wood. My ideal system is to have three branches of each age—nine in all. On the newly set plants all wood usually is young enough to bear. Later, the three-year-old wood will be a deep brownish red in color, the two-year-old somewhat lighter, while the one-year-old is a grayish green.

The Bramble Fruits. Red raspberries and apples require about the same climate, while dewberries, blackberries and black raspberries will thrive where peaches grow. In milder climates of the South, the youngberry and boysenberry varieties of blackberry produce rich globs of sweetness that are the envy of every Northern gardener.

Although they are grown in as many ways as there are varieties of brambles, most home gardeners prefer to grow them on trellises that prevent the canes' whipping in the wind. I know of no nastier injury resulting from gardening than the tears caused by a raspberry or blackberry cane brushing against one's face or arm.

For the blackcaps and purplecaps (which are just other names for black and purple raspberries) the trellis need be only a single wire suspended 24 inches above the soil line. Wooden posts set every 15 feet will give plenty of support if firmly anchored. For red raspberries, blackberries, dewberries and loganberries, a wire at 12 inches and another one at 48 inches are used.

As the canes grow, they are tied to these wires to prevent whipping. If only a few plants are grown, they can be tied to individual stakes.

Dewberries, boysenberries and youngberries do not ordinarily bear fruit where winter temperatures drop much lower than 10 degrees above zero. They can be grown farther north if laid down and covered with earth in winter. However, the chore of handling the long canes makes this job hardly worth the effort.

Red raspberries should be planted 24 to 36 inches apart. Blackberries, black- and purplecaps and dewberries should be set 36 to 42 inches apart. Youngberries and boysenberries need at least five feet between plants.

The suckers that spring up around the mother plant of red raspberries can be used to set new rows. Old plantings of this fruit tend to grow so thick and matted that they are difficult to care for. It is easier to start a new row every third year and kill out the old immediately after harvest the following year.

Most other brambles are propagated by tip layers. The long branches arch over to the ground and root at the ends. Some blackberries and dewberries, however, also sucker. If they do not, covering the end of an arching cane with soil will produce a new plant in a hurry.

All the brambles require a moist soil, and a heavy mulch does much to keep them growing well. In midsummer, feed liberally with a chemical fertilizer, being sure to soak this through the mulch with water.

Harvesting and pruning of the brambles are the same as for *groseilles*, except that all fruiting canes are cut away, since they will die the next winter. One point to remember is that the autumn-bearing varieties of red raspberries produce the fall crop on wood of the current year's growth. For this reason it is not necessary to save the old canes, as some suppose. The quicker all fruiting wood is removed following harvest, the stronger will be next year's canes.

Blueberries for the Home Garden. The modern cultivated blueberry (*Vaccinium*) has come in for criticism from diehards, who claim it lacks flavor and quality. Although this may be true of the commercial blueberry picked before it is dead-ripe and shipped to a distant market, I defy anyone to match the luscious richness of a modern variety like 'Earliblue' or 'Bluecrop' picked at full maturity and eaten within an hour.

Where naturally acid soils are available, the cultivated blueberry is one of our finest fruits. Too, the bush on which these fruits are produced makes a lovely ornamental.

Blueberries do best if there is some acid peat in the soil. In planting, a mixture of one-third peat and two-thirds soil is about right. Be sure the peat is really acid, however. Many domestic peats are alkaline in reaction. To be safe, insist upon a Swedish or German peat. When mixing the soil, add a handful of ammonium sulfate and a teaspoonful of chelated iron to each peck.

Set the plant a little deeper than it grew in the nursery. It will grow rather large, so allow at least 48-by-48-inch spacing. Once planted, mulch heavily and be sure the soil stays moist.

Although blueberries are often found growing in swamps, they do not like water standing around their roots. They grow on hummocks, which keep them in well-drained soil while supplying adequate moisture. Here is a clue to their moisture needs: A soil high in organic matter, mulched with oak leaves, pine needles or peat moss and kept constantly moist but never wet will produce the best crops.

Feed the bushes about mid-August when they are setting next year's flower buds. Use only an ammonium form of nitrogen such as ammonium sulfate, ammonium nitrate or diammonium phosphate.

Like grapes, blueberry varieties are hard to recommend for general planting. North of Maryland, the new U.S.D.A. varieties 'Blueray,' 'Berkeley,' 'Bluecrop,' 'Herbert' and 'Coville' are among the best. For the South Atlantic Coast, the new crosses between Northern varieties and the rabbit-eye blueberry are best.

For Michigan and adjacent states, recommendations of the State Experiment Station at South Haven should be followed.

One important point to remember is that all varieties are self-sterile. For this reason, at least two varieties should be planted to insure cross-pollination. Otherwise little or no fruit will be set.

Fruit is borne only on the short side branches of last year's growth. As soon as these laterals have borne, cut them away. At the same time, shorten some of the current year's growth to produce larger berries.

Every year, cut away one-third of the old wood entirely. In this way, the plant renews all its stems at least every three years. Since the best fruit is borne on younger wood, this insures high quality.

Dwarf Apples for the Home Garden. Most dwarf apple trees are budded or grafted on one of the so-called Malling understocks. These were selected in England at the East Malling Station, since moved to Merton. Not all of them produce dwarf trees, but several are well known for their ability to do so. Of these, the one known as Malling IX produces the smallest tree, sometimes no taller than five to six feet. Unfortunately, "Number 9," as it is known in the trade, is a weak grower. It does not produce a good union between root and top. As a result the tree is likely to snap off in a good breeze, usually when loaded with fruit. This tendency can be partially overcome by staking. However, the tree is short-lived, seldom surviving longer than ten years.

The type known as Malling VII makes a much more satisfactory tree. If allowed to grow without restrictive pruning, it will attain a height of 15 to 18 feet. However, by proper training it can be held down to 10 to 12 feet. This is not too large for the small property.

Dwarf pears can also be had, although they are not as predictable in growth as apples. Pear understocks have not been standardized, but are grown from seeds. For this reason, pears are considered more difficult to grow as dwarfs, although the same advantages apply.

Dwarf peaches, apricots, plums and cherries are also available. There are at least two naturally dwarf sour cherries which require little corrective pruning to keep them down in height. In the case of other stone fruits, the understocks used determine size, usually six to ten feet at maturity.

Perennial knot garden is hedged with 18-inch-high boxwood, Buxus microphylla koreana, *and features lavender and various scented types of mint. Instead of boxwood, the hedging might also be worked out in green and gray santolina, perennial (and evergreen, also) candytuft* (Iberis sempervirens) *or germander.*

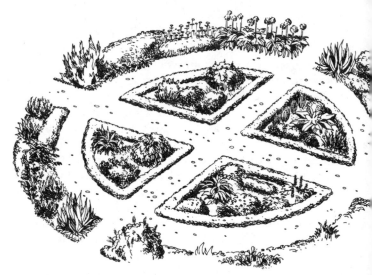

ABOVE: *A less complex version of a knot garden is hedged with parsley, which is kept trimmed, and features most of the popular kitchen herbs—among them, tarragon, rosemary, chives, chervil, dill. For color, several varieties of marigold have been planted, along with deep-toned basils and apple-scented geraniums. Walks between beds may be grass or small pebbles. Foliage plants such as germander, santolina and nepeta were originally used for ribbon effect in knot gardens.* BELOW: *Three small, modern knot gardens. Simple, these feature a few herbs with attractive foliage, such as silvery sage, rosemary, wormwood, purple basil, parsley, chervil and useful tender perennialis such as lemon-verbena, sweet bay and scented geraniums.*

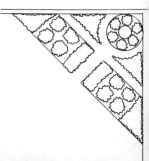

9. Gardens for Seasonings and Fragrance

Anything from a small green window box perched above a busy street to a secluded, quiet half-acre, neatly hedged and green-ribboned, can be a herb garden. Most herbs need only two things: a not overly rich soil and sunshine. There are many lovely plants to grow in shady gardens, but few of these are the culinary herbs.

Unassuming, fragrant, pleasant, tough, herbs have had many household uses since before the Bible was written down. The culinary herbs make first claim on modern herb gardeners. After edibles, and very close to them, come the herbs we grow for fragrance. Some are useful for both cooking and fragrance.

Culinary Herbs

The commonest of the culinary herbs form the core of any herb garden, large or small, decorative or utilitarian. Chives, parsley, dill, basil, rosemary and mint are perhaps the first in any list. Then follow, depending on the scope of the garden, marjoram, sage, oregano and burnet; thyme, anise and caraway; savory, coriander and balm; angelica, fennel, chervil, horseradish and tarragon.

Then follow plants for fragrance. Lavender and lemon balm perhaps should head this list. Next bee balm, the fragrant-leaved geraniums, sweet cicely, lavender-cotton, orris root, the sweet old-fashioned nasturtiums, violets, lemon verbena, sweet woodruff and tansy. Any herb gardener will have already seen that some of the culinary plants also have a place in a fragrant list. From these two categories, we go on to the decorative medicinal herbs, among which are larkspur, monkshood, gasplant (dictamnus), poppies, some of the roses, lungwort, hore-hound and borage.

The beginner is likely to buy too many seeds and too few plants. But since many of the seeds are annuals or biennials, time will take care of the surplus. When the perennials, either from seeds or purchased plants, become firmly established and begin to spread alarmingly, admiring friends and other gardeners will be delighted to have the extras.

Begin, then, with packets of seeds and at least a few small, nursery-grown plants. The simplest way to start your herb garden, if space is available, is to plant in rows both seeds and plants, making what is really a cutting garden. Then, in the first season, while purchased perennials are getting established as plants, and seedlings of annuals, perennials and biennials are making their growth, you can lay out the herb garden itself.

The charm of the herb garden lies not in showy, enormous blooms nor in gorgeous beds of brilliant color, but in the cool gray-greens of varied foliage and in the gentle, fragrant charm of unassuming but useful plants. There is much to please in the simple informal garden, in the tidy, neat precision of the formal garden or the intricate texture of a good knot garden.

A specific plan for your herb garden will depend on your personal preferences, the location available, the adjacent architecture and the surrounding gardens. Consider first the formal herb garden. A stone retaining wall may offer a gray, serene background, or a tall hedge of evergreens can be used to screen the carefully planned herb beds from other less formal gardens. This hedge may stand at one side of the herb garden or it may be an enclosing evergreen wall of hemlock, box, yew or holly. Traditionally, the hedge of box is most often used. But where the climate is too cold for box to thrive, other evergreens such as Carolina hemlock or arborvitae will make beautiful and effective hedges. All must be kept within bounds by careful and regular shearing once or twice a year. If the time needed to establish a handsome hedge seems too long, or if the expense, which is considerable, seems too much, a low picket fence or a woven chestnut fence will make effective and pleasant substitutes.

Within this enclosure, place the individual herb beds or borders. One of the simplest plans consists of four narrow borders that are arranged to enclose four smaller, central beds, all to be separated by inviting grass walks that ease weeding and upkeep. In the center, an old sundial, orrery or small pool may provide a focal ornament. Low hedges of slow-growing box, *Euonymus fortunei minimus*, germander (*Teucrium chamaedrys*), hyssop, lavender-cotton (*Santolina chamaecyparissus*) or perennial candytuft (*Iberis sempervirens*) make fine bed edgings, and all lend themselves well to shearing.

TRADITIONAL AND CONTEMPORARY PLANTING SCHEMES FOR HERBS.

BRICKS WITH HERBS

SCENTED HERB COLLECTION

The herb-garden plans here suggest either traditional or contemporary settings. Brick and flue-tile beds can be repeated to make as large a collection as desired. Scented herb garden might include mints, basil, savory, chervil and marjoram; tree might be a standard scented geranium or heliotrope.

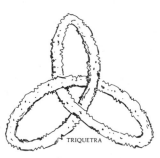

GOOSEFOOT HERB GARDEN

MODULAR GARDEN

SQUARE

TRIQUETRA

Goosefoot garden is made in raised beds banked with 8-inch-high planks. Squares, plain or interlaced, the Segment planting bed and the Sector are suited to modern landscapes, while Triquetra and Guilloche are traditional patterns used in knot gardens.

THE GUILLOCHE (CURVED SEGMENTS)

THE SEGMENT

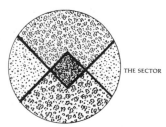

THE SECTOR

The Herb Garden Surround

The approach to the herb garden helps to suggest and determine its style. An old house, with large grounds and tall shade trees nearby but not near enough to obscure the indispensable full sun, will make a charming setting for a formal herb garden. So may a contemporary house, where you may walk from a terrace, patio or poolside into a geometrically balanced herb garden. Here, crisp rectangular beds and an interesting modern metal orrery can combine to make an orderly, harmonious effect. Garden furniture in the herb garden near an old house should of course be relevant in style. A decorative bench of stone or wood or a cast metal seat, placed where some shade will fall on it, makes a hospitable accent.

Another simple but dignified arrangement is that of a rather narrow brick wall between brick-edged beds of selected herbs, placing the taller-growing sorts to the back, giving the lower annuals and perennials a place near the front. Or the gardener may prefer to separate annuals and perennials in different beds, thus making his maintenance simpler by far. These small brick-edged beds are especially useful for growing annuals.

There may be curves as well as lines and angles in the formal herb garden. The beds themselves may form a large circle, broken only by low hedges or intervening grass walks. Walks may be made of pebbles, colored gravel, flagstones or bricks, if the gardener for any reason prefers these materials to grass. And the beds themselves may be edged with brick. Only the difficulties of upkeep need restrain the imaginative resourcefulness of the planning gardener. The matter of upkeep must be carefully considered since there should be time and leisure to enjoy the garden as well as time to work in it.

When it comes to planning an informal herb garden, there is a wide range of possibilities. The simplest type is the old-fashioned kitchen garden, where one steps literally out of the house into an array of useful and fragrant herbs. Here a grass, brick or flagstone walk may lead in straight lines or in a winding path between long, deep borders of varied herbs. The informal garden may be contained within a low brick wall or picket fence, dividing it from other parts of the grounds and yet leaving it an entity where small beds of plants approximate the orderliness and the simplicity of a vegetable plot. This kitchen garden admittedly has elements of formality in its design, but it seems to belong in the informal category if only because it is so simple. Here those vegetables that are eaten for themselves, as well as being used for seasoning, may be grown. Carrots, lettuce, parsley, celery, finocchio, onions, leeks and their relatives may be planted to advantage beside basil, thyme, dill, savory, marjoram and other herbs.

An informal herb garden also may combine flowering plants that are decorative in themselves, as well as being medicinal or fragrant. Nothing is more charming than larkspurs, lavenders and pinks growing in profusion in front of a picket fence in a deep and billowy border. Within this enclosure of fence and taller perennials, small beds can be cut into turf, each having assigned to it a single herb. Planted in rows in these beds, such herbs as burnet, basil, wood strawberries, parsley and borage are very attractive. A close picket fence will serve not only to enclose and frame the garden, but also to restrain the cats and dogs of the household and of the neighborhood generally. It will not keep out rabbits. Only a wire mesh fence, set a few inches below ground and partly concealed by the prettier picket fence, can exclude rabbits.

For decorative and very tall plants that lend dignity and stature at the back of herb beds and borders, consider these: elecampane (*Inula helenium*), with enormous gray-green leaves topped by gay, daisylike flowers; lilies, of many heights and types; delphiniums, preferably the long-lasting, sturdy garden strains with their strong, dark blues; monkshood (*Aconitum*), with sprays of hooded bloom in blue, lavender or blue-and-white; artemisias, gray, feathery and graceful; tansy (*Tanacetum*), tall and pungent, with pretty, yellow, buttonlike flowers; costmary (*Chrysanthemum balsamita*), with handsome, dark green, abundant leaves, shrubby habit of growth and golden-yellow flowers in August; angelica, handsome, imposing and architectural in effect; lovage (*Levisticum officinalis*), sturdy, with dark green, celerylike leaves. And do not forget the sturdy shrub roses (the Damask, Cabbage, Moss, Bourbon and Musk) that lend charm and fragrance in the herb border and make a fine green background for other plants.

Growing Herbs Indoors

Herbs will grow well indoors in the same conditions that yield thriving geraniums. They need a sunny place with temperatures ranging between 50 and 75 degrees. Try to provide an airy, moist atmosphere. It helps to set the pots in trays filled with an inch or two of moist sand or pebbles. Wash the foliage frequently in tepid tap water; this cleans the leaves and discourages insects. Container-grown herbs need well-drained soil, always nicely moist but never dripping wet for more than a few hours. Any prepackaged potting soil recommended for geraniums will suffice, or you can mix equal parts garden loam, sand and peat moss.

If you have no sunny window for herbs, then you can grow them under fluorescent lights. You will need a 48-inch industrial fixture that houses two 40-watt bulbs, one daylight and one natural white, or one daylight and one Gro-Lux Wide Spectrum. This size setup will accommodate 36 three-inch pots or 20 four-inch pots of fresh herbs. The fluorescent tubes should be about five inches from the tops of the foliage and turned on 14 to 18 hours daily.

Harvesting Your Herb Crop

Harvest of leafy herbs can begin early in the season, and because cutting encourages fresh new growth, it can continue almost until frost. The most flavoring power seems to be locked in leaves and tips just before the blooms form. Kinds include basil, chervil, lovage, marjoram, myrrh, parsley, rosemary, savory, tarragon, thyme and lemon verbena.

The best time of day to harvest the leafy herbs is early on a sunny day, after the dew is off but before the temperature warms to the point of volatilizing the oil in the leaves. Before spreading the leaves and tips to dry, wash them quickly to remove any traces of dust and insects. Avoid washing too much or in water that is warm, because this will bruise leaves and release the oils.

Quick drying is usually the best procedure, and this can be done by spreading the leaves thinly on a wire-mesh rack that is placed in a slow oven (100° to 150°). Leave the oven door open, and stand by because the leaves will be chip-dry in a few minutes.

Herbs are sometimes cut in bunches and hung to dry in a shaded, airy place, such as an open garage, porch or attic. This works well if the atmosphere is sufficiently dry to preserve the herbs before they are covered with dust. Another version of this method, not so picturesque but dust-free, is to hang the herbs to dry inside roomy brown-paper bags. Herbs that dry well in bunches include lemon balm, basil, horehound, marjoram, mint, oregano, sage and savory.

Keep the popular herb basil, Ocimum basilicum, *growing and encourage its branching habit by pruning as shown: Far left, remove tips of young plant at a uniform height; as plant matures, near left, crop as black bars show, to create rounded shape. Leafy clippings (but not flowering stems) can be used for seasoning. Besides being available in a dwarf form with green leaves, there is also a sweet basil with purple leaves called 'Dark Opal.' Basil grows well in pots, indoors or outdoors.*

How to harvest angelica: Cut stems 6 to 8 inches long. Soak in cold water, then cook until transparent. Make syrup of sugar and water and cook pieces until glazed. Place on tray and cut into leaf shapes for decorating pastry. May be stored in air-tight tins.

Storing the Herb Harvest

When the leaves are chip-dry, they are ready to be stored in labeled clean glass jars with screw tops. It is important to take care of the bottling as quickly as possible. Whole leaves retain the most in scenting and flavoring ability.

Once they're bottled, it is important to watch for any signs of condensation. If any moisture shows in a jar, empty the contents at once and dry again. Otherwise the entire lot will mold. Bottled herbs keep best in a dark, cool place. Refrigeration isn't necessary, but a shelf over or near the stove isn't the best place, however convenient it may seem.

When properly harvested, dried and stored, leafy herbs grown in your garden will remain flavorful for at least a year. They should be kept from sunlight.

The newest way to keep leafy herbs in an arrested state of garden freshness is to put a supply in the deep-freeze. Some that keep especially well this way include salad burnet, chervil, chives, dill leaves, mint and tarragon. After rinsing in cold water and lightly blotting dry, store portions of each kind in plastic sandwich bags. Label and staple several together; this keeps order in the freezer and makes it easy to remove one portion at a time. Freeze without blanching. Mincing can be done on a chopping board at the time of use; this works better than if it is done before freezing.

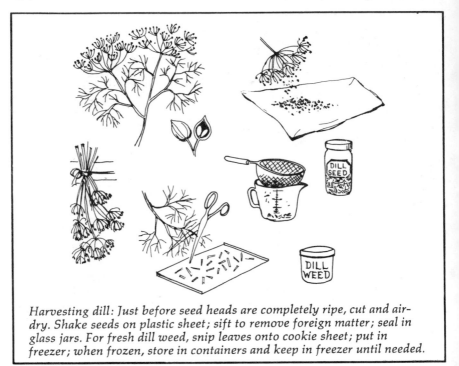

Harvesting dill: Just before seed heads are completely ripe, cut and air-dry. Shake seeds on plastic sheet; sift to remove foreign matter; seal in glass jars. For fresh dill weed, snip leaves onto cookie sheet; put in freezer; when frozen, store in containers and keep in freezer until needed.

To harvest the seeds of coriander, cumin, caraway, dill and fennel, it is necessary to watch the seedheads closely as they begin to ripen; cut just before the seeds begin to drop. Cut entire plants and place, seedheads down, in a paper bag. Hang to dry in an airy, warm place in the shade. When dry, shake the bag, and the seeds will fall to the bottom. Chaff can be removed by winnowing in an airy place. Then store the cleaned seeds as you would leafy herbs.

Potpourri and Decorations

Herb flowers and fragrant, sometimes colorful leaves are today harvested and dried with at least two general uses in mind. First is the making of potpourri, sweet bags and pillows. The second is for long-lasting, natural floral decorations.

Herbs that dry easily and well for wreaths and arrangements include artemisia, bachelor's-button (nearly-open buds), broom, delphinium, dock, globe amaranth, lavender, mullein, statice, strawflower, tansy, teasel and yarrow. Simply cut these when the leaves, flowers or seedheads (as the case may be) are in peak condition and hang to dry, tops down, in an airy, warm, dry, dark place.

A simple method of preparing a potpourri is to pick the flowers (or petals) when they are young and spread them on paper in a dry, airy room away from the sun. Turn them over every day. Let dry completely—it may take a week. Then store the petals in an airtight glass or ceramic jar. To each quart add 1 ounce orris-root, which acts as a fixative, helping to retain the scent and, to some extent, the color. If you wish, you may also add ½ teaspoon of such spices as cinnamon, coriander, or mace.

Petals for potpourri must be fresh; fading roses from a vase have few of the volatile oils that help to create the scent of a potpourri. Pick the flowers after the dew has dried but before the sun is quite hot, and select flowers that are just coming into bloom. Rosebuds, dried, are charming in a potpourri, but have little scent to contribute. Roses noted for their fragrance include 'Charlotte Armstrong,' 'Crimson Glory,' 'Mexicana,' 'Neige Parfum,' 'Oklahoma,' 'Petite de Hollande,' 'De Meaux,' 'General Jacqueminot.'

The word potpourri is French and means, literally, a potful of rotting floral materials, which is what potpourri actually is. In the Middle Ages it was made by alternating in an open-mouthed jar layers of petals and salt and allowing these to age. In time they fermented and dried, forming the powdery cakes that gave off the haunting fragrance associated with potpourri. This method of making "sweet bowls" is called the moist method, while the system described earlier is known as the dry method.

To use a modern version of the moist method for making potpourri, dry fresh rose petals 24 hours on screens in the shade and layer ½ inch deep in a 1-quart bowl or crock with a wide mouth. Cover the petals with a thin layer of salt. Repeat the process daily until the crock is more than half full, stirring well after each addition. Mix in ½ cup of patchouli and another of powdered orris-root, ¼ cup each of oil of rose and oil of rose geranium or other scents. You may also add a teaspoon each of two or three spices such as cloves, grated nutmeg and anise. When the mixture begins to ferment, stir and allow to stay in the crock for ten days, or until a cake forms.

This potpourri recipe calls for rose petals but can be made with lavender, lemon verbena or rose geranium. After drying about 15 ounces of petals on a screen or newspaper in a dry, sunless, warm place for 10 days, mix in the following ingredients: 13 ounces orris-root, ⅛ ounce of oil of rose, ¼ ounce oil of rose geranium, ⅛ ounce oil of sandalwood, ½ ounce oil of bergamot, ½ ounce tincture of musk, 1 ounce yellow sandalwood in chips. Allow the mixture to mellow for about six weeks in a tightly covered jar, then place in glass bottles. If the bottles are opened only when it is time to scent the room, the fragrance from this modern potpourri will last for years.

ABOVE: *Container plants are used with great style in this tiny back-yard garden in San Francisco. Note uniformity of pot plants on ledge behind seating, right. A collection of bonsai grows on the bench in front of the round dining table. Pots of carefully pruned geraniums give an abundance of flowers. For another view of this garden, see page 202.* RIGHT: *Crocus are among the easiest of the hardy spring bulbs to grow in containers. Here the boxes are constructed (by the owner) of garden grade redwood (because it is naturally rot-resistant). In autumn plant two dozen crocus bulbs in each 12-inch box.*

10. Container Gardening Outdoors

Before the coming of Christ, the Egyptians and Romans were gardening in containers. The technique became a fine art in the Orient, where dwarfed bonsai trees were passed on from one generation to another. Today, limited by time and space, we are using container gardens in ways never dreamed of by the ancients. Plants and containers become accessories to complement exterior living. Not only can container plantings be changed from season to season for nonstop color, but they can be arranged, moved, mixed and matched as the occasion may require. The same pots of roses used to decorate a terrace for Sunday brunch can line a front walk to welcome guests in the evening. The possibilities are numerous. But success depends upon choosing plants and containers that work well separately, in groupings and in various locations.

Since nurseries everywhere cultivate trees, shrubs and flowers in containers, it's easy to shop for suitable plants to grow this way. While it may be difficult to envision a gangly bareroot rosebush in a decorative terra-cotta pot, it is a simple matter to buy a rose already growing in a pot or can and transplant it at home to a container of your choice. Other shrubby plants for containers in the sun include allamanda, Chinese hibiscus, bougainvillea, dwarf crape-myrtle and hydrangea. For a partially shaded place, select from camellias, gardenias, pieris and azaleas.

Almost any tree that normally grows in your area can be grown in a container. The general rule in fitting a tree to a container is to let the diameter of the container equal one-fourth to one-third the height of the tree. By this guide, a flowering crab 6 feet tall will need a tub 18 inches to 24 inches in diameter. Other trees suitable for container gardens include pine, beech, deodar cedar, juniper, Japanese maple, podocarpus,

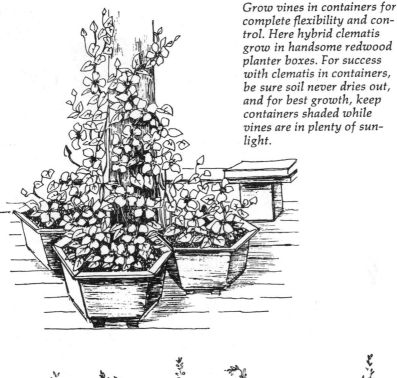

Grow vines in containers for complete flexibility and control. Here hybrid clematis grow in handsome redwood planter boxes. For success with clematis in containers, be sure soil never dries out, and for best growth, keep containers shaded while vines are in plenty of sunlight.

ABOVE: *Some strong-growing vines or shrubs, such as the pyracantha, are useful to cover an expanse of plain wall. If there is no access to the ground, growing in attractive containers is the answer.*
OPPOSITE: *Back-yard garden in San Francisco as seen from second floor. Note careful placement of container plants for accent color; see also page 200.*

Twelve indoor-outdoor plants to help green your thumb—and your environment. All need shade outdoors in warm weather, but several hours sun indoors in winter. They are: (1) holly fern, (2) screw-pine, (3) clivia, (4) spider plant, (5) hoya, (6) ficus, (7) ponytail or beaucarnea, (8) hatrack or euphorbia, (9) Swedish-ivy or plectranthus, (10) Aechmea fasciata 'Silver King,' a bromeliad, (11) peace-lily or spathiphyllum and (12) butterfly palm.

spruce, fig, the dwarf 'Bonanza' peach, any of the ornamental flowering fruits such as Japanese cherry, plum, quince and peach, and espalier-trained apples.

One magnificent plant can add much more to the design of your home than half a dozen pots on the windowsill. And if the plant tub for "the magnificent specimen" is properly designed, your showpiece can live in it for years without transplanting, and can look as good against the soft furnishings of your living room in winter as against more rugged textures of nature on your summer terrace. The tub for "the long pull" should be large enough to accommodate the plant for a good many years, to prevent the setbacks caused by constant repotting. It should be planned with the drainage problem in mind. If no drip-pan arrangement is provided, it should be waterproofed and planted with several inches of loose aggregate at the bottom. It should be raised off the floor on legs, partly to prevent increased drying out at the bottom from radiant-heated floors, and partly to protect the floors against unseen seepage from the tub.

Flowers for Containers

Most annual flowers will do well in containers located in a sunny place outdoors, but the naturally neat kinds are the most satisfactory. Select from 'Thumbelina' zinnias, dwarf and hedge-type marigolds, ageratum, flowering kale and ornamental cabbage, 'Dwarf White Bedder' nicotiana, petunias, salvias and periwinkles. The best tender perennials for a place in the summer sun are geraniums, wax begonias, caladiums, lobelias, lantanas and pentas.

For flowering plants in shady locations, use impatiens, wax and tuberous begonias, browallia, torenia, fuchsia, achimenes and gloxinias. For colorful foliage in a shaded place, rely on caladiums and coleus.

Vegetables that respond well to container culture are sweet and hot peppers, eggplant, cucumbers and tomatoes. Favorite herbs for pots include basil, dill, sage, mint, thyme, chives, sweet marjoram, oregano, savory, rosemary, sweet bay and lemon verbena.

Select containers on the basis of size, color, site and availability. The classic shapes and earthy colors of clay and terra-cotta pots make them useful in virtually any setting. Some of today's best contemporary containers are done in ceramics and fiber glass with clean architectural lines. Wooden planters can be as handsome and natural in appearance as clay pots. If you do not like the design of those commercially available, make your own, using 1-inch redwood or cedar. Soil for a container garden should drain well, but should contain sufficient humusy material so that it doesn't dry out too rapidly. One excellent medium can be made by mixing equal parts by volume of garden loam, vermiculite and milled

Vegetables and herbs can be productive—and quite beautiful—in container gardens. LEFT: Small-fruited tomatoes will thrive in hanging baskets. When laden with clusters of ripe fruit they are highly ornamental. BELOW: Redwood boxes on rooftop or patio provide growing space for a variety of choice vegetables, strawberries and grapes. Choice herbs grow in pots on a shelf. Research for all drawings this page, Ortho.

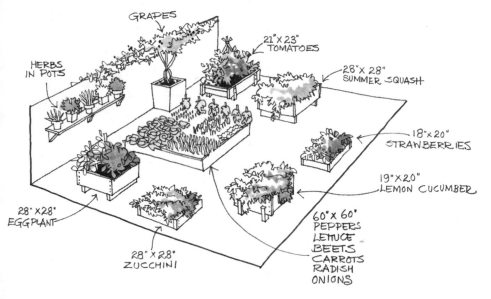

GRAPES

HERBS IN POTS

21"X 23" TOMATOES

28"X 28" SUMMER SQUASH

18"X 20" STRAWBERRIES

19"X 20" LEMON CUCUMBER

28"X 28" EGGPLANT

28"X 28" ZUCCHINI

60"X 60" PEPPERS LETTUCE BEETS CARROTS RADISH ONIONS

LEFT: Vegetables and herbs in particular, but also flowers grown in pots outdoors will do better in hot weather given the double-pot treatment. Moist moss between two pots keeps soil and roots cooler. BELOW: For a collection of smaller pots in hot weather, group them in redwood box with moist bark chips.

sphagnum moss (or wet peat moss). Water containers often enough to keep the soil moist. Twice a day, morning and evening, may be needed in hottest weather. When you go away on vacation, or if you garden only on weekends, hire a local youngster who is interested in gardening to be your water boy. Most containers will have drainage holes, but if not, add a layer of pebbles to a depth of about 2 inches before planting. After heavy rains, drain off excess water by tipping containers that have no drainage holes. Feed plants every week or two. Use plant food, following the manufacturer's directions.

Basket Gardening

The name "basket plant" suggests a rather specific type of plant in a specific kind of container. In actual fact, (1) any small, colorful plant is a good basket plant, although trailers such as ivy geraniums, fuchsias, tuberous begonias and balcony petunias are the favorites; and (2) any container that can be hung from chains or wires above the ground makes an excellent "basket."

If you use the conventional wire basket (the lightest type of container), line it first with sphagnum moss (florists' "sheet moss") and then fill it with soil. To slow the otherwise rapid evaporation of moisture (in hot, breezy weather, plants in wire baskets often need to be watered two or three times a day) place a clay saucer over the moss in the bottom.

Other containers also lose moisture more rapidly than usual when they are hanging. But here again you can retard evaporation somewhat by lining the containers with sphagnum moss.

For hanging baskets in a hot, sunny location, plant 'Cascade' petunias, sedums, creeping thyme, ivy-leaf geraniums, variegated flowering maple, Joseph's-coat, shrimp plant, lantana, mesembryanthemum and pentas. For baskets in a shaded location, possibly with sun in early morning or late afternoon, use achimenes, basket tuberous begonias, chlorophytum, ferns, episcias, fuchsias, English ivy, asparagus-fern, *Campanula isophylla* and donkey-tail sedum (*Sedum morganianum*).

OPPOSITE: *Proper initial planting and day-to-day watering are the keys to success with basket gardens. Where baskets are wanted up high, a pulley arrangement may be used for ease in lowering for watering and grooming. To plant a wire basket, first line with sheet moss, then a layer of plastic film with a few drainage holes punched in it, and, finally humus-rich, moisture-retentive soil. Water wire baskets by immersing in a pail of water, then drain before returning to original position. Baskets not easily taken down may be enclosed in plastic clipped in place to catch excess moisture, or by placing a few icecubes on the surface; soil absorbs moisture as they melt. For a sphere shape, fill two wire baskets with moss and soil; wire together with piece of plywood between. Insert rooted cuttings all around. Where feasible, permanently mounted metal brackets at various heights help display baskets attractively.*

To make fern ball, wire together two wire hanging baskets after each half
has been stuffed with unmilled sphagnum moss and planted with ferns.
Pack the ferns into each cage from the bottom up, interlacing them with
strands of moist moss. Clip the cages together and keep moist in a lightly
shaded place. Fern balls are generally made with "feet" ferns, the davallias,
but begonias and small-leaved ivy are grown this way also.

Achimenes grow well in a wire hanging basket lined
with sheet moss. Plant rhizomes 1 inch deep. When
plants are 2 inches tall, pinch out tips to promote
branching.

Drainage for pots keeps plants from becoming water logged. It is easily added by placing a couple of inches of broken clay pot or coarse pebbles at the bottom of the container before adding the potting soil.

Large potted plants thrive if top-dressed occasionally. Remove an inch or two of the old topsoil with as little damage to the surface roots as possible. Replace the old soil with a rich mixture of fresh potting soil. This is really a lazy person's way of giving a large pot plant a new lease on life without going to the trouble of completely repotting. It also saves shocking the plant.

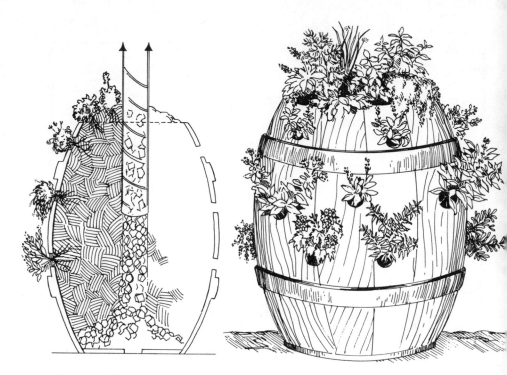

How To Plant a Strawberry Barrel

Barrel gardening refers to growing plants in a barrel, strawberry-jar fashion. Cut 2- to 4-inch-diameter holes in the sides of a tight barrel, and drill smaller drain holes in the bottom. Add a 6-inch-deep layer of coarse aggregate or broken crock in the bottom for drainage and cover with fine aggregate as a filter. Stand a 6-inch-diameter stove pipe or other cylinder (rolled, heavy paper) in the middle. Fill around the pipe with soil mix, fill the pipe with small aggregate and, finally, withdraw the tube, leaving the column of aggregate which facilitates watering. The fill compost is Basic Potting Mixture (see Chapter 1) fortified with composted manure, bone meal or other slow-acting fertilizer. Plants to grow in the barrel include strawberries, sempervivums, sedums, the small bush herbs and the tougher rock-garden plants.

Strawberry jars are basically the same as strawberry barrels. They usually have little pouchlike openings in the side for the plants, which may be inserted from the outside. Standard strawberry jars are usually 18 to 24 inches tall, of a size that will accommodate dwarf-growing runnerless strawberries, miniature roses or rose-moss (portulaca). The miniature strawberry jars sold planted with pre-cooled crocus bulbs, ready for forcing, may be used after the crocus are gone for planting rooted cuttings of miniature English ivy or miniature cultivars of African violets.

ABOVE, LEFT: Container plants mix beautifully with those growing in the ground.

ABOVE, UPPER: Roses, especially compact-growing floribundas, do well in pots and tubs.

ABOVE, LOWER: Color for shaded corners comes from fancy-leaved caladiums, browallias, impatiens and many different begonias.

LEFT: Small clay pots and tubs hold flowers in this terrace garden; small trees grow in tubs.

How to make a simple compost pile:
ABOVE, LEFT: *In an out-of-the-way part of the garden alternate 6-inch layers of garden refuse (leaves, grass clippings, plant tops, straw, old hay, sod) with 2-inch layers of earth and manure, or earth mixed with fertilizer (*ABOVE RIGHT*). Repeat refuse and earth layers until the pile is 4 to 5 feet tall, or until autumn.* LEFT: *To accelerate the composting process, add a sprinkling of sulfate of ammonia and superphosphate of lime.* BELOW, LEFT: *Keep pile well moistened.* BELOW, RIGHT: *When weeds or grass clippings are added directly to the garden as mulch, they rob the soil of nitrogen. It is better first to put weeds and grass clippings through the composting process. However, leafmold and peat moss can be added directly to the soil with good results.*

11. Gardening the Organic Way

Quickening ecological concern in the late sixties and early seventies has focused attention on organic gardening. Certain prudent gardeners have probably utilized organic methods since the very beginning of agriculture, but in modern times popularity of the practice dates from early in this century, when Sir Albert Howard, an English agricultural advisor to the Indian state of Indore, first developed a method of farming which did not include synthetic chemicals but relied entirely upon available natural materials.

To begin gardening organically one needs to know the pH or "potential of hydrogen" of the soil to be used. On a scale from 1 to 14, 1 is acid and 14 is alkaline, with about 6.1 to 6.9 (or slightly acid) being best for most plants. To measure acidity or alkalinity of soil one may use a portable, home testing kit or send samples to a commercial soil-testing laboratory, an Agricultural Experiment Station, a State Agricultural College or the County Agricultural Agent.

In native forests and prairies there is a permanent state of soil fertility. All that is produced by the soil eventually dies, decays and goes back into the soil as humus. Man and agriculture disrupt this cycle. The organic gardener perceives a balance in nature and tries to maintain it in his own gardening.

How To Make Compost

To be an organic gardener, you will want to make and use compost—organic matter, usually garden debris, that has been allowed or encouraged to decay. Compost is useful in improving fertility and texture of planting beds (including lawns) and is an important constituent of

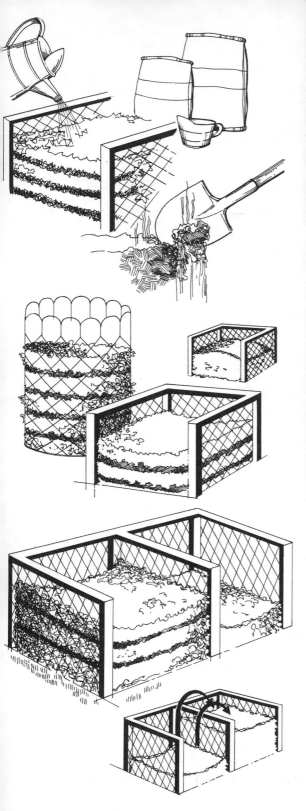

ABOVE: *When you maintain your own compost pile, you will have plenty of good humus to return to the soil. Here a rotary tiller is being used to turn a dressing of well-rotted compost into the earth between rows of beets. In flower beds a shovel or trowel can be used.*

LEFT, UPPER: *Elements that make compost are organic refuse layered with soil, manure and/or commercial fertilizers. The heap is stacked, in this system, into a wire bin in layers and is watered and turned often.*

LEFT, CENTER: *Mounded, or convex-shaped compost pile will shed water and is wrong; concave heap holds water and will compost far more quickly. Circular bin is tidier system.*

LEFT, BOTTOM: *Two-bin system makes turning the pile a relatively easy job.*

greenhouse and potting soils. Its nutritive qualities depend on the fertilizers and other nutrient-containing materials added to the compost pile as it decomposes. The value to the average gardener of a composted supply of humus is hard to beat, and most amateur gardeners today compost in some form. Compost to which nutritive elements have been added is used as rotted manure is used; compost that isn't enriched is used as humus only.

The best-quality garden loam for all purposes includes one-third humus. It makes the soil spongy, airy and light, and retentive of moisture. Sandy soils lacking humus allow rainfall to wash the nutritive ingredients down and out, and a clay soil without humus will bake so hard it is almost impervious to water and to the rootlets trying to work their way toward food and moisture.

Although something of a mystery is made of composting and much has been written about it, the truth is that anything organic left to the elements will compost (decompose). Leaves, grass clippings, plant tops, straw, old hay, sod are some of the materials you can use to make compost. Kitchen refuse, too. But bones, branches and diseased garden materials aren't desirable.

Many gardeners have made it a practice to add humus in the form of raw organic materials—weeds, for instance—to the soil without composting them, by digging them into borders and around plantings. While the theory is sound enough—the practice does add humus to the soil— raw organic matter causes soil bacteria to speed up their activities and this robs the soil of nitrogen and often causes the leaves of the growing plants around to yellow. It is better for the plants to remove weeds to the compost heap and return them to the soil when they have become compost. Leafmold and peat moss are two forms of organic matter that can be added to the soil without composting, as they are already composted.

There are any number of methods, simple and complex, to build a compost pile. A simple leaf pile, or a series of them located at convenient points around the garden may be encased in 15 ft. or so of snow fencing wired into a circle. In time, two years or more depending on your weather, the leaves will turn into compost without any effort on your part. Miscellaneous leaves composted provide an excellent source of supplemental potting humus, but little in the way of nutrients. Beech and oak leaves are acid, and after composting are excellent additional humus to place around acid-loving broad-leaved evergreens.

To build a less casual and more nutritive compost pile, select a site away from house views and strip sods from a rectangle 4 ft. by 6 ft. Use a portion of the sods to make a low wall around the rectangle and save the rest to top the pile later. Dig earth from inside the rectangle and make a mound of it close by. If you can get manure, pile it next to the soil. If no manure is available plan to use commercial fertilizers in the proportions directed on the package.

As garden refuse and other organic materials become available, use them to make a layer 6 in. deep inside the sod rectangle. Cover this with 2 in. of earth and manure, or earth mixed with fertilizer. Make the layer concave so it will hold rainwater, as humidity is essential to decomposition. Repeat the refuse and earth layers until the compost pile is 4 to 5 ft. tall, or until fall. In autumn, cover the pile with the sods saved, making sure the concavity is retained, and leave it all to time and the elements. Depending on your climate, the pile will become a spongy, fertile humus in one to three years.

You can hasten the process by turning the compost. Some advocates call for a turning every month. A pitchfork is the easiest tool for the purpose. Keep heaping the solids toward the center. Compost piles heat to as much as 150° in the center as the materials decompose, but as decomposition takes place, the heat lessens. The turning keeps fresh raw materials in the center "working" and makes the composting process faster.

Gardeners use decay accelerators to hasten the composting process. One compost recipe using an accelerator calls for preparation as described above but prescribes a pile 3 ft. square. To a layer of garden debris 3 ft. deep, add one-half ounce each of sulfate of ammonia and of superphosphate of lime. Over this goes a layer of manure, fresh or dried, 2 in. deep. Instead of ammonia and superphosphate of lime, a decay accelerator may be used. Cover with 2 in. of garden soil and after six weeks turn the pile completely. It may be turned again in six weeks, or left to its own to decompose.

While there are advantages to quick composting, less ambitious gardeners can create a continuous supply with little effort using a three-pile system. The first season, make compost pile one, and allow it to decompose through the next season. The second season make compost pile two, and allow it to decompose through the following season. That third season, pile one will be ready to use, pile two will be curing, and you can make pile three. When pile one is gone, make pile four in its place, and the perennial cycle is under way.

Feeding the Organic Way

Instead of using chemical fertilizers, the organic gardener uses compost and animal manure which is rich not only in nitrogen but also in phosphorus and potassium. When contrasted with chemical fertilizers, the chief virtue of manure is that it adds valuable humus-forming matter to the soil. Manure is expensive (unless you raise animals or poultry), but a little goes a long way. Seasoned manure that has been mixed with straw should be used at the rate of about ½ ton per 1,000 sq. ft., spread evenly on the garden early in the spring, and dug under about a week before planting.

Composted manure is also a useful supplement in planting holes beneath newly set shrubs and trees.

Manure—from chickens and sheep—that is not mixed with straw is more likely than other types to burn plants. It is therefore safer to apply it as a liquid side-dressing. If it is used dry, the garden should not be planted for several months.

One safe rule to follow in the use of all manure is: Let it season at least a few weeks. If possible, compost it with straw, leaves or other vegetable waste.

The manures most commonly used in the U.S. are:

Cattle manure. Dried and shredded or ground, several proprietary formulations (mixed with peat moss or similar materials) are available at seed stores. It has much the same values as fresh manure, but generates less heat. Often sold as dried steer manure.

Chicken manure. Very rich in all three elements but needs to be mixed with straw to make much humus. Very hot—it ought to be allowed to dry several weeks before application.

Cow manure. Low in chemical content. Can be used soon after it is produced, because it contains less straw. Slower acting than horse manure. Best for making liquid manure (normal preparation: 1 qt. manure steeped in 3 gal. water). Especially recommended for water-lilies (placed beneath surface soil in potting boxes) and greenhouse soil.

Fish emulsion. This natural plant food prepared from fish is available almost everywhere plants are sold. It is the preferred fertilizer of some of the best house and greenhouse gardeners, especially growers who specialize in begonias and gesneriads.

Green manure. A crop that is grown and turned under expressly to improve the soil by the addition of humus-forming matter, and, in some cases, nitrogen compounds. It is probably the least expensive, yet an effective means of adding organic matter to poor land. Successive plantings of buckwheat in spring and summer may be allowed to grow to about 8 inches, then plowed under and, after a week or ten days, disked and readied for further planting. Where they grow well, oats are preferable to buckwheat. While buckwheat will grow in the most impoverished soil, it will add only humus. For this reason, nitrogen-gathering legumes, such as soybeans, cowpeas or vetch, will be more useful. However, to grow well, all the legumes must be sown in fairly good soil. After October 1, winter rye or wheat should be planted instead of buckwheat. This will become established before the ground freezes, and can be plowed under early the next spring.

Guano. Bird droppings equivalent to chicken manure, but not widely available in the U.S.

Horse manure. Not so rich in plant foods as some other types, but decomposes fastest. Best for hotbed use because it generates more heat. Should not be applied until the straw in it has decomposed.

Liquid manure. A dilute mixture of rotted or dried manure (*not* fresh manure) and water. Less important since the development of good soluble fertilizers, but still considered valuable for feeding plants, especially just before they come into flower or fruit. Particularly good for potted plants, because it helps replace nutrients leached out in ordinary watering. Liquid manure works most effectively when applied no more often than one-week to ten-day intervals, and only to the roots, since it may burn the foliage. If the mixture becomes too strong, dilute it. For best results, suspend the manure in a sack in water for three or four days. The standard formulas are as follows:

Cow or cattle manure—1 qt. (dry) to 3 gal. water.
Horse manure—1 qt. (dry) to 2½ gal. water.
Sheep manure—1 qt. (dry) to 4 gal. water.
Chicken manure or guano—1 lb. (dry) to 5 gal. water.

Sewage sludge. Not so rich as other manures, but useful. You may be able to get treated sludge from your local sewage plant. But dried sludge—also processed for sale—is widely available at seed stores. It is relatively odorless, easy and safe to use.

Sheep manure. Compares with chicken manure in richness. When fresh, it produces as much heat as horse manure. The fresh variety is not very widely available. Use dried manure if fresh is not available.

Mulching is used by many organic gardeners. A layer of mulch material is placed around growing plants to moderate soil temperature, to decay and add fertility, to keep the soil loose and eliminate need for cultivation, to conserve moisture and to protect ripening fruit. Some useful mulch materials are: grass clippings, leaves, stones, hulls and shells, sawdust and wood chips, shredded cornstalks, straw, alfalfa or other hay.

Organic gardeners are generally opposed to the use of chlorinated hydrocarbons such as DDT for the control of pests. These hard chemicals do not deteriorate or disappear but travel up the natural food chain from insect to man. They are of a broad-spectrum type, killing off from 100 to 1,000 species of insects, some of which are beneficial, including natural predators and parasites of insects the gardener wants to eliminate. Also, harmful insects are capable of quickly developing strains resistant to hard chemicals.

Preventive measures can often head off trouble. Select seeds and plants of highly resistant varieties. Destroy diseased plants by burning or placing them deep in the hot center of a compost pile. Avoid monoculture. Rotation of crops discourages disease.

In this plan consider companion planting, the growing of different species in close proximity for the benefit of one of them. Chives planted among roses tend to keep aphids away. Some growers have found that marigolds planted with beans prevent Mexican bean bettle infestation. (See accompanying chart for lists of plants which help each other.)

If pests have already invaded, one still need not use hard chemicals. Make use of a pest's natural enemies. Ladybugs can be purchased by the gallon for control of aphids, mites and scale insects. The trichogramma, a parasitic wasp, eats the eggs of many moths and butterflies which are leaf eaters in their larval stage.

Birds may be encouraged to help with pest control by feeding them during seasons when insects are not plentiful, by providing them with water and nesting materials. Toads are also allies of the gardener. They like a shallow pan filled with water and a toad house made by breaking a small hole in a clay flowerpot and turning it upside down.

Some gardeners have successfully used insect disease to control pests. For instance, *Bacillus thuringiensis* is effective against some 60 or more insect pests. It is highly selective and will not harm beneficial insects. It is also nontoxic to humans and other warm-blooded animals.

Dry powders or dusts desiccate and thus kill pests. Some effective dusts are: lime, talc, silica and diatomaceous earth. Ground green shallot onions mixed with water in equal parts are effective against aphids. Hot-pepper spray eliminates cabbage worms. Organic gardeners also approve pyrethrum, ryania and rotenone; all are plant-derived pesticides.

For the gardener who would avoid poison sprays and synthetic fertilizers, natural organic materials are readily available. Organic gardeners are in harmony with the growing belief that a closed system is needed, in which resources are husbanded and recycled, to replace the current open-end economy in which resources are squandered.

Companion and compatible plantings are also among the weapons in the organic gardener's arsenal. Following are lists of plants which help each other in various ways and some which are inimical. A companion plant is one that assists another plant in the control of a disease or of an insect pest. Marigolds, asters, chrysanthemums, cosmos and coreopsis are among the flowers whose scent is repellent to assorted insects. Most aromatic herbs also achieve this highly desirable effect. Among these are: basil, anise, coriander, rosemary and sage. Organic gardeners recommend either planting these insect-repelling flowers and herbs in the vegetable garden and annual or perennial beds, or using them as an edging in these situations.

Plants which complement each other because of their height, root spread or cultural needs are called compatible plants. Some, according to organic gardeners, are actually mutually beneficial. Dr. Ehrenfried Pfeiffer, in his book *Bio-dynamic Farming and Gardening*, lists such plants, as well as some which mutually distress each other. Following are lists based on his findings:

Compatible Plants

Beets and onions
Cabbage and beans
Carrots and peas
Celeriac and leeks
Celery and bush beans or leeks
Corn and peas
Cucumber and bush or pole beans
Early potatoes and corn, beans or horseradish
Kohlrabi and beets
Leeks and beans
Onions and beans
Potatoes and corn
Radishes between rows of lettuce
Tomatoes and parsley or basil
Turnips and peas

Incompatible Plants

Pole beans and beets or kohlrabi
Red and black raspberries
Tomatoes and fennel or kohlrabi

COMPANION PLANTING CHART

PLANT	COMPANION	TO REPEL
Asparagus	Tomatoes	Asparagus beetles
Beans	Potatoes	Mexican bean beetle
	Marigolds	Mexican bean beetle
	Nasturtiums	Mexican bean beetle
Broccoli	Nasturtiums	Aphids
Cabbage	Sage	Cabbage butterfly
	Tansy	Cabbage worm and cutworm
	Tomatoes	Cabbage butterfly
	Mint	Cabbage maggot
	Rosemary	Cabbage maggot
Corn	Larkspur	Japanese beetles
	Soybeans	Japanese bettles and chinch bugs
Cucumbers	Marigolds	Cucumber beetles
	Nasturtiums	Striped cucumber and squash bug
	Radishes	Striped or spotted cucumber beetles
Grapes	Geraniums	Japanese beetles
Lettuce	Chives	Aphids
Peach tree	Garlic	Peach tree borer
Peas	Chives	Aphids
Potatoes	Beans	Colorado potato beetles
	Horseradish	Potato bugs
Roses	Geraniums	Japanese beetles
	Chives	Aphids
	Parsley	Rose beetles
	Garlic	Black spot, mildew and aphids
Squash	Radishes	Squash bugs
Any plant	Marigolds	Nematodes
Any plant	Onions	Cutworms
Any plant	Radishes	Attract root maggots. Plant them as a trap crop

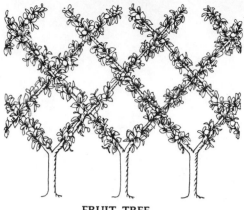

**FRUIT TREE
BELGIAN FENCE**

**FLOWERING SHRUB
ARCURE METHOD**

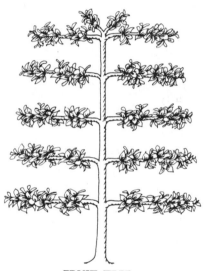

**FRUIT TREE
HORIZONTAL-T**

An "espalier" is the training trellis or wall against which espaliered trees are grown, but the word has also come to mean a plant trained in this manner. On this and the following pages are depicted the most common methods, formal and informal, for training espaliers. The stylized, clearly patterned shapes are best suited to situations where the visual demands made by their outstanding appearance can be appreciated: a blank modern wall, a dull clapboard garage corner, a two-story formal entrance. The Belgian Fence and the Arcure Method of espaliering are frequently used on a small lot to encourage the production of a lot of many types of fruit. They are highly decorative both in blossom and later, too, when fruit is ripening.

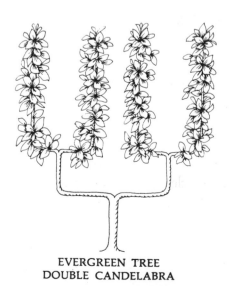

**EVERGREEN TREE
DOUBLE CANDELABRA**

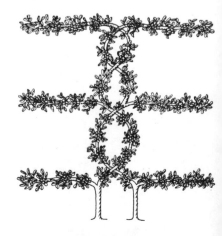

**FLOWERING SHRUB
BRAIDED TREE**

12. Gardening Techniques for Artistic Expression

Highly specialized plant training techniques are the natural outgrowth of a country's cultural maturity. Espaliering, topiary and standard trees originated in Europe, bonsai in the Orient. All have been practiced in the United States for many years, but only recently have they become popular. To succeed with any one of these art forms, it helps in the beginning if you are a knowledgeable and successful gardener. However, as art forms, they often appeal to people who are not necessarily gardeners, but who are willing to learn gardening basics in order to work with plants as a medium for artistic expression.

Espalier: Two-Dimensional Plants

Espalier became an artistic garden form in Europe during the Middle Ages, but the original purpose in pruning fruit trees severely was to produce better fruit in less space against warm, south-facing walls in cold climates.

The technique requires a support for the tree, and in home gardens in Europe the support is a stone wall whose warmth lingers after the sun has set and so helps the fruit to ripen early. In the U.S., where summer heat is more intense than in Europe, there is less incentive to espalier against a support that retains warmth. However, interest in the technique has undergone a revival here because the stylized forms add interest to the bare walls of modern architecture. And because espalier is an interesting project for the gardener.

Any woody shrub or small tree can be trained to an espalier shape. A few to try are the juniper, cotoneaster, yew. Plants that grow profusely, as the forsythia, make handsome espaliers, but the habit of lush and fast growth also makes greater demands on the gardener.

The best way to understand the technique is to follow the steps necessary to create one classic espalier shape; then you will be able to apply the basic rules to other patterns and designs. The Double U Candelabra is one of the most popular classical forms. Here is how to achieve it.

Choosing a tree: Dwarf apples, pears, peaches and nectarines are popular espalier subjects: they produce early, bear well, and don't try to grow more than 8 or 10 feet tall. Ask your local nursery for a one-year-old whip, and follow their recommendations on species and varieties that are successful in your area. Since many fruit trees will not bear unless they are pollinated by another variety of their own species, it would be wise to choose a fruit already established near you.

Where to plant: A 1- by 8-foot border of humusy, slightly acid, well-drained soil next to a wall facing southwest is ideal. A southeast wall is fine too, though the rising sun can damage buds if you have late spring frosts. In areas where summer temperatures go into the 90's, a wall facing squarely south may get hot enough to damage the tree.

The soil usually has enough humus if it feels spongy and rakes smooth easily. To add humus, mix in compost or rotted manure. Peat moss, spoiled hay or sawdust are good too, providing you add half a pound of ammonium nitrate per bushel to maintain the nitrogen balance. If drainage is poor, line bottom of trench with a few inches of gravel.

The permanent trellis: The permanent trellis for a Double U Candelabra should be about 6 feet high by 8 feet wide. For posts use 4- by 4-inch by 8-foot redwood, or rough-barked cedar saplings that size—whichever blends best with your background wall. Set the posts at either end of your border and bury them in holes 2 feet deep, 8 inches from the wall. Fasten the tops securely to the wall with expansion bolts or brackets. Stretch a 14-gauge galvanized wire horizontally between the posts 12 inches from the ground and tie so securely that no slack can develop. The next wire goes in one foot high, and so on to the top of the posts.

How to plant: When the ground is workable in early spring and before the tree leafs out, if possible, dig a hole that will place the trunk of the tree in the exact center of your trellis and just in front of the horizontal wires. This hole should be roomy and deep enough so that the tree can be set as deep (but no deeper) as it was at the nursery. A change in color on the bark will tell you where that was. Fill the hole two-thirds full,

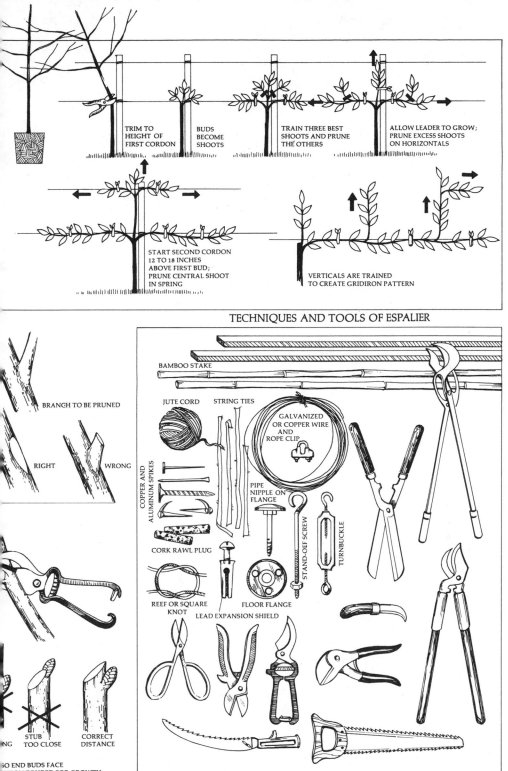

TRIM TO
HEIGHT OF
FIRST CORDON

BUDS
BECOME
SHOOTS

TRAIN THREE BEST
SHOOTS AND PRUNE
THE OTHERS

ALLOW LEADER TO GROW;
PRUNE EXCESS SHOOTS
ON HORIZONTALS

START SECOND CORDON
12 TO 18 INCHES
ABOVE FIRST BUD;
PRUNE CENTRAL SHOOT
IN SPRING

VERTICALS ARE TRAINED
TO CREATE GRIDIRON PATTERN

TECHNIQUES AND TOOLS OF ESPALIER

BRANCH TO BE PRUNED

RIGHT

WRONG

STUB
TOO CLOSE

CORRECT
DISTANCE

SO END BUDS FACE
CTION DESIRED FOR GROWTH

BAMBOO STAKE

JUTE CORD

STRING TIES

GALVANIZED
OR COPPER WIRE
AND
ROPE CLIP

COPPER AND ALUMINUM SPIKES

CORK RAWL PLUG

PIPE
NIPPLE ON
FLANGE

STAND-OFF SCREW

TURNBUCKLE

REEF OR SQUARE
KNOT

LEAD EXPANSION SHIELD

FLOOR FLANGE

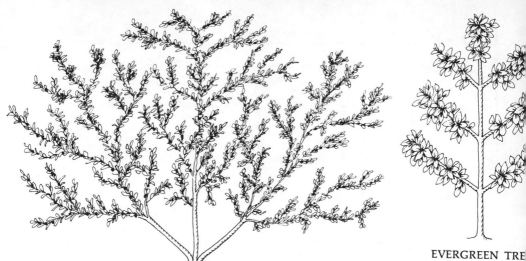

EVERGREEN SHRUB
JAPANESE HOLLY

EVERGREEN TRE
PALMETTE OBLIQ

FLOWERING SHRUB
PALMETTE VERRIER

While fruit trees are perhaps the most popular subjects for espaliering in lands where the technique originated, in North America many flowering shrubs and evergreen climbers and shrubs are used in espalier as landscape accents. Among the most successful are English ivy, firethorn, Japanese holly, Hick's yew. Although these ornamental espaliers are most often planned in the formal espalier shapes developed in earlier centuries, modern gardeners find some of the more informal shapes highly effective against the masonry or wooden walls of modernistic homes. Among the forms that require the least maintenance once the basic shape has been achieved are evergreen trees in Free Form, in an Informal U-Shape or in an Informal Fan, the evergreen shown here in Fan Shape and the flowering shrub in Informal. The Simple Upright Cordon, below right, is another easy and effective espalier.

FLOWERING SHRUB
INFORMAL

FIRETHORN
SIMPLE UPRIGHT CORDON

firm the earth and pour in a bucket of water containing a nitrogen-phosphorous-potash liquid fertilizer at one-half strength. When the water has soaked away fill the hole and firm again. In late spring, mulch the entire border with anything from peat moss to grass clippings and keep the mulch 2 inches deep. Espaliered fruit trees require slightly less feeding than bigger trees. The spraying schedules for espaliered fruit trees are the same as for orchard-grown trees.

Shaping a candelabra: Never be afraid to cut wood from your tree, but be sure the plant is dormant and the cutting purposeful. After you have planted the tree prune it back to just above a pair of buds on opposite sides of the trunk 12 inches from the ground. Let the two shoots that develop from these buds grow free all summer; in the fall they will be bent and tied to a temporary U-shaped training trellis made of bamboo canes or wood strips.

To make the temporary training trellis for an apple or a pear tree, cut a bamboo cane 30 inches long, center it on the lowest horizontal wire of the permanent trellis and tie it there securely. For peaches and nectarines the cane should measure 60 inches. Next, cut two shorter canes, 14 inches each, and tie each at right angles to either end of the long cane. The tops of the shorter canes are now ready to be lashed to the next wire up on the permanent trellis. When summer growth is over, bend the two young shoots down so that they extend along either side of the base of the training trellis. Tie them to it with raffia or cloth strips. The ends of the shoots should protrude beyond the bamboo, and these you now bend up and tie firmly to the uprights of the U. The following spring, while the plant is still dormant, prune the tips of each upright back to a sturdy pair of buds near the second wire and remove all other shoots. This procedure will be repeated in autumn when you are ready to develop the second, or top, layer of the candelabra. Shoots from the pair of buds you left on each upright will become the two upper U's. These must be shaped and tied to two bamboo trellises that are narrower than the base U—12 inches across for apples and pears, 24 inches for peaches and nectarines. To induce growth the following spring, prune the tips of all four uprights back to a bud headed upward. Prune all other growth.

To extend the candelabra in following years, select the best upward-growing shoot at the upper end of each arm and tie it to the wire above. In spring, prune each tip back to a bud as before. All other shoots you must prune back to stubs containing three buds. These stubs will produce leaves and provide places for fruit buds to form.

Pinching: Even when your espalier is mature, it will require pruning and pinching to maintain its shape and to induce fruiting. Starting in May,

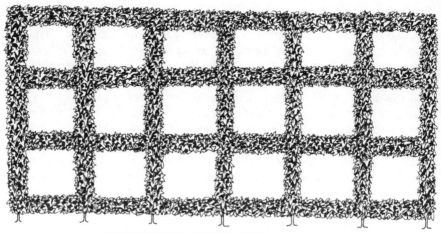

ENGLISH IVY SCREEN, TREILLAGE

ENGLISH IVY
SIMPLE HORIZONTAL CORDON

English ivy in its nearly countless varieties is highly suitable for espalier training. One special advantage is that some forms are cold-hardy far into the North. Screen, ABOVE, *can be trained on wire or on a wall. Cordon,* LEFT, *needs simple wire or lath support. The patterns* OPPOSITE *are trained on a fence; "garland" is possible on the other side of the fence with either V- or diamond pattern providing the roots.*

pinch off about half of every side shoot 12 inches or longer. The stubs will put out new growth. In midsummer pinch the new growth back to its last two leaves. In a good growth year you may have to repeat the operation. Your purpose is to make the shoots form fruit spurs.

Pruning and pinching are a nuisance to some, but remember that just a little effort on your part is likely to produce so much fruit that you may have to thin the crop. Do this after the fruit has started to round out.

Many dwarfs are so eager to produce that you may have to remove fruit buds the first year to preserve their strength, but you can let them set fruit the second year. By the fourth you should harvest two bushels and more—a handsome by-product of one of the most elegant of garden ornaments.

Bonsai: Trees and Shrubs in Miniature

Bonsai are dwarf potted plants—usually trees, sometimes shrubs—cultivated for centuries by the Japanese and Chinese. Since World War II the art has become popular in the U.S. Development of a bonsai is a time-

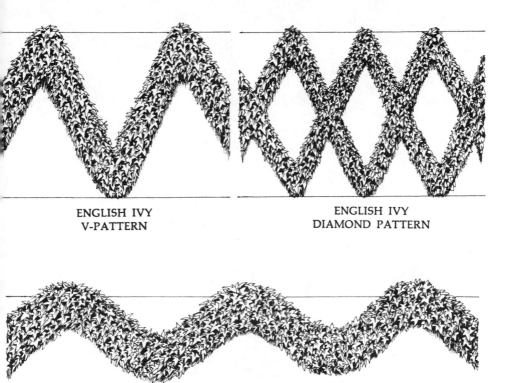

ENGLISH IVY
V-PATTERN

ENGLISH IVY
DIAMOND PATTERN

ENGLISH IVY GARLAND

consuming process requiring care and patience and considerable artistic skill. There is more to it than the nurture and training of a plant, for a successful bonsai might well be described as the marriage of a plant and a container to create a delightful picture of nature in miniature.

Although the true bonsai is a hardy tree or shrub that is grown outdoors (in a pot), woody tropical plants such as dwarf pomegranate may also be developed as bonsai. Only fairly small-leaved species should be used; otherwise, the foliage will be out of scale with the rest of the plant. Zelkova, ginkgo, some of the pines and maples can become outstanding bonsai. As a rule, the most interesting bonsai are developed out of already runty plants with substantial, tapering trunks and naturally twisted or gnarled branches, or from young but otherwise normal plants. These may be found in the wild or in a nursery.

Bonsai pots—an important part of a bonsai—come in many designs. They range from 2 to about 25 inches in diameter; from 1 to 10 inches deep. Some are made of porous red clay; others are glazed. All should have drainage holes.

Soil mixtures vary, but in all cases should be capable of holding

A small pine trained to windswept shape of a traditional bonsai rises from rock, soil and moss formed to resemble a cliffside. It is generally believed that the first bonsai were plants dwarfed and stunted by cruel weather conditions in Japanese mountains and brought to cities as a reminder of nature in its wilder state. Professional growers began to develop bonsai from native and nursery materials, and learned to create the ancient-seeming twisted and unusual shapes we now associate with this art form. By the bonsai here are the tools of the art —a rake, a dibbler, clippers of various sizes and a small pointed saw.

moisture and food while providing excellent drainage and aeration. Bonsai experts normally arrange the soil in layers, starting with a fairly coarse mixture at the bottom of the pot, generally working up to a fine mixture. The soil is topped off with moss, small ground-cover plants such as *Helxine soleirolii* or fine pebbles.

In potting up a bonsai for the first time, you should pick the soil away from the outside of the rootball and shear the roots rather severely. Then cut the top of the plant back to the same degree. (That is, if you reduce the rootball one-third in size, the top of the plant should also be reduced a third.) Then place the plant in the pot and pack the soil in firmly around it. Water well and set in light shade outdoors for two or three weeks. Then gradually move the plant into full sun.

The best time to start developing a bonsai is in the spring.

Repotting will be required as the plant becomes established and starts to grow. Some bonsai need repotting twice a year; others only every few years. The average is once a year. The process followed is the same as for the original potting.

No simple set of directions can be given for training bonsai. In general, it is a process of hard, selective pruning and thinning and of pinching out new growths. To control the direction of growth and to give the plant interesting warped lines, you may wrap fairly stiff copper or steel wire around the trunk and branches and then bend; or you may tie the stems to stiff, preshaped wires and rods.

For the uninitiated, thoughts of developing a bonsai can be discouraging and almost frightening. The art of bonsai in the past was surrounded with mystery. The idea that a bonsai takes endless years of patience before it can mature into a beautiful tree is not true. Fine bonsai can be developed in a few hours following these simple procedures.

1. Trim out all dead wood, shorten long branches and eliminate branches growing at the same levels around the trunk. Leave clean cuts, no stumps.

2. Trees with excess branches should have a few removed, leaving three at the lowest level of the trunk. An ideal bonsai reveals the trunk line for two-thirds of the distance up the trunk. The first third is completely bare of branches; the next third is bare of branches in front and framed by branches at the sides and back; the top third has branches all around. The side that displays the trunk is the front.

The main terminal of certain of the informal styles always bends to the front. Other branches toward the top should be left closer together.

The first three branches are No.1, No. 2 and No. 3. No. 1 is the lowest, No. 2 is a little higher up on the opposite side of the trunk and No. 3 is at the back and a bit higher than No. 2 or between 1 and 2.

3. Root structure is part of overall design and should be allowed to

HOW TO START
A BONSAI

Trim out dead wood, shorten branches and eliminate others at the same level on the trunk. Cuts must be clean.

Insert wire in soil behind base of trunk, wrapping wire in even spirals. Use one heavy- or two medium-gauge wires.

Root structure is part of the design and should show. Pull away the soil and expose main surface roots using a chopstick.

Wire the side branches, gently shaping them to the desired style before potting. Use a lighter wire to strengthen the natural direction of small branches. Expose the roots and prune them to fit the shape of the container you are using.

Lower third of tree must be bare; the next third should have only side and back limbs; the top third, limbs all around.

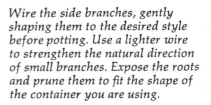

Cover the drain holes in the container with plastic mesh and thread and anchor wires through both holes and mesh. Put in the first layer of coarse soil.

In all, three grades of granular soil have been used to complete the potting. Now finish off by placing wet moss over the dry soil surface. Perhaps the placement of a stone might be a suitable touch to complete the artistic composition.

Settle the tree roots in the soil by giving it a gentle twist. Cross the anchor wires over the roots, twist ends together and hide them in the root mass.

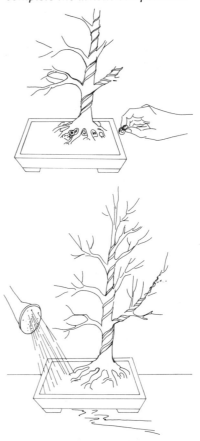

Add a less coarse grade of soil to the pot, working it in carefully around the roots with a chopstick. Care must be taken to firm the soil well, tamping it to fill the air holes. Finish filling with a third layer of still finer soil.

Now the bonsai is ready for watering. Plunge the pot in a basin full of water to reach just below its rim. Water from above with the fine rosette on a watering can. Display your handiwork on a table in good light and enjoy it. In hot dry climate, shade it.

show. Pull away soil and expose main large surface roots. Pointed chopsticks are best for this chore.

4. Start wiring with heaviest wire at base of trunk, inserting end in soil behind the base of the trunk and spacing spirals evenly. For the beginner, it's better to use two wires of medium gauge than one very heavy one.

5. Neat wiring is essential to the appearance of the tree. Bend branches with opposed fingers and thumbs. Use lighter-gauge wires to shape or strengthen natural direction of lesser branches and twigs. After wiring the tree, gently shape the branches to the desired style before placing in the container.

6. In a container of the correct size for the tree, with drain holes covered with plastic mesh, thread anchor wires through holes and mesh. Put a layer of the coarsest soil into the bottom of the pot.

7. Expose roots of the tree by breaking the earth away with chopsticks. Shorten the roots to the general shape of the container. Settle the tree into the soil with a gentle twisting motion to eliminate air pockets.

8. Cross the anchor wires over the surface of the roots, twist the opposite ends together to tie them and tuck the ends back into the main root mass.

9. Put more soil of a less coarse texture into the pot. Work the soil into and around the roots with a jabbing motion of the chopsticks to fill all the air holes, and top with the finest soil mix. Then place moss (wet first in water) as desired on the dry surface of the soil. Add a stone if it seems to improve the composition, then place the whole bonsai into a basin full of water that will reach to just below the rim of the pot. Water from above with a fine spray from a watering can. Be sure you have watered the plant on all four sides and thoroughly.

To keep bonsai healthy, give them fresh soil every year. Feed often. Water regularly. Keep the plant outdoors and in the sun (except in midsummer and immediately after potting or repotting). However, in winter, in cold climates, store true bonsai on a cool (about 40°), bright sun porch or the equivalent. Never bring a true bonsai into a warm house except in moderate weather—and then only for a day or two. (Tropical bonsai plants, of course, are handled like house plants.)

Topiary: Sculpting Live Plants

Topiary is the art of pruning or otherwise training shrubs and trees to geometric or representational forms. Topiary was done by the Romans and reached its peak of popularity in England, where innumerable fine examples still exist, including whole gardens, as at Levens Hall. There is less topiary in the United States, because this is work that requires time and patience. However, there are specimens in some of the old gardens

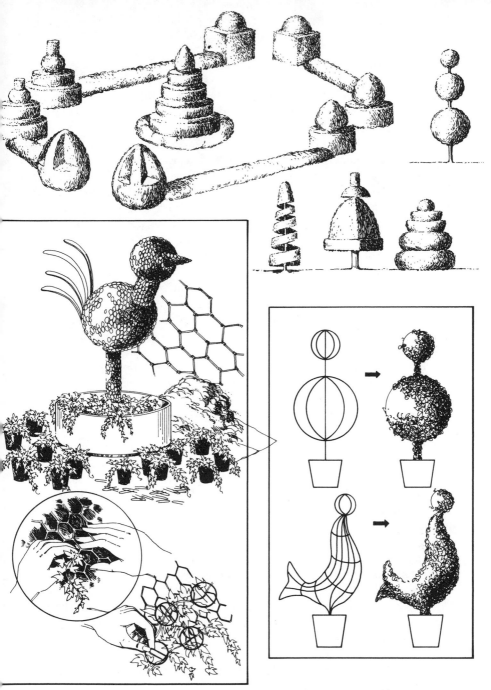

The upper sketches show classic, true topiary, which derive their shapes entirely from artful clipping and pruning. No wire frames are used, although individual branches may be wire-trained, as in bonsai. The lower sketches show the technique for "instant" topiary, trained on wire armatures—which may be made at home or purchased ready-made. Form for fanciful bird is stuffed with moist sphagnum moss, then planted with rooted cuttings of English ivy.

and large estates in the East (Williamsburg, the Philadelphia area, Long Island, and the Brayton Estate in Rhode Island), and to some extent, on the West Coast (San Mateo, California).

There is a less exacting form of topiary that has met with favor because it is ornamental, easy to move and relatively quick to make. You may be acquainted with one very common form: a hoya (the wax-plant) or crown-of-thorns (*Euphorbia milii*) trained on an arched wire support, inserted in the pot. This is a simple method, but it is topiary. You can grow any small, pliable climber this way. Home gardeners have long resorted to this method, partly because it can be artistic, partly because the plant trained like this takes up less space.

For a more complicated topiary, you need to build an armature, or frame, on which to train your plant. You can buy ready-made frames, but that takes half the fun out of your creation.

To make the armature, bend and cut a piece of chicken wire to the desired form. This form does not have to be a finished work of art, as it will not show in the final product.

At this point, you have two ways to go. One is to pack the wire frame with moist sphagnum moss and insert numerous rooted cuttings of small-leaved English ivy until the bird is completed. You will have to keep the sphagnum moist, or the ivy will die. (Creeping fig, *Ficus pumila*, is also suitable.)

The second way is to anchor a form in a pot of growing ivy (the more shoots, the better). Do this by setting the frame over metal stakes driven into the soil on either side of the pot. Let stakes extend 2 or 3 inches above the pot rim to provide good anchorage for the topiary. Then train the ivy over the form, tying lightly where needed. Guide the ivy as it grows and clip side shoots that threaten to spoil the looks of the figure you are making.

You may also use 8-gauge iron or aluminum wire to make the form you want. For unusual forms, it will be necessary to tie or solder pieces of wire together and bend them to desired lines.

Regardless of the armature you decide on, the plants need the good care you would give any house plant. Start them in good soil and water regularly. Feed them with a soluble fertilizer when you start the topiary; after that, only as needed, your guide being the rate of growth. This should not be so fast, nor so much, that plants become problems and unmanageable.

Ivy is the most satisfactory plant for this type of topiary, but you might also like to experiment with ceropegia, grape-ivy, jasmine or pothos for topiaries.

If you are a dedicated gardener and want to make topiaries in your outdoor garden, there are several plants you can use, evergreens being the most satisfactory: boxwood, yew, juniper, holly. Privet is good in colder areas, but it is deciduous and there is not much to be said for a leafless bird, animal or human figure.

Actually, any clipped hedge may be considered a form of topiary. Sixteenth-century knot gardens started the vogue. These were small gardens of flowers, intricately laid out, and surrounded by low hedges of clipped boxwood. Yew came to be preferred after the Restoration of Charles II in 1660. From simple beginnings, the art proceeded to overwhelming hedges, roofed allees and figures. Birds have always been popular, especially peacocks, but there have been such animals as giraffes, bears and, in Disneyland, an elephant standing on his feet.

Topiary implies formality and fixed design. There are more or less naturally shaped globe and pyramid forms available of yew and arborvitae. These are the easiest ones to use for a formal effect, as you have little pruning to do to keep them in shape. If you want something fanciful, here are basic steps to follow:

1. Visualize the completed form and select a plant that will lend itself to evolving into what you want.
2. Have a plan. Topiary does not work just anywhere. It must have a specific setting for proper show.
3. Provide full sun. Shade affects plant growth, which, in turn, spoils the shape.
4. Choose large plants to start with, if money is no object.
5. Choose small plants if budget is limited, and expect results in seven to ten years.
6. Provide good, rich soil, 2 or 3 feet deep. (The plant stays there for years.)
7. Plant in fall if not too cold; otherwise in April or May.
8. Bend and secure branches if necessary, to get them into the form you want. This will be a rough outline at first.
9. Resist clipping until the second year, when the plant is well established.
10. Clip new top and lateral tip growth to make a compact, dense base— whatever the superstructure may be.
11. Clip lightly several times the first few years. After the form is well set, clip once a year after new growth is completed.

The forms you can make are limited only by your own ingenuity. You will need wire, bamboo, wood stakes or forms made of these materials to guide growth the way you want it.

You might want to start with a spiral, which is relatively easy. Choose a young plant and trim it to a single shoot. Drive a heavy stake into the soil at the base of the trunk and train the shoot spirally around the stake. Secure the shoot with plastic-coated wire, but never so tightly as to cut into the shoot. Prune the shoot as it grows, so as to force the side shoots into thick growth. Keep side growth clipped for neatness and to give depth to the ascending layers of the spiral.

For an archway over a path, set two plants opposite each other, install a bent metal form and train the plants, by tying and clipping, until they meet on the frame.

To make an animal, set four yews in a rectangle. These will be the legs. Prune the tops to make them bush out and give you the material for shaping into a cat, dog, bear, or whatever suits your fancy.

For large, complicated forms, you will need heavy supports or whole armatures. Proceed to these from the simpler forms and experience will be your guide.

How To Train a Standard

In horticulture the word standard usually refers to trees with a single straight stem topped by a compact head of foliage. Familiar examples are weeping mulberry and tree rose, both of which require grafting. However, there are many plants which can be trained to standard form without the complication of grafting. These include geranium, English ivy, fatshedera, fuchsia, heliotrope, lantana, azalea, coleus, myrtle (*Myrtus communis*) and rosemary. Start with a rooted cutting or seedling in a pot, with a bamboo pole or other stake the height you have in mind for your finished tree. Develop a single stem by pinching out all side shoots as they form. As the plant grows, tie the stem firmly (but not so tight it becomes constricted) to the stake. When the main stem is at the desired height—perhaps between 2 and 6 feet—pinch out the tip and allow branches to develop only at the top. As the branches grow, continue pinching out each to encourage maximum branching and fullness.

Opposite, left, top: *Four-inch geranium tip cutting roots readily. Cut just below leaf node; trim away lower leaves as shown, then root in moist, sandy soil.*
Right: *Geranium in standard tree form. At 4 feet begin pinching back all tips to encourage bushiness; this also tends to promote flowering.*
Right, bottom: *As standard grows, keep all leaves pruned away from the trunk, as black bars indicate, except for those at the top.*
Left, bottom: *Standard may require two or three seasons to develop, so pot it in successively larger containers. With good care, it will live for years.*

SPECIAL WAYS WITH CHRYSANTHEMUMS

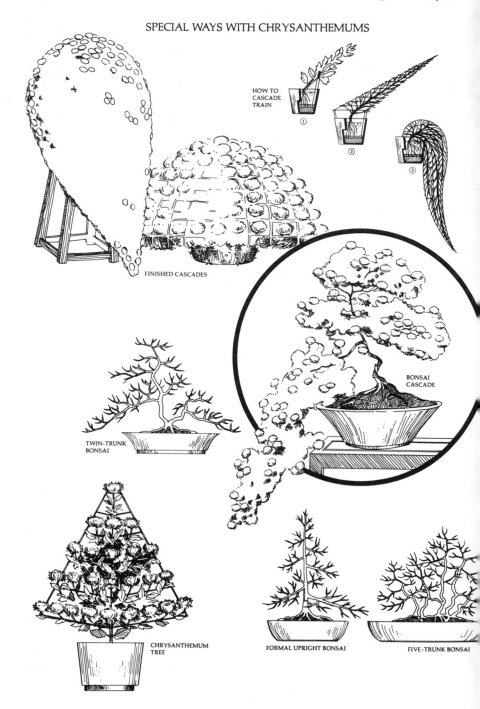

HOW TO
CASCADE
TRAIN
①
②
③

FINISHED CASCADES

TWIN-TRUNK
BONSAI

BONSAI
CASCADE

CHRYSANTHEMUM
TREE

FORMAL UPRIGHT BONSAI

FIVE-TRUNK BONSAI

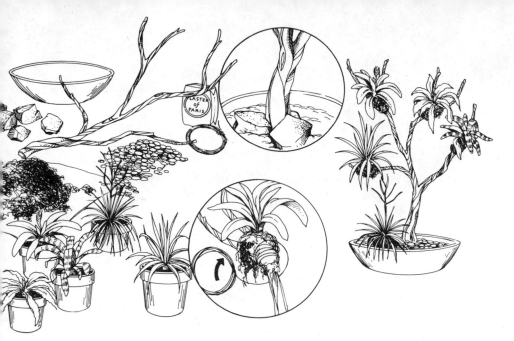

OPPOSITE: *Chrysanthemum stems are flexible enough to be trained. For a cascade of blossoms on one side of a pot, prune the plant to a single stem; gradually bend it to fall over the side. For fountain effect, train many stems in the same way. For bonsai effect, wind stems with soft wire so they will keep desired shape. A combination of bonsai and cascade is accomplished by letting one stem grow down while the rest of the plant grows upright. Use wire frame to train small-flowered chrysanthemum as an espalier.*

ABOVE: *Epiphytic bromeliads, accustomed as they are to perching in real trees in their native haunts, may be cultivated in a similar manner indoors in a bright, moist atmosphere. The technique is simple. Select a dried tree branch of suitable size and shape. Using plaster of paris, anchor it in a pot or tub, hiding the white surface with moss or pebbles. Wrap a generous handful of moist sphagnum moss around the roots of each bromeliad and tie it to a tree branch with nylon thread. Mist plants and moss daily.*

BELOW: *Fuchsias bloom on new wood and will keep blooming if branch tips are pinched back often to encourage bushy growth. Rest plants in winter, and in spring cut back after leaf buds show to the dark lines shown here, trimming away growth represented by the lighter line. Sketches show what to cut back on, left to right, a hanging-basket fuchsia, a tree fuchsia, an espalier fuchsia and an upright fuchsia to encourage growth and maintain form. Some fuchsias are naturally trailing, others more upright.*

13. Basic Garden Construction

Steps, walks and walls add enormously to the visual interest of the landscape. The combination of brick, stone and pebble textures and shapes with the basic greens and browns of a garden is often needed to heighten the interest of borders and foundation plantings. For the gardener with even a little aptitude for do-it-yourself, construction jobs involved aren't difficult. An understanding of the materials is important; once grasped, practice with the methods will quickly make the amateur proficient enough to achieve satisfying results.

Wood in the Garden

The most difficult problem in using wood in the garden—for fences, trellises and other structures—is to prevent decay. Redwood and cypress are the most resistant to attack by decay fungi and termites. But pine, cedar, fir and other woods are just as frequently used because of their economy. No matter which wood you use, the secret of long life lies in the application of a wood preservative and in proper construction methods.

Preventing rot. First step in building any outside wood structure is to treat the wood with a preservative. A variety of chemicals are used (creosote, copper naphthenate, zinc naphthenate) but the standard is pentachlorophenol. This is a clear liquid which does not affect the grain structure of the wood, and may be painted over.

For maximum impregnation, all preservatives should be applied under pressure at the factory or lumberyard after the lumber has been cut to size. You can, however, achieve adequate protection by painting or dipping the lumber yourself. Make two applications, the second several days after the first has dried. It is important that all cutting, surfacing and notching of the wood be done *before* the treatment is made. Special care should be taken to ensure that the ends of each piece of lumber are treated.

Wood that is to be buried in the ground should be most carefully treated. You may use pentachlorophenol or similar transparent compound, or apply several coats of creosote. Although exposure to moisture is not so prolonged, wood above ground should also be treated—not only to prevent rot but also to forestall weathering and splitting and to discourage termites.

Cold Frames and Hotbeds

These can be made of wood or concrete. If you use wood, make sure it has been pressure-treated with a wood preservative (but not creosote); otherwise it will rot out in a year or two.

Poured concrete is better. The walls should be 6 inches thick. How far they extend below ground level depends on how deeply you want to work the soil. Minimum depth is 12 inches; maximum (if you put in a deep manure bed), 36 inches. The low front wall should be at least 12 inches above ground; the high back wall 6 inches higher.

To provide a hinge strip for the sash, bolt a wood 2 by 4 treated with preservative to the top of the high wall along the outside edge. Insert the bolts 4 feet apart in the concrete, head down, before it has set. They should project 2 inches above the concrete.

Drains and Their Construction

Marshy land and other low, wet spots can usually be transformed into more useful lawn and garden areas by simple drainage methods. Just digging a trench from the wet spot to some lower-lying runoff point will often accomplish the purpose. Or, you can install drain tile.

Drains should be buried about 6 inches below the surface and laid at enough pitch to permit the water to flow off. The number of drain lines required will depend on the size of the area to be drained, the composition of the soil and the amount of water to be removed. A wet spot in the neighborhood of 100 square feet, for example, can probably be drained by a single line. But to take care of large areas it may be necessary to install several lines or even to install a radial system with branch lines feeding into a central line.

Two types of drain pipe may be used. Both are 4-inch diameter. The old standby is clay tile, which comes in short lengths. The tiles are spaced about ½ inch apart and the joints covered with loose strips of tar paper to keep out dirt.

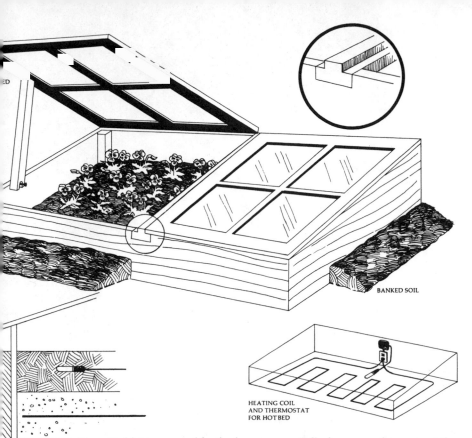

BANKED SOIL

HEATING COIL
AND THERMOSTAT
FOR HOT BED

CROSS-SECTION
OF HEATING COIL
INSTALLATION

Top: *Cold frames and hotbeds are essentially boxes used to extend the season, and are similar in construction. The cold frame is heated only by the sun whereas a hotbed receives artificial heat provided by a heating cable. Suitable materials include concrete, brick or wood. Sash covers are always wood. Note mounding of earth to act as insulating against cold.*

Center: *Details of electric heating installation for a hotbed. Drawing at left shows a cross-section of soil beneath the hotbed with heating cable imbedded in a layer of gravel. Drawing at right shows typical layout at the heating coil in a hotbed. Thermostat regulates temperature.*

Bottom: *Winter and summer use of a cold frame. Lathing is used in summer to shade plants. In cooler season, cold frame with sash may be used to force bulbs, start seedlings, harden off started seedlings, grow lettuce. Drawing at right shows typical layering of soil.*

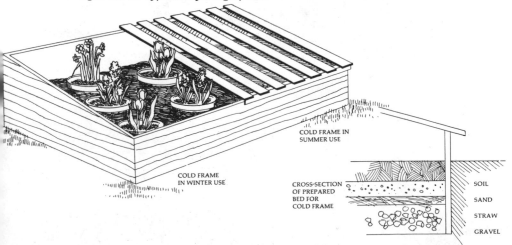

COLD FRAME IN
SUMMER USE

COLD FRAME
IN WINTER USE

CROSS-SECTION
OF PREPARED
BED FOR
COLD FRAME

SOIL

SAND

STRAW

GRAVEL

New composition pipe is easier to handle because it is very light in weight and comes in lengths up to 10 feet. For drainage purposes, use pipes which are perforated along one side. Install the perforated side down. Join lengths of pipe with tight-fitting plastic sleeves, which keep out tree roots.

Fences and How To Build

Posts. Wood posts are generally 4 by 4s, but may be larger (metal posts are smaller). They should be pressure-treated at the mill with a wood preservative, and the top shaped so that water runs off easily.

Sink posts in the ground about 18 to 24 inches. This will vary depending on the consistency of the soil, the height and weight of the fence and whether it is exposed to unusually high winds. If the soil is heavy and packs solidly, all you usually have to do is dig a hole, toss in a couple of inches of gravel for drainage, set in the post and backfill with the soil. If the soil is very loose, however, make the hole about three times the width of the post and fill in around the post with concrete. Metal posts should almost always be set in concrete.

In setting posts use a carpenter's level to make sure they are straight up and down.

Rails and stringers. These are usually 8 feet long, but in a rail fence are more likely to be 10 feet. The wood need not be treated with preservative, but it will last longer and hold paint better if it is.

For strength, mortise rails and stringers into the posts or support them with special metal brackets attached to the posts. Screws will hold better than nails.

Use a carpenter's level to make sure rails and stringers are level. But on sloping land, they may follow the contours of the land.

Gates. Hang them on posts set deep into the ground and embedded in concrete. Use diagonal crossbracing to support wide gates. Very wide gates usually also need to be supported with a wire or chain stretching from the outside upper corner of the gate to the top of a gatepost that is 4 to 6 feet higher than the gate itself.

If a gate is to swing from a masonry post, hinge it to a wood 2 by 4 and then attach the 2 by 4 to the masonry with lead expansion anchors and long screws.

Steps and Their Construction

Choice of materials for garden steps lies among stone, brick, concrete and heavy timbers. The first two are esthetically pleasing, durable and

OPPOSITE: *This garden and outdoor living area is filled with projects that can be built by the amateur: benches for seating, wooden table and fence, and spacious terrace.*

relatively easy to handle. Concrete is even more durable and easy to work with, but even when the steps are designed by an expert, they have a cold, formal quality unsuited to many gardens. Wood (half-logs or railroad ties) looks good in informal surroundings, but will not last as long, even when treated with preservative, and affords more precarious footing.

There are only a few rules for making garden steps that cannot be broken one way or another. Among them, these two are paramount: Never permit a step to wobble even slightly; never place in immediate sequence steps that are appreciably different in height of riser or width of tread. For every kind of stair, a dozen variants are possible, but certain generalizations may be helpful. Wood steps of open construction are likely to last longer without rotting than wood in contact with the ground, but they may give way at the joints. Turf steps require more fussy upkeep than any others. Poured-concrete steps may be built wherever cement, sand and gravel may be obtained, but ledge stone and formal masonry are practical only where materials and qualified labor are available. Bricks are obtainable everywhere, of course, but the ability to lay them well comes only with a nice blend of patience and aptitude or with long practice. Everything from the simplest flagstone path to solid-masonry stairs requires a real foundation, to give trouble-free, long-term service.

Whatever materials are used, garden steps should be only about 6 inches high; the treads, 12 or more inches deep. Such approximate dimensions give the steps a sweep and a restful quality that are compatible with gardens.

Timber steps are built simply by setting the timbers into the slope. If the timbers are partially buried along the front edge, they should be perfectly safe—at least on gentle slopes. But to give positive protection against tipping under weight and against sliding in wet weather, you should drive two or three creosoted stakes deep into the earth against the front edges of the steps.

Be sure that railroad ties, or any wood treated with creosote, are completely dry before using. Otherwise, unsightly oily spots appear that are slippery underfoot and injurious to plant material that may come in contact with them.

Walks, Terraces and How To Build

Brick. Excavate 4 inches deep and firm the soil. Pour in a 2-inch layer of sand or hard cinders, and roll smooth. Stretch strings for the edges of the walk. Then lay in the brick. (When laying a terrace, start from one corner and work toward the center.) Leave ¼ to ½ inch space between each brick and fill with sand, or sand mixed with a little cement.

A dry brick walk made in this way rarely heaves with the frost, and is easy to repair if it does. Under certain circumstances, however, solid brick masonry may be desired. In this case, excavate 6 inches deep and pour in a 2-inch layer of sand or hard cinders. Then pour a 1½-inch slab of concrete. After this has set, coat the surface with a grout of ½ sack cement and 3 gallons water. Then immediately spread on a ½-inch layer of concrete mortar and set the bricks in place. After the mortar bed has set for about three hours spray the bricks lightly but thoroughly with water. Then fill the joints between bricks with a liquid mixture of 1 part cement and 2 to 3 parts sand.

Concrete. To prevent cracking, lay the walk over a well-drained base. In some areas, where the soil is sandy or gravelly, all you have to do is scoop out the ground about 2 inches deep and tamp the base firm. If the soil is dense, however, dig it out 8 inches deep and pour a 6-inch layer of sand, gravel or fine, hard cinders into the trench, and tamp it.

A walk may be any width. It is desirable, however, to make a front walk 4 to 5 feet wide. Side and back walks may be from 1½ to 3 feet wide. The pavement should be 4 to 6 inches thick to bring it 2 inches above ground level.

Pour concrete for a walk in oiled wood forms. Along the sides, lay boards—preferably 2 by 4s—at least 4 inches wide. Hold in place vertically with stakes. The top edges of the lumber should be 2 inches above the surrounding ground. To permit runoff of water, slope the walk about ½ inches to one side.

Provide expansion joints at 4- to 6-foot intervals along the length of the walk. These are made with ¾-inch boards set vertically between the side rails. Place a layer of tar paper on both sides of these.

Pour the concrete into each section, tamp well and level with a "strike-board" resting on the top edges of the side rails. Work the strike-board back and forth in sawlike fashion as you move from one end of the walk to the other. After the concrete has set for about 1 hour, finish with a wood float. For an even smoother finish, let the concrete set another 30 to 60 minutes, then finish with a steel trowel.

After the walk has dried for several days, remove the wood divider strips and side rails. Do not bother to take out the tar paper in the expansion joints. (If the divider strips are difficult to remove, don't worry about them.)

Stone. Excavate well-drained gravelly soil 4 inches deep; heavier soils to 6 inches. Smooth and tamp well. Then fill with enough sand, gravel or hard cinders to bring the stones to grade. Firm. Set in stones and level. Then fill cracks with sand. In a flagstone walk, use stones that are 1½ inches thick. Thinner stones are likely to break.

If stones are to be laid in mortar, and if you are using heavy field-stones, dig out the ground deep enough to accommodate a 4-inch layer of sand, hard cinders or gravel under the stones. Level and tamp. Place stones in position. Then trowel mortar into the joints and smooth level with the edges of the stones. Keep covered with wet burlap for four days.

If you are paving with flagstones laid level with the ground, excavate 6 inches deep, tamp, and fill with a 4-inch layer of sand, gravel or hard cinders. Over this pour a 3-inch bed of concrete. Let set for 24 hours.

Then lay out on the concrete about 9 square feet of the flagstones (1-inch thickness is adequate). Number them with chalk and make a diagram on paper so you can return them to the same places. Then remove the stones and brush onto the concrete base a grout of ½ sack cement to 3 gallons water. Over this immediately place a ½-inch layer of concrete made of 1 part cement and 3 parts sand. Then set the flagstones in place and press down. Fill the cracks between the stones with the same mortar, and trowel level with the edges. Cover paving with wet burlap for four days.

To make concrete flagstones for a walk, build wood forms of any shape and size you like. Make them 1½ inches deep. Coat the wood with oil or automobile grease. Then pour in a mixture of 1 part cement, 2¼ parts sand and 3 parts coarse aggregate. Trowel smooth, cover with damp burlap and allow to set for 48 hours.

Wood block. Cypress or redwood blocks will last longest. They may be cut in any shape or sliced off the end of a tree trunk. They should be 2 to 3 inches thick. Before laying, saturate them with wood preservative.

Excavate ground 4 inches deep, tamp and spread in a 2-inch layer of sand. Then set blocks in place and fill joints with sand.

Walls and How To Build

Brick. (See also directions for using and maintaining brick.) Brick walls may be one, two or three tiers thick, depending on their layout, height and exposure to winds. If you are building a straight wall which is not subjected to unusual wind pressure, you may choose among the following designs:

If less than 4 feet high, build a wall one tier (4 inches) thick. Reinforce every 15 feet with brick piers 12 inches square.

If the wall is 4 to 6 feet high, build a one-tier wall reinforced every 15 feet with brick piers 16 inches square. Or build a two-tier (8-inch) wall without piers.

If the wall is 6 to 9 feet high, build a three-tier (12-inch) wall. No piers are required.

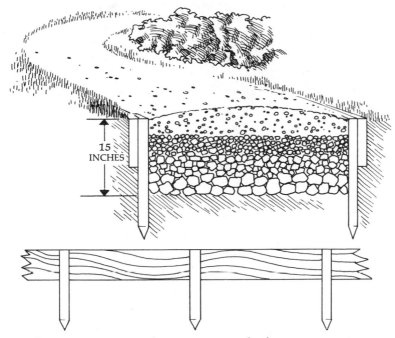

Construction of gravel or aggregate path, shown in cross-section: Soil, to a depth of 15 inches, has been replaced by rocks and coarse gravel, topped with finer materials. Top is slightly crowned, to improve surface drainage. Boards anchor sides of path.

By careful design a children's sand box and play area has been quietly integrated into this garden. Redwood frames the area and also provides seating. Upright poles are set securely in concrete anchor posts. When children outgrow the play area, the uprights can be sawed off at ground level, or pillar roses trained on them. With benches removed, the area can be filled with soil and thus converted to a raised planter bed for flowers, bulbs, roses or shrubs.

Dry stone wall gives an attractive finish to an embankment that terminates abruptly. This type of construction allows for the planting of small subjects and gives an informal, rather than formal, look to the landscape. Drawing at right shows how flat stones for a dry wall are set into the embankment to hold it and to brace the wall against the hillside's slope.

ABOVE: Redwood planks create planting pockets on a steep hillside and provide steps from level to level. Planks are tilted, edge up, against the slope of the hill and are braced by sturdy 4-foot stakes, driven into the ground at either end of each plank.

BELOW: Earthen embankment loses seeds and soil to rains until nature has had a chance to mature a ground cover. A cloth mesh placed over the slope keeps soil from washing away while seeds, sown beneath cloth, germinate and become established.

If a straight wall is exposed to high winds, follow the directions above, but in all cases reduce the height of the wall at least 18 inches below the maximums.

If a one-tier wall is curved or laid out in serpentine fashion, the use of piers is not essential. The wall should not exceed 4 feet in height. A two-tier wall may be built in the same manner to about 8 feet.

Do not use brick walls as retaining walls unless they are under 3 feet high and the ground behind them is stable.

Concrete. No matter how high the wall is to be, excavate the ground at least 12 inches to assure a firm foundation. In cold climates, dig to below frost level.

Unless the wall is very low, provide a concrete footing. This should be as deep as the wall is wide, and extend 6 inches beyond both the front and the back of the wall. Leave surface rough so that the concrete of the wall will stick to it. Just before pouring the wall, coat the top of the footing with cement grout made in the proportion of ½ sack cement to 3 gallons water.

The wall itself should be at least 6 inches thick. Reinforcing is not required unless the wall is over 6 feet high. Build the forms of ¾-inch fir plywood nailed to 2 by 4s. To keep the plywood panels the proper distance apart, place wood spacers at frequent intervals between them. These are removed as the concrete is poured. To prevent the plywood panels from spreading apart, nail wood braces across the top, and wire the panels together through the middle with steel baling wire. Pull out the wires after the concrete has set but not hardened, or you may leave them in the forms and cut them off flush with the face of the wall later.

To build a dry stone wall, excavate the ground to a depth of 6 inches or more and fill the trench with large stones or stone rubble. The wall should be at least 2 feet thick. Three feet is a safe maximum height. Use small slivers of stone to wedge and balance the large ones. To give the wall stability and lock the two sides together, set a few long stones at right angles to the wall so that they run from front to back.

To lift heavy stones, use a crowbar and raise the stones a few inches at a time on a crib of 2 by 4s. Another way to do the job is to lay a pair of heavy timbers or 4-inch tree trunks side by side from the ground to the top of the wall. Skid the stones up these.

Watering Systems

To simplify the job of watering, every garden should be equipped with several faucets. And in dry climates, installation of an underground sprinkling system is advisable.

Today, thanks to the plastics industry, almost anyone can install this type of equipment easily and at reasonable cost.

ABOVE, LEFT: *Attractive brick walkways and garden houses are construction projects with the potential of adding beauty and convenience to the landscape.* ABOVE, RIGHT: *The most attractive garden work centers blend in with existing architecture. Plan carefully so that there is a space allotted for every tool, accessory and supply you need for gardening. Build a potting bench at the height most comfortable for you. It will help keep the place tidy if you can hose off the floor.*

The faucets should be connected to the home water-supply system with long, flexible coils of tough, lightweight, noncorroding, nonclogging plastic pipe. Because this material rarely cracks when frozen, it need be buried only about a foot deep, or just deep enough to keep from cutting into it with a spade.

At the house end, the pipe is connected to the cold-water pipes with standard metal pipe fittings or threaded plastic fittings. A valve should be installed at this point so that the water can be cut off in winter.

At the faucet end, the pipe should be equipped with a 90-degree elbow buried about 12 inches below the soil surface. From the elbow, a length of metal pipe runs vertically to the faucet. The pipe should be strapped to a post or wall to prevent it from wobbling.

In most gardens, ½-inch plastic pipe is large enough to provide a steady supply of water at adequate pressure from all faucets.

Underground sprinkling systems vary somewhat in design, but all are installed in much the same way as just described. Flexible plastic pipe is run underground from the house to the sprinkler heads. The heads are placed on a deep bed of gravel so that they are flush with the surface of the soil. The heads must, of course, be located so that all sections of the lawn or garden will receive water.

There are do-it-yourself kits for installing underground watering systems, but you will be happier in the long run if you negotiate for a professional job.

Water in the Landscape

Garden pools are simple to maintain and can be easy enough to build if the gardener has any of the handyman's talents. An old bathtub, a wash boiler, even a plastic wading pool can be set into the ground and landscaped to make a reflecting pool or a small water garden. Make sure the sides are level as otherwise the water will appear to run uphill. Formal, larger pools are built, as swimming pools are, of concrete or stone masonry and usually are designed and handled by professional pool builders.

Design and Location. The pool can be formal or informal. Choice of design and materials is usually dictated by the landscape. A naturalized landscape would look too wild if a formal water garden were set nearby; a formal landscape might lose some of its style if a rough little woodland pool appeared in its midst. Symmetrical shapes are most often associated with formality; a circular, oval, rectangular or square shape creates an element of formality and looks best when made of materials such as concrete and edged with brick, marble or concrete. An informal pool can

If you have a greenhouse, valuable growing space inside can be saved by storing pots, potting mixtures and other materials in an adjoining work room or garden work center like this one. The design here provides several bins for the storage and sifting of various soil mixture ingredients—well-rotted compost, peat moss, soil, sand, gravel and leafmold.

be developed from a precast container such as the tub or a wading pool suggested above, edged with stones set into concrete, or it can be built from concrete in a free-form shape and edged with stones or pebbles.

One way to decide what location and what pool shape will be most attractive in your landscape is to cut out sheets of light-colored paper in the shape and size you think you will prefer, and to spread the paper on the ground in various locations, studying each placement to see what views of the pool will be afforded from the house, the terraces and other popular areas on your grounds.

While the location of the pool will depend on where the gardener believes it will be most attractive, there are other considerations in the positioning of the pool. The site should be sunny; most of the plants that do well in pools require a fair amount of sunlight. The pool should not be set under trees or shrubs that will deposit catkins in spring and leaves throughout summer and fall.

It should also be in a well-drained site. Damp, boggy places accumulate water pressure under the pool in wet seasons and this sometimes develops enough force to heave the pool from its setting. Ponds are suitable water gardens for boggy places, but not pools.

The pool also should be near a source of water so that it is easy to fill and so that the water level, which is lowered daily by evaporation, can be maintained. It should also, ideally, be near a slight down-slope that will allow the pool to drain down to a nearby ditch or dry well.

Depth. The depth of a garden pool generally is between 2 inches and 2 feet. A 2-inch pool is a reflecting pool and probably will not be suited to the growing of many aquatic plants, but it creates sufficient depth to reflect the light and is as effective for this purpose as a deeper pool would be. A pool 12 inches deep holds enough water to allow for the raising of fish as well as many water plants. A 2-foot-deep pool is required for some of the very large-rooted water plants and some water-lilies. As a rule, the shallower the pool the less expensive and costly it will be to build.

Drainage. Two important aspects to keep in mind if you are planning to build the pool yourself are that water will be required to fill it and to keep it filled and that it will be necessary occasionally to empty it. Small bathtub or playpool installations may be filled and drained by hose, but a more important installation will require underground pipes to fill the pool and to keep up with water lost by evaporation. Drains to empty the pool generally are located in the bottom, to one side.

The easiest way to provide drainage for a pool is to excavate the ground beneath it an extra 12 inches, fill this excavation with coarse gravel or crushed stone and install a drain pipe into it. This drainage layer must be tamped very firmly before the concrete is poured. If you

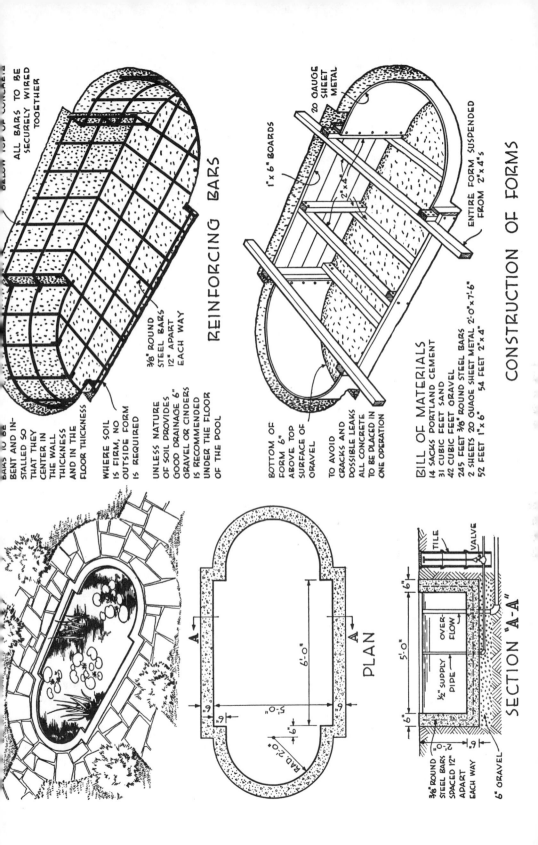

CONSTRUCTION OF FORMS

BELOW TOP OF CONCRETE

ALL BARS TO BE SECURELY WIRED TOGETHER

REINFORCING BARS

3/8" ROUND STEEL BARS 12" APART EACH WAY

BARS TO BE BENT AND INSTALLED SO THAT THEY CENTER IN THE WALL THICKNESS AND IN THE FLOOR THICKNESS

WHERE SOIL IS FIRM, NO OUTSIDE FORM IS REQUIRED

UNLESS NATURE OF SOIL PROVIDES GOOD DRAINAGE 6" GRAVEL OR CINDERS IS RECOMMENDED UNDER THE FLOOR OF THE POOL

20 GAUGE SHEET METAL

1" x 6" BOARDS

2" x 4"

ENTIRE FORM SUSPENDED FROM 2" x 4"'s

BOTTOM OF FORM 6" ABOVE TOP SURFACE OF GRAVEL

TO AVOID CRACKS AND POSSIBLE LEAKS ALL CONCRETE TO BE PLACED IN ONE OPERATION

BILL OF MATERIALS
14 SACKS PORTLAND CEMENT
31 CUBIC FEET SAND
42 CUBIC FEET GRAVEL
245 FEET 3/8" ROUND STEEL BARS
2 SHEETS 20 GUAGE SHEET METAL 2'-0" x 7'-6"
52 FEET 1" x 6"   54 FEET 2" x 4"

PLAN

A

A

6'-0"

5'-0"

6"

6"

6"

RAD. 2'-6"

SECTION "A-A"

TILE

VALVE

OVER-FLOW

5'-0"

6"

1/2" SUPPLY PIPE

6"

3/8" ROUND STEEL BARS SPACED 12" APART EACH WAY

6" GRAVEL

2'-0"

are building on a slope, however, it may be equally easy to extend a 1-inch drain pipe from the pool outlet to a low runoff point.

The drain pipe in the pool should be 1 to 2 inches in diameter and of brass. Wire it into place before the concrete is poured. The pipe may be cut off on the underside of the pool so that it drains directly into a gravel bed, or it may be connected with a long runoff pipe.

Into the top of the drain, screw a vertical standby pipe extending just above the water level. If the pool is overfilled or flooded by rain, the standby pipe will empty the excess water down the drain. In winter, when the pool is to be drained, simply unscrew the standby pipe from the drain.

Construction. The usual cement mixture for pools is one part cement, two parts sand and three parts half-inch gravel. Before concrete is poured, the floor of the excavation should be lined with 6 inches of stones or gravel, and forms of wood or metal should be constructed to hold enough concrete to make walls 6 inches thick. Pour the pond floor first, the walls right after, so that the two are firmly joined. In dry weather, and depending on the humidity of the local climate, concrete usually sets up enough over a 48-hour period so that the forms for the walls may be removed. A thin coat of finer cement mix may be applied to give a more attractive finish, or the whole may be rubbed with a stone or a brick to smooth rough spots. The new concrete will require 10 to 20 days to cure and during this period should be kept moist by covering it with a tarpaulin that is given an occasional light soaking.

If the pool is to have a stone coping (surround) this is cemented into place after the walls have been poured and the forms removed.

Reinforced-concrete Pool. A reinforced-concrete pool gives excellent year-in, year-out service. The directions below are for a pool which is roughly saucer-shaped and formed in one continuous process. It is a much easier pool to build than one with straight sides.

First, dig in the ground at the pool site a saucer-shaped depression that approximates the pool you have in mind but is 4 inches deeper and wider all around. When the digging is finished, use a shovel or a spade to firm and smooth the soil; keeping it wet makes shaping easier.

Build a form of wood around the top edges of the pool to help level the structure to be made, and to hold the reinforcement in position.

To reinforce the pool, line the sides and bottom with medium-weight (No. 10 or heavier) steel mesh. Bend this to conform with the excavation. If the pool is irregular, it may be easier to cut the mesh into triangles, which are wired together after they are placed. If you use the triangle mesh method, make sure each triangle overlaps the one next to it. Block the mesh up from the bottom and sides of the excavation with 2-inch pieces of brick or with stones.

The next step is to add the concrete. Add just enough water to make a damp-dry mixture. Spade the concrete into the excavation, starting at the bottom and working up evenly on all sides. The cement should be 4 to 5 inches thick. You will probably want to use your hands as well as a shovel and trowel to pack the cement firmly and to smooth it off. Cement is hard on the skin, so wear heavy work gloves. Be sure the cement is worked down into and under the mesh to form a firm, solid base.

Planting the Pool. Before planting, the pool must be cured; that is, rid of the alkaline salts water leaches from cement. To cure the pool, fill it four times to the brim, allow the water to rest there four days, then empty it completely. At the fifth filling, the pool should be ready for planting.

Water depths over plants are adjusted by raising the tubs in which aquatic plants are set from the floor of the pool on concrete blocks or bricks or stones. Tubs resting on the bottom of 24-inch pools would be at the right depth for most water-lilies; to grow water arum, the tubs would be raised from the floor of the pool by the height of one row of bricks.

Soil for water plants should be loam enriched with dried cow manure, 1 part manure to 10 parts loam. The muck found in some ponds and bogs is suitable for many aquatic plants though it is not recommended for water-lilies or lotus.

Keeping the Water Clear. It is impossible to keep pool water clear unless there is a continuous flow. If it is planted, it is not possible to clear pool water by the addition of chemicals. However, some degree of sanitation can be maintained by the addition of fish and algae-eating snails. Covering the bottom of the pool and the soil in the tubs with coarse pebbles helps keep the water clear when there are fish in the pond.

Winter Protection of Plants. Except in very warm climates, tropical water-lilies and lotus should be dug up at frost time and stored indoors. Hardy water-lilies are safe if the roots are planted below the frost line; if not, either they should be dug up or the pool should be covered with boards, straw and leaves. Other aquatics are left to take their chance with the winter and can be replaced if they don't survive.

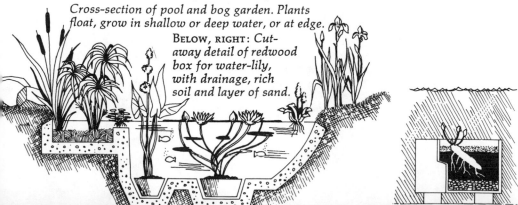

Cross-section of pool and bog garden. Plants float, grow in shallow or deep water, or at edge.

BELOW, RIGHT: *Cutaway detail of redwood box for water-lily, with drainage, rich soil and layer of sand.*

Nine sure-fire ways to attract insect-eating allies: in the top third of the sketch are a purple-martin apartment house, trees for shelter, a gourd home for hummingbirds; center, a roofed seed and suet station, blueberries, a birdbath; in the foreground, pyracantha berries, string for the nest building and a suet bag.

14. How To Cope with Garden Problems

All kinds of plants grown in and around the home and garden are attacked by insect pests and diseases. Fortunately, each plant is attacked by relatively few pests. There are about 10,000 types of injurious insects and 80,000 different plant diseases. Together, these pests cause an average annual loss of about $9 billion in the United States and Canada.

Insect and disease attack, on wild and cultivated plants alike, should be considered a *normal* part of nature and one of numerous ecological factors that help keep the hundreds of thousands of living plants and animals in balance with each other. Pests are just one of many hazards that must be considered when man carefully selects and grows plants. In many cases we have taken plants out of their natural environment, selected for genetic uniformity, and grown them closely together under what are abnormal conditions. Also, many of our valuable crop and ornamental plants are very susceptible to insects and diseases and would have difficulty surviving without man's help.

This chapter is designed *not* to frighten you about the many thousands of pests you will never see or have, but to help you recognize and control the more common garden insects and diseases. You should be able to prevent most pest damage to your lawn, trees, shrubs, flowers, house plants, vegetables and fruits by spending less than an hour each week.

Insects and Mites

Insects and mites have inhabited our planet for over 50 million years. They have caused injury or death to plants that have provided man with food, clothing, shelter, fiber and beauty for many thousands of years.

The mouth parts of insects and mites limit how and where they feed and the type of damage they do. Chewing insects, such as beetles and caterpillars, simply bite off and eat parts of leaves, flowers, stems and roots. Chewing insects are generally much easier to kill than are sucking insects, though many insecticides cope with both equally well. Insects, especially sucking types—such as aphids or plant lice and leaf-hoppers—are important in transmitting microorganisms and viruses that cause plant diseases.

Beneficial Insects

Many insects do not feed on plants or animals and are beneficial to man. Some are predators and feed on other insects, and we depend on pollinating insects, especially bees, for pollen transference from flower to flower. The more common predator insects which attack insect pests include the adults and larvae of lady beetles. They feed on aphids, spider mites, scales and mealybugs. Aphid lions, the immature stage of green lacewings, have an elongated, tapered body and sickle-shaped jaws. They feed on aphids, mealybugs and thrips. Damsel bugs (not to be confused with the also predacious damsel flies) and assassin bugs are similar, light brown, long-legged and angular-shaped bugs with front legs shaped to capture insects. These predators feed on a variety of immature insects which infest plants. Praying mantises, both nymphs and adults of over a dozen species, attack and feed on other insects. Generally, praying mantises have a large abdomen, slender thorax and an angular movable head. The front legs are large and held in a "praying" position of attack. Immature mantises feed on aphids as well as on other mantis nymphs. The adults attack and feed on many species of insects.

Other beneficial insects include syrphid fly larvae, ground beetles, dragonflies, robber flies, spiders and predacious mites. Many species of wasps are beneficial in controlling garden insects. Some wasps are parasitic in that they lay eggs in the bodies of insects such as aphids and caterpillars; the newly hatched wasp larvae feed on and kill the host insect. Others simply attack and sting their prey, paralyzing and eventually killing the pest.

Biological-supply houses are among the sources for acquiring a supply of beneficial insects such as lady beetles, praying-mantis eggs, aphid lions and others. Probably more important than purchasing these insects is managing the population of beneficial insects already present in the garden area. Suggestions for maintaining or increasing beneficial insect populations include:

Use only short residual sprays or dusts, e.g., malathion, dylox, diazinon, or carbaryl (Sevin) for controlling insect pests on plants.

Apply insecticides *only* when there is a pest problem. Learn to recognize beneficial insects. If they are present in moderate numbers, avoid using an insecticide. Observe overwintering habits of beneficial insects and provide a favorable environment for them. For example, lady beetles usually overwinter as adults under leaves and other debris; praying mantises overwinter as eggs in a case on tree limbs.

Beneficial insects are only part of pest management. Other important parts are cultural practices, sanitation, fertilization, resistant varieties, insecticides.

Diseases

Fossil records prove that plants were diseased 250 million years before man appeared on earth. The Bible and other early writings mention blast, mildews, rusts and blights. These and other diseases have caused famines and great economic hardships.

Plant diseases can be divided into two large groups: (A) those that are infectious, and (B) disorders caused by unfavorable growing conditions. Infectious diseases are caused by several types of microorganisms (i.e., fungi, bacteria and mycoplasmas); viruses; nematodes; and a few flowering seed plants—dodder, mistletoes, broomrapes and striga.

Physiogenic Noninfectious Diseases

These are caused by an excess, deficiency or imbalance of water, light, temperature, air currents and humidity, or essential soil nutrients (e.g., nitrogen, phosphorus, potassium, manganese, magnesium, iron, zinc, calcium, boron, sulfur); extremes in soil acidity or alkalinity; injury from pesticides and fertilizers, air pollutants, water-soluble salts, hail, lightning, tools and equipment; changes in the soil grade or water table; girdling roots; and unfavorable storage.

Controlling Insects and Diseases

Successful pest control is based on accurate diagnosis. The charts below will help you decide the cause. Control should start with buying the *best* seed or planting stock, continue in the seedbed, throughout the growing season, and after harvest until the product is used or disposed of. Dusting and spraying are only a *small* part of an overall, integrated pest-control program.

1. Select and grow only varieties and types of plants adapted to *your* locality and recommended by your State Agricultural Experiment Station and Cooperative Extension Service, or reputable seedsmen and nurserymen.
2. Buy planting materials certified to be insect- and disease-free.

3. Before planting, treat the seed of flowers and vegetables with a seed protectant containing Captan or thiram plus diazinon, to guard against seed decay, seedling blights (damping-off) and insects that feed on the seed and young seedlings.
4. Plant at the correct depth in a moist, fertile, well-prepared and well-drained seedbed.
5. Where feasible, follow a recommended rotation. Exclude growing the same or closely related plants in the same area for several successive years. Many soil-borne pests survive from one season to the next in plant refuse or soil.
6. Control weeds, especially perennials and biennials. Weeds harbor insects, mites, viruses, mycoplasmas and other disease-producing agents.
7. Avoid excessively close and deep cultivations that prune roots. Cultivator wounds make entrances for fungi and bacteria.
8. Control rodents that girdle trees, shrubs and brambles and eat bulbs and corms. Check with your local County Agricultural Agent regarding the latest controls for rodents.
9. Compost or turn under plant refuse at season's end. Disease- or insect-infested plant parts should be carefully collected in a paper sack *as they appear* and put in the garbage can.
10. Destroy worthless alternate hosts of important rust diseases.
11. Follow other cultural practices recommended for your area and plants grown, including fertilization, watering, pruning, spacing and cultivation.
12. If the above practices do *not* provide suitable pest control, timely application(s) of a recommended pesticide may be needed. Here it is important to follow label directions and apply the *right* chemical in the *right* amount at the *right* time in the *right* way. Follow a regularly scheduled program of treating plants to protect against disease during wet periods, when most infections occur. Insecticides and miticides should be applied on a planned schedule *before* large numbers appear and damage occurs. Repeat applications after extended rains. Sprays are usually effective for seven to ten days; dusts last three to seven days.

Spray or Dust

Most modern pesticides may be applied as sprays or dusts. Insecticides and miticides are sold as liquid concentrates or wettable powders for spraying plants, in aerosol cans for space treatments, and as granules for special uses. Disease-control chemicals are generally wettable powders or dusts; a few are liquids.

Sprays are preferred by most gardeners because of the ease of covering *all* surfaces of the "target" plant with little waste and drift. In spraying, use a fine mist and wet all aboveground parts to the runoff point. Keep the spray stream moving and the spray mix in suspension. A quart of spray is enough to cover a 50-foot row of vegetables and flowers when plants are young; 20 to 25 feet when mature.

Dusts are quickly and easily applied, but are wasteful of material. To be effective, apply dusts when air is calm and plant surfaces are damp. One ounce of dust is sufficient for 50 feet of row early in the season; 2 to 3 ounces when plants are full grown.

Precautions

1. Always read and understand the entire package label before purchase. Follow *all* precautions regarding safe handling, frequency and rates of application, time interval between treatment and harvest, and plants approved.
2. Store pesticides in a *locked* cabinet outside the home, closed to children.
3. Keep only original containers; destroy unlabeled chemicals. Wash out empty containers thoroughly and pour on a gravel drive or in a hole in waste soil.
4. Never breathe dusts, mists or vapors of pesticides. Avoid spilling on shoes or clothing. If an accident occurs, immediately remove contaminated clothing and wash contacted body areas.
5. Never smoke, drink or eat while mixing or applying pesticides. Afterward, wash hands and face thoroughly before eating or smoking.
6. Use a set of household measuring spoons and cups exclusively for mixing pesticides.
7. Use a *separate* sprayer for applying weed-killers.
8. Minimize loss of pollinating and other beneficial insects by applying pesticides in late afternoon, early evening or early morning, when such insects are *not* present or when flowers are closed.
9. Use wettable powder formulations or prepared dusts when combining insecticides and plant-disease chemicals. Do *not* mix liquid concentrates with wettable powders. Keep dusts, wettable powders and granules dry and liquids from freezing.
10. Do *not* apply any spray or dust when the temperature is above 85° or below 45°.

Soil Fumigants

These chemicals are released in soil and disperse as gases to kill pests such as nematodes, soil insects, weed seeds and fungi. Certain "fast-moving" ones must be confined under a gasproof plastic cover. The manufacturer's directions must be carefully followed. Treatment is made at least three to four weeks before planting, when soil moisture is adequate for planting and the soil temperature 4 to 6 inches deep is 55° to 85°. In the South, many gardens are treated each year with DD, ethylene dibromide (EDB) or DBCP (Nemagon or Fumazone) to control nematodes. DBCP is unique in that it is safe to apply around many actively growing plants to control nematodes. Other useful soil fumigants include formaldehyde (controls soil fungi, insects, many weed seeds); Vapam or V.P.M. (controls nematodes, soil fungi, soil insects, weed seeds); and DMTT (Mylone, Soil Fumigant M, Barber Preplant 50-D, Miller Mico-Fume 25-D) (controls nematodes, soil fungi, soil insects, weed seeds).

Sprayers

Most sprayers have a number of accessories and fittings available. These include adjustable nozzles, extension rods or tubes, extra hose, spray booms, pressure tanks and special rubber-tired carts. Rust-free models —stainless steel, brass, copper or fiber glass—last longer than lower-cost models. For covering fruit and shade trees you will need high pressures. Power sprayers are excellent for these jobs.

Have a *separate* sprayer, properly labeled, just for chemically controlling weeds.

Clogging of spray nozzles can often be prevented by stirring wettable powders to a thin, smooth batter of water and powder, then washing through a fine screen or nylon stocking into the spray tank.

Pressurized spray cans are handy for treating indoor plants. *Warning:* To avoid injury, hold the can 12 to 18 inches away and operate in short bursts.

Household sprayers are low-priced, versatile, easy to operate, but limited to small jobs. Buy a type with a fully adjustable nozzle which shoots a continuous spray, has spray chamber and nozzle made of non-corrosive material, and can be easily drained.

Compressed-air sprayers are popular, inexpensive and easy to operate. Useful for many jobs around the home, yard and garden. Air is compressed into tank above the spray by a hand-operated air pump. Choose model with open or funnel-type mouth, pressure-release top, chemical-resistant hose, curved extension rod and adjustable nozzle. Can be carried by shoulder strap or by pump handle. Some models have (or will fit) a cart with rubber wheels. Operating pressure is maintained by occasional pumping. Shake frequently.

Knapsack sprayers are very useful for large gardens and estates, but are heavy for a lady to carry. This type straps onto the back, with a side handle for pumping. Adjustable nozzle delivers fine, continuous spray that carries farther than compressed-air type.

Slide pump or slide sprayers are relatively inexpensive, smooth, durable, telescoping pumps that spray continuously. High-pressure spray is delivered from ground level to tops of 25-foot trees. Some models come with half-gallon jar (plastic or glass) attached; others with weighted hose for use in a pail. Buy type with rust-resistant metal, an extension and adjustable nozzle.

Wheelbarrow, cart and barrel sprayers provide many advantages of power sprayers—portability, continuous high pressure and big capacity. Can use to spray medium-sized trees with convenient lever-type piston pump. Spraying is easier with two persons.

Hose-end sprayers, as the name indicates, are screwed to the end of a garden hose and operated by water pressure. The spray gun meters out liquid or solid spray material from the jar by suction and mixes it with water from the hose. A quart jar of concentrated spray makes several gallons of diluted spray. Since dosage control is difficult, material is often *not* applied at an even rate. Hose pressure may not be sufficient to break spray into a fine mist. Adding detergent to spray will help. *Inconveniences:* Use is limited to area reached with the hose.

Small power sprayers include wheelbarrow or estate types, which vary greatly in design and special features. A gasoline engine or electric motor with powerful hydraulic pump generally delivers 1 to 5 gallons of spray per minute at constant pressure. Wheel- or skid-mounted. Get large-wheeled, easily maneuverable model with an extra 25 to 50 feet of chemical-resistant hose, agitator, trigger-type spray gun and adjustable, fog-to-steam nozzle. Excellent for small orchards, large gardens, parks and estates.

Dusters

Dusters are of simpler construction than comparable sprayers, with fewer parts. For maximum protection and safety, dust only when air is calm and plants are damp. Select duster large enough so refilling does not become a nuisance. Order an extension tube and use with the dust flowing *up*.

Plunger dusters are lightweight, inexpensive, easy to operate and treat small areas with little waste. Choose one with dust chamber made of metal or glass. Larger models with extension tube and adjustable nozzle or deflector cap are much hardier. *Avoid* "salt shaker," flick, plastic squeeze and telescoping cardboard-carton types.

Small bellows, crank or rotary dusters are easy to use and give better coverage than plunger type. Ideal for continuous dusting of small or large gardens.

Capacity dusters are suitable for large gardens and estates and throw a fine cloud of dust. They cover large areas rapidly without refilling, are lightweight and simple to use. General types: *bellows* or *knapsack* (strapped on back) and *rotary-fan* or *crank* (carried in front by shoulder straps). Both operated with hand crank. Delivery tubes and nozzles are adjustable for height and direction. Buy type with long extension tube, flaring "fish-tail" nozzles and agitating device.

Small power dusters are practical for large gardens, small orchards or estates. Small gasoline-engine models (weighing 40 to 67 pounds) are carried on the back; larger ones may be powered by tractor. If desired, duster may be mounted on tractor, trailer or truck. The feed regulator may be adjusted to apply up to 50 or 100 pounds of dust per acre. Covers large areas rapidly without refilling. Wasteful of material, as dust often blows onto other plants. Buy type with an agitator.

MULTIPURPOSE SPRAYS AND DUSTS

Flowers, Trees and Shrubs
1. methoxychlor, Sevin or rotenone
2. malathion, diazinon or Kelthane
3. Captan, zineb, maneb, thiram, folpet or chlorothalonil
4. Karathane or sulfur

Vegetables
1. methoxychlor or Sevin
2. rotenone or malathion
3. zineb or maneb

Fruits
1. methoxychlor or Sevin
2. malathion
3. Captan or thiram

Granular Applicators

Applicators are available for applying granular or pelleted insecticides, fungicides and nematicides for controlling lawn and soil pests.

Hand-crank granular applicators are usually small box- or tanklike units supported by straps and carried in front. A rotary fan is turned by a hand crank as the operator walks across the lawn or soil area.

Cart-type granular applicators are usually mounted on two wheels, with a tank or box holding the pesticide. The granules are distributed by gravity flow or by a rotary fan. Most granular packages have instructions on the label for proper settings for various makes of applicators. *Do not use granular insecticide-fertilizer combinations for insect control.*

Keeping House Plants Healthy

When bringing in new potted plants from a nursery, florist shop or friend, isolate them for two weeks and observe for pest activity. If insects or mites are present, treat before putting with your other plants.

The most common insect pests affecting house plants are lice, mealybugs, scales and whiteflies. All of them may be controlled by a malathion, pyrethrum or rotenone aerosol spray. Or make a spray of diazinon or pyrethrum and soap. Many small insect pests are simply controlled by washing them off the foliage. Two teaspoons of detergent per gallon of water (¼ teaspoonful per pint) will aid in removal.

Caterpillars, slugs and other insects may be hand-picked. Another method is to invert the plant and dip in a mixture of insecticide and water. Use 2 teaspoons of malathion per gallon of water for insect control and 1 teaspoon of dicofol (Kelthane) per gallon for control of mites. To keep soil from spilling, cut a circular cardboard disk to fit around the plant and over the pot rim. Or wrap soil and pot surface tightly with plastic. *Keep bare hands out of dip.*

Commercial, ready-to-use sprays are available in pressurized spray cans. These give effective insect control on house plants. Check the label on the can to determine if it can be used on your specific plants.

Foliage diseases, caused by fungi and bacteria, are not a problem on plants growing in a home, apartment or office environment. Damage from nematodes, viruses, mycoplasmas, soil fungi and bacteria, as well as noninfectious diseases, are controlled by the following practices:

1. *Use the right soil mix.* Many foliage plants—gloxinia, African violet, gardenia, tuberous begonia and azalea—do best with a high organic-matter content. Cacti and many other succulents require less organic matter and more sand in the mix. Special mixes may be desirable for certain plants such as orchids and bromeliads. For most house plants, see Basic Potting Mixture, page 21.

2. *Disinfect the soil mix* before planting, to kill weed seeds, insects, nematodes as well as destructive fungi and bacteria. This is easily done by this method: Place moist (but *not* wet) soil mix, up to 4 inches deep, in a baking pan, roaster or other container. Bury a raw, 1½-inch potato in the center. Then cover the container with heavy aluminum foil and seal down the edges. Punch a small hole in the foil and insert the bulb end of a candy or meat thermometer into the center of the soil mix. Place in a 180° to 200° oven and hold for 30 minutes *after* the soil temperature reaches 180°. The potato should be well cooked. Then remove the soil and let cool for 24 hours before using. Do *not* let the oven temperature exceed 200°.

3. *Keep the soil uniformly moist* (not *wet*). Overwatering is a common problem in growing house plants. Too much water may produce wilting, sudden leaf drop, yellowing or spotting of leaves and a soft, dark rotting of stems and roots. Lack of water causes wilting, leaf scorch, leaf and flower drop, root injury and stunting. A general rule—apply water when the topsoil feels dry. Use water of room temperature and wet the soil mass thoroughly from top to bottom. Do *not* water again until the topsoil feels dry. A drainage hole should be in the bottom of the container.

4. *Fertilize lightly,* but *only* when plants are making active growth.

Avoid overfertilizing—it can cause yellowing, scorching, stunting and dropping of leaves, slow growth, wilting and dieback. Generally a complete fertilizer is suggested at three- or four-month intervals, though some plants may be fed weekly or monthly. You may also use a fraction of the dosage in each watering. Put a level tablespoon of fertilizer, such as 5-10-5, 10-6-4 or 7-7-7, in a quart of water. Before adding fertilizer let the water stand overnight if you are in an area where the water is chlorinated. Do *not* use fertilizer high in nitrogen when plants normally bloom or flowers may not develop. A level teaspoon of a complete fertilizer to a quart of soil mix or a 6-inch pot *before* planting is usually sufficient.

5. *Avoid soluble-salt injury.* Salts build up as water evaporates, from overfertilization and using organic matter from places where salts have accumulated. Look for a whitish crust on the surface of the soil and container. Excess salts may produce leaf scorching or bronzing, stunting, root dieback or wilting and yellowing of the foliage. To avoid soluble salts from accumulating, periodically put the pots in the bathtub or outside and flush them out with soft water equivalent to five or six times the soil volume.

6. *Keep the humidity up.* The humidity in an apartment, home or office may be only 10 to 30 per cent—too low for good plant growth. Symptoms include scorching or spotting of leaves, which drop early. Flowers may suddenly wither and fall off. Increase the humidity around sensitive plants (e.g., African violets, begonias, ferns, gardenias and rubber plants). Buy a humidifier and install a humidistat or build your own "humidifier": (A) Set potted plants on bricks or inverted pots over a large pan of water, (B) place in a glass or plastic case or (C) a planter filled with sphagnum moss, sand, pebbles, vermiculite or perlite kept thoroughly wet. A range of 40 to 60 per cent relative humidity satisfies most potted plants.

Best for plants *and* people is a temperature below 72° with a humidity of about 50 per cent.

7. *Know the light and temperature requirements.* House plants vary greatly in their light and temperature needs. Some thrive best in direct sun, others require partial to moderate shade. Excess light may produce yellowish-brown or silvery spots on leaves; lack of light leads to spindly growth, pale green leaves and leaf or flower drop. A sudden change in light intensity or temperature may cause leaves and flowers to suddenly drop off.

Most plants do best if the day temperature is about 70° and it is 60° to 65° at night. Others require a night temperature of 50° to 60°.

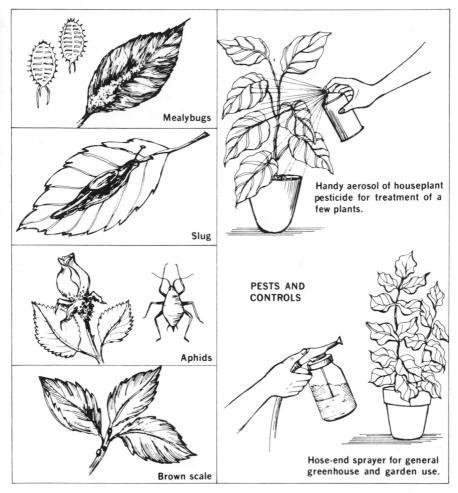

Mealybugs

Slug

Aphids

Brown scale

Handy aerosol of houseplant pesticide for treatment of a few plants.

PESTS AND CONTROLS

Hose-end sprayer for general greenhouse and garden use.

ABOVE: *Sketches show some of the more common house and greenhouse plant pests. One effective, safe way to cope with scale or mealybugs is to wipe them off leaf surfaces and stems at 10-day intervals using tissues moistened in baby oil or rubbing alcohol.* LEFT: *The screw-pine (Pandanus veitchii) is one nearly pest-free house plant.*

Air-pollutant Damage to Plants

Some 250 million tons of air pollutants are released into the air over the United States and Canada each year. The pollutants come largely from automobiles, trucks and airplanes; electric power plants; a wide range of industries; plus space-heating and refuse-burning. Injury to all types of cultivated and wild plants is increasing each year, especially in and near densely populated areas, major highway complexes, factories, power plants and refuse dumps.

The major plant-toxic pollutants are sulfur dioxide, fluorine, ozone and peroxyacetyl nitrate (PAN).

Sulfur dioxide comes chiefly from industries and other sources that burn soft coal, high-sulfur oil and coke. Sulfur dioxide is toxic to many susceptible plants at concentrations as low as 0.25 part per million (ppm) parts of air for several hours or longer.

Fluorine injury is common near smelters, refineries and factories producing fertilizers, glass, brick, aluminum and ceramics. Fluorine is even more toxic to sensitive plants than sulfur dioxide, since this element is accumulated by plant leaves.

Ozone and PAN injury is evident in and near major cities. Exhaust gases from internal-combustion engines contain large amounts of unsaturated hydrocarbons. Minor sources of similar hydrocarbons include refuse-burning and combustion of fossil fuels. Ozone, PAN and other oxidizing chemicals form when sunlight combines with nitrogen oxides and hydrocarbons, resulting in "smog." This pollutant complex is damaging to susceptible garden plants, farmer's crops and forests many miles from its source. Ozone and PAN damage sensitive plants at levels of 0.01 to 0.05 ppm for several hours.

Air pollutants cause leaf-mottling, scorching of margins and tips, early leaf and blossom drop, die-back of twigs, suppression of growth, delayed maturity, abortion of flowers, reduced vigor and lowered yield or quality. Injury from air pollution is easily confused with disease and insect or mite damage, nutritional deficiencies or toxicities, misuse of pesticides or other chemicals and the adverse effects of temperature, water and wind.

Control. Drastic steps are needed to curb air-pollutant damage. These will involve legislation at local, state and federal levels; control devices on motor vehicles, airplanes and at factories; selection and breeding of resistant plants, or growing of less-susceptible plants; carbon filtration of greenhouse air.

How To Keep Ahead of the Weeds

Weeding is the dullest of garden chores. The only satisfaction is the knowledge that, by eradicating the weeds, you enable your good plants to grow better. This, of course, is the primary reason for weeding: to keep the weeds from crowding out your favorite plants. Weeds have tougher constitutions and can grow under even the least favorable conditions.

The method you use for getting rid of weeds depends on where the weed is growing, its type, and—even though this should not be a significant point—how energetic you feel. Here are some of the tried-and-true weeding techniques:

Pulling. Often the best method. But you must pull the weed before it goes to seed, and with perennial species, you must get out all the root. In a vegetable garden or flower border, use a pronged cultivator or hoe; in a lawn, a knife or, for deep-rooted weeds such as dandelion, an asparagus knife.

Cultivating. Just hoe out the weeds and leave them on the surface so the roots dry in the sun. The job goes fast, especially if you use a sharp scuffle hoe, also called Dutch hoe, but the debris is unattractive until it dries up.

Cutting off the tops of weeds regularly will discourage their growth and ultimately kill them. Some large, rank-growing, deep-rooted weeds can be handled only in this way. A scuffle hoe or Dutch hoe is a specific tool for this purpose.

Burying. An alternative to hoeing out weeds and leaving them on the top of the soil is to plow or dig them under as deep as you can. The advantage is that this adds humus to the soil. But of course you can dig weeds under only in open areas.

Mulching. The same idea as burying—except that the weeds need not be touched. Just cover them with a heavy layer of straw, leaves, peat or mulching paper.

Poisoning. With new herbicides chemical control can be extremely effective. In many cases, there is a risk that careless application may poison desirable plants growing nearby. Manufacturers' directions should be followed carefully.

Using the above techniques, here are the best ways to tackle the weeds in the various garden areas:

In flower beds, a combination of pulling and cultivating is the only solution. If the weeds are removed with a hoe or cultivator, leave them on the surface only until they're dead; then dig them under. But it's really just as easy to rake them all up right after they're removed and add them to the compost pile.

In vegetable gardens, remove weeds by cutting, cultivating or plowing. A scuffle hoe is an excellent tool to use here, because it trims off the tops of weeds and tills the soil at the same time. Around the roots of vegetables, of course, you must resort to pulling or very careful hand cultivating.

In shrubbery borders, pulling is most effective. Cutting off the tops is also good if you are careful not to injure the roots of the shrubs. Perhaps the easiest method is simply to smother the weeds with a mulch of leaves or peat.

In lawns. The hard way but the best is to pull every weed you see when you see it. Thus you get rid of them gradually; they never have a chance to spread, and you give the grass a chance to fill up the spaces that are left.

But even the pull-as-you-see method is not easy. The alternative, therefore, is to apply one of the so-called selective herbicides. These are of two types: pre-emergence killers, which destroy weed seeds before they germinate, and post-emergence killers, which kill weeds that have sprouted and are growing vigorously. The pre-emergence materials are applied as a dust in early spring or in late summer before a lawn is to be remade. They are used primarily against crabgrass and annual bluegrass, but some kill a variety of weeds. The post-emergence weed-killers, such as silvex, are applied as sprays or dusts whenever necessary (but preferably when the weeds are young). They control a wide assortment of weeds, but are not very effective against crabgrass. Unfortunately, they may also kill or injure good plants.

Herbicides must be applied with great care in accordance with the manufacturer's directions.

In gravel paths and driveways. Poisoning is the practical solution, but it involves some danger. Good plants along the edges may be killed or injured if you use a spray; or if you apply a dry chemical to the gravel, it may reach the roots of wanted plants. A number of weed poisons are available. Rock salt is still among the best and cheapest.

In flagstone walks and terraces and the like, weeding is especially difficult because the roots grow under the stones. Pulling with the help of a knife or trowel may get some of them. But it's usually necessary to spray with 2,4-D or to apply sulfate of iron to the crown of each plant.

Poisonous weeds, such as poison ivy, and other woody weeds present a special problem because they grow mostly in the wild or intermixed with valuable trees and shrubs. But they won't survive very long if you dig them out—being sure to get all the root. Or in the wild, if you don't mind damaging surrounding vegetation, you can use strong weed-killers.

Coping with Rabbits and Deer

The rabbit—a charming but destructive wild animal much attracted to gardens. To keep rabbits from girdling small trees, wrap the trunks in 2-

foot-high cylinders of wire mesh. To protect the vegetable and cutting garden, build a 3-foot wire fence around the entire garden. The wire should be sunk slightly into the ground to discourage burrowing. Most repellents are limited in effectiveness, but Arasan 42-S applied as a spray with a spreader-sticker does a good job for several months. Dried blood (blood meal) has been tried with mixed results. Dogs and cats discourage resident rabbits.

If rabbits visit your garden, chances are they will be the first to discover fresh green shoots of spring bulbs. Unless you take positive action, leaves and buds will be nibbled to the ground—and in short order. Fortunately, this problem has a humane solution, suggested by Seth L. Kelsey, who manages an estate garden in Kennett Square, Pennsylvania.

Mr. Kelsey recommends the use of a harmless chemical taste repellent to divert rabbits to other available food sources. He writes, "We spray large drifts of young bulb shoots with thiram fungicide and repellent in the early spring and have no rabbit damage at all. Yet we have no shortage of rabbits.

"There are a number of sprays that contain an effective taste repellent—Arasan 42-S thiram fungicide and repellent. Or, you can mix 1 quart Rhoplex AC-33 or Latex 512R in 2 quarts of water, then mix thoroughly with one quart Arasan 42-S. A single application from a knapsack sprayer or by brush on a small bed of bulbs will last the entire season."

Deer have a special liking for yews, tulips and vegetable gardens. To some extent, spraying with a harmless commercial deer repellent is helpful. Many gardeners swear by dried blood as a deer deterrent. It adds nutrients to the soil and wards off some other pests that plague woodland gardens. Dried blood is available at most local garden centers. Other deterrents that work for some gardeners are a scattering of moth balls and hearty doses of black pepper. These should be placed at strategic spots approaching the areas to be protected or around the plants themselves.

A dog will keep deer away. However, dogs often learn to "run" deer, that is, chase the deer until it drops of exhaustion, and attack it. Dogs that get into the habit of running deer are likely to continue and in some states the law allows farmers to shoot such dogs. For this reason it is best to chain watchdogs in areas where deer are a problem.

What To Do About Moles

The common Eastern mole makes long tunnels through the yard; Western species throw up large mounds of dirt. The mole does so while doing you the favor of eating grubs that destroy your lawn. Probably the

To keep birds from your supply of berries, use airy scarecrows and can tops, cover tall berry bushes and low-growing strawberries with netting, or netting resting on wire cages. Protect newly sown seeds with a network of crossed string attached to wooden stakes.

best way to get rid of moles is to grubproof the lawn with diazinon and to kill the insects moles enjoy eating. Or a direct assault can be made on the pests by setting large spring traps athwart the main tunnel. They are very leery of traps, however, and you will need to camouflage the trap under a mound of soil. In addition, there are various fumigant poisons available which can be placed in the main tunnel. Cyanogas or paradichlorobenzene placed in the runs at 6-foot intervals and then each portion blocked with soil is one method used. However, these techniques should be used with extreme care, and probably as a last resort. If it is possible to bring a car close enough, a hose can be attached to the exhaust and the fumes piped into the run.

More humane methods include scattering camphor balls and castor beans in and around the runs. One organic-gardening method involves sinking bottles in sand so they can be tilted to catch the wind. The sound of the wind hooting in them is said to send moles packing.

Birds—To Encourage or Discourage

Whatever you may think of birds, they belong in gardens. We need them, especially to help keep down the insect population, and they supply sound, movement and color to the landscape.

To attract birds, it is necessary to protect them from their own natural enemies (mostly cats), to provide nesting places, and to maintain an ample supply of food and water. Trees, plus a few sensible birdhouses, will answer the nesting problem. A good "bird tangle"—a thorny thicket or hedge—is particularly welcome to most birds.

Water should be made available in stone or concrete birdbaths, preferably raised above ground and set in an open place.

In summer, birds usually prefer the seeds and fruits nature provides. Particular favorites include *Amelanchier* (shadbush, Juneberry), *Aster*, bayberry, blackberry, *Centaurea*, chokeberry, dogwood, elderberry, inkberry, mulberry, *Myosotis*, poppy, *Portulaca*, raspberry, spicebush, sunflower, *Viburnum* and *Zinnia*. Winter food can be purchased from almost any seed, hardware or grocery store. Sunflower seed and millet make a suitable mixture.

To discourage birds from feeding on valuable fruits, the best protection is a net of plastic mesh, cheesecloth or wire over the plants. This need not be an elaborate structure; just lay the cloth directly over the plants while the fruit ripens.

Another safeguard against birds—but by no means perfect—is to plant some fruits that are useless to man but that will ripen and attract birds just before and during the time your valuable fruit is ready to be picked. Among such fruits are some of those noted above, as well as dwarf apple, hawthorn, holly, honeysuckle, mountain ash and sumac.

15. Indoor Gardening

The growing of plants in the house is one form of gardening that everyone can—and almost everyone does—enjoy. The urge seems strongest for city dwellers, and while today's new establishment may not long for traditional furnishings, crystal and silver, plants are among the first acquisitions. Indeed, there is hardly a wedding or housewarming gift more welcome than a tree-size pot plant or a lush-growing hanging basket. The reason is simple. Living, thriving house plants bring to man's contemporary habitat that elusive and wonderful sense of being close to nature. And as urbanization takes more and more of us away from the land, our need for the beauty of plants increases.

The Indoor Climate

Your success with indoor gardening depends on "weather" conditions— no less than if you were gardening outdoors. Sunlight, temperature, soil, moisture and plants work together. Even beneath the roof of your house or in your apartment each room has its own climate. You can grow the plants suited to that climate, or you can change the climate to fit the plants' needs.

Get acquainted with your indoor weather. Study the amount of light that comes through your doors and windows. How much moisture is there in the air? How warm do you keep the various rooms in your house? The more you know about your indoor climate, the better you will be able to choose plants that will thrive with a minimum of care, in the places you'd like most to beautify.

Opposite: *Grape-ivy* (Cissus rhombifolia) *thrives in bright light, needs little sun. Shower leaves frequently, but avoid overwatering.*

Light comes first. Photosynthesis, the process by which plants grow, is triggered by light. Plants vary in the amount they need, but most perform satisfactorily in a wide range of intensities. For indoor gardening, here are four suggested basic light categories:

Shady areas receive no sunlight, but have light strong enough to cast a shadow.

Semishady places have bright, open light but little or no direct sunlight.

Semisunny locations receive two to five hours of sun each day in winter. Windows facing east or west belong here.

Sunny areas receive at least five hours of direct sunlight in winter. Usually a window facing southeast, south or southwest admits this amount of light.

Know how much light you have. Many factors affect the amount of light that comes in your windows. Where you live is important. For example, in the Rocky Mountains, winter sunlight is much more intense than in New England. Smoke from local industries may make sunny days hazy. Trees and shrubs cut down on light—can make a south, east or west window suitable for shade-loving plants. A white house or apartment building next door, or a cement driveway, will give reflected light. Clean windows mean more light. And don't forget—screens reduce light up to 30 per cent.

When the right plant is selected for a place indoors, it can be the delight of both decorator and gardener. The following lists represent important selections of plants that can be grown indoors in various light situations. There are plants for full sun and full shade. Knowing a plant's natural habitat is a valuable clue to where you place it in your home. For instance, if you were to trace the ancestry of the plants suggested for semishade and shade, you would find that most of them came from the tropics, where they carpeted the floors of rain forests or grew as small, shrubby plants under canopies of vines and shade trees. Heights vary from thumb-size miniatures to towering palms. Leaf textures may be bold, lush and tropical; delicate, airy or fernlike; or stiff and starkly dramatic. If yours is the common plight of no sun, in these two groupings you will discover an abundance of plain green plants, a wealth of those with richly hued foliage and a few that yield flowers.

Plants for Shaded Areas. Many foliage plants will grow in an area that receives no sunlight. But there should be enough light to cast a shadow when you pass your hand across the area in which the plant will be placed. It is a good idea to rotate plants kept in poor light—give them a week or two of bright light, even two hours of morning sun; then let them have a sojourn in the dimly lighted place.

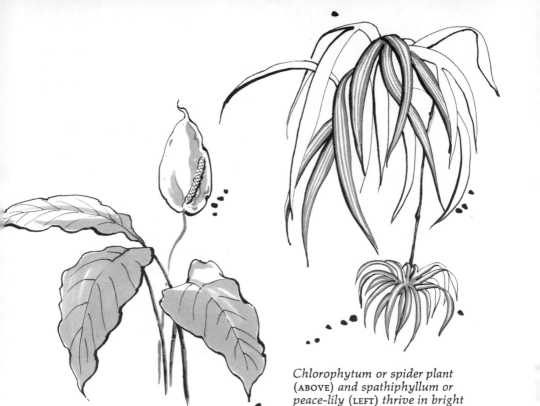

Chlorophytum or spider plant (ABOVE) *and spathiphyllum or peace-lily* (LEFT) *thrive in bright light, need no sun.*

PLANTS FOR SHADED AREAS

BOTANICAL NAME	COMMON NAME
Aglaonema	Chinese evergreen
Asparagus	Asparagus-fern
Aspidistra	Cast-iron plant
Brassaia	Schefflera
Chamaedorea	Palm
Chlorophytum	Spider plant
Dieffenbachia	Dumb cane
Ficus	Fig or rubber plant
Hedera helix	English ivy
Monstera	Swiss cheese plant
Nephrolepis	Boston fern
Ophiopogon	Mondo-grass or dwarf lilyturf
Philodendron	(Same)
Podocarpus	(Same)
Polystichum	Fern
Sansevieria	Snake plant
Scindapsus	Pothos, devil's-ivy
Spathiphyllum	Peace-lily
Syngonium	Nephthytis

Plants for a Semishady Location. Plants in this grouping thrive in bright, open light, but need little or no direct sunlight. They will succeed in a warm, slightly moist atmosphere. Most are for foliage.

BOTANICAL NAME	COMMON NAME
Acorus	Chinese sweet flag
Aglaonema	Chinese evergreen
Araucaria	Norfolk Island pine
Ardisia	Coral berry
Asparagus	Asparagus-fern
Aspidistra	Cast-iron plant
Brassaia	Schefflera
Chlorophytum	Spider or airplane plant
Chrysalidocarpus	Butterfly and other palms
Cissus	Grape-ivy
Coccoloba	Sea-grape
Cryptanthus	Bromeliad
Cyrtomium	Holly fern
Davallia	Fern
Dieffenbachia	Dumb cane
Dracaena	(Same)
Dyckia	Bromeliad
Fatshedera	Aralia
Fittonia	(Same)
Hedera helix	English ivy
Ipomoea batatas	Sweet potato
Kaempferia	(Same)
Leea	(Same)
Maranta	Prayer plant
Monstera	Swiss cheese plant
Myrtus communis	Classic myrtle
Neoregelia	Bromeliad
Oreopanax	(Same)
Osmanthus fragrans	Sweet-olive
Pellionia	(Same)
Pilea	Aluminum plant; artillery-fern
Polypodium	Polypody fern
Pteris	Table fern or brake fern
Sansevieria	Snake plant
Scindapsus	Pothos, devil's-ivy
Spathiphyllum	Peace-lily
Syngonium	Nephthytis

Cyrtomium or holly fern (ABOVE) and chrysalidocarpus or butterfly palm (LEFT) need bright, open light. Some direct sun is beneficial, especially in winter.

Plants for a Semisunny Location. Plants suggested in this category need two to five hours of sunlight in winter. In warm weather, they will do well in bright light with little or no direct sun. Provide a warm (60 to 80 degrees), moist (humidity 20 per cent or more) atmosphere. These plants can be grown in an area that receives full sun if they are protected by a curtain or if a sun-loving plant rises up to give them some shade. In summer, they do well in bright light with little or no direct sun.

BOTANICAL NAME	COMMON NAME
Achimenes	Magic flower
Aechmea	Living vase plant
Aeschynanthus	Lipstick vine
Allophyton	Mexican foxglove
Begonia	(Same)
Beloperone	Shrimp plant
Billbergia	Pitcher plant
Brunfelsia	Yesterday-today-tomorrow
Calliandra	Powderpuff
Ceropegia	Rosary vine
Chlorophytum	Spider or airplane plant
Chrysalidocarpus	Butterfly and other palms
Cleistocactus	Silver torch
Clivia	Kafir-lily
Codiaeum	Croton

Four plants for a semisunny location, LEFT *to* RIGHT: *ficus, aechmea, clivia and the howea or kentia palm.*

BOTANICAL NAME	COMMON NAME
Coleus	(Same)
Cyanotis	Pussy ears
Cymbalaria	Kenilworth-ivy
Faucaria	Tiger jaws
Ficus	Fig or rubber plant
Haemanthus	Blood-lily
Haworthia	Aristocrat plant
Impatiens	Patience plant
Kalanchoe	(Same)
Lippia	Lemon verbena
Malpighia	Miniature holly
Mimosa pudica	Sensitive plant
Musa	Banana
Nerine	Guernsey-lily
Ophiopogon	Dwarf lilyturf
Oxalis	Wood sorrel
Peperomia	Watermelon-begonia
Portulacaria	Elephant bush
Rivinia	Rouge plant
Saintpaulia	African violet
Sansevieria	Snake plant
Saxifraga sarmentosa	Strawberry-begonia
Schlumbergera	Easter or crab cactus
Selenicereus	Night-blooming cereus
Sinningia	Gloxinia
Tradescantia	Wandering Jew
Zygocactus	Christmas cactus

Plants for a Sunny Place. Plants listed in this category need at least five hours of direct sunlight in winter. They will thrive in average house temperatures and a reasonably moist atmosphere (humidity of 20 to 30 per cent).

BOTANICAL NAME	COMMON NAME
Abutilon	Flowering-maple
Acalypha	Chenille plant
Agave	Century plant
Begonia semperflorens	Wax begonia
Bougainvillea	(Same)
Campanula	Star of Bethlehem
Capsicum	Bird pepper
Cereus	(Same)
Ceropegia	Rosary vine
Cestrum	Perfumed night jasmine
Citrus	Orange, lemon, lime
Gloriosa	Glory-lily
Hibiscus	Rose of China
Hippeastrum	Amaryllis
Hoya	Wax plant
Ixora	Jungle flame
Lantana	(Same)
Neomarica	House iris
Oleander	(Same)
Oxalis	Wood sorrel
Pandanus	Screw-pine
Pelargonium	Geranium
Pentas	Star clusters
Portulacaria	Elephant bush
Punica	Dwarf pomegranate
Rechsteineria	Helmet plant
Rosa	Miniature rose
Sinningia	Gloxinia

Day length affects plants. When days are longest, plants will do noticeably better in your house; east- and west-facing windows will qualify as being sunny, while south-facing locations will need to be curtained so they do not admit too much sun. Day length also determines when certain plants bloom. Poinsettias and Christmas cacti set flower buds in autumn when days begin to shorten. Calceolarias and tuberous begonias set buds when days are increasing in length.

If you have no area indoors bright enough to grow plants or sunny enough to grow flowering kinds, an artificially lighted garden is the answer. Fluorescent lights make it possible to have thriving plants where you will enjoy them most. Even your basement or attic can be filled with beautiful flowers. The basic setup is a standard industrial, preheat fixture with two 48-inch, 40-watt tubes (one daylight and one natural white; or one daylight with one plant-growth lamp such as Gro-Lux) and reflector suspended about 18 inches above the surface of a bench or table on which potted plants are placed. When these lamps burn from fourteen to sixteen hours out of every twenty-four, most plants respond by growing compactly and luxuriantly and by blooming well over a long season.

Fluorescent lights can turn wasted space into a place to grow plants. Here an outmoded dumbwaiter at the rear of a kitchen has been converted into a greenhouse for herbs, foliage and flowering house plants. These standard industrial fixtures are 24 inches long and each holds two 20-watt fluorescent lamps. They are plugged into a timer for automatic "sun-up" at 8 a.m., "sun-down" at 11 p.m., or 15 hours of good-growing light daily.

The Air Surrounding Your Plants

Fresh, moist air helps plants thrive indoors. Excessive dryness in a room not only is harmful to plants, but can damage furniture and make human occupants uncomfortable. Use a humidity indicator (an accurate hygrometer can be purchased for under $10) to determine how much moisture is present. Humidity ranging from 30 to 60 per cent is agreeable to most plants. Using a cool-vapor humidifier is an excellent way to increase humidity in a room or small apartment. The smallest of these dispense about two gallons of water in twelve hours. Larger units, which cut off and on automatically, add up to eight gallons of water to the atmosphere of the house or apartment in a 24-hour period. You may also have a humidifier installed as a part of your home's heating system.

The majority of foliage plants, especially those with glossy or thick leaves, manage to live in surroundings where humidity is low, but dry air is best corrected to some extent. One way is to conceal containers of water among the plants. Standing plants in saucers holding an inch of pebbles and water is another (some of the water evaporates to form humidity around the plant; some is absorbed into the soil in the pot). Syringing the plants' tops with a fine mist of water several times weekly is another means of adding humidity.

Most common house plants will grow in a temperature range of 65 to 75 degrees. A few degrees above or below these figures shouldn't be harmful. Plants from the tropics suffer when the temperature drops below 60 degrees. On the other hand, plants such as cinerarias and camellias do best with a maximum temperature of 65 degrees. For these cool-loving plants, you may be able to keep a sunny bedroom cool. Or perhaps you have a sun porch that is cool—but not freezing in winter.

Where winters are severely cold, tender plants close to windows may freeze. At night, put a piece of cardboard between plants and windows, or move plants to a warmer, interior part of the room.

Fumes from manufactured gas cause plants such as African violets to drop their flower buds and geranium leaves to turn yellow and fall off. Natural gas is not harmful to plants, but many don't grow well in air that is frequently heavy with fumes from industrial and gasoline engines.

Water for Indoor Gardening

If you can drink the water where you live, then it is safe for pot plants. You may blame your city water department for retarding the growth of your house plants or even killing them, but how you use the water is far more vital to plant life than is the chemical content.

Two kinds of purifier are common in city water systems: free chlorine and chloramine. Free chlorine will evaporate from water left standing overnight. Chloramine will not evaporate, even when water is boiled. However, the amount of either chemical in drinking water is so small that it benefits rather than harms plant life. If the chlorine content were sufficient to injure plants, the water would be undrinkable.

Softened water may be harmful to plants. Water softeners of the zeolite type can injure them. This kind of softener replaces the calcium in water with sodium, which does not settle out, evaporate or become harmless. It will accumulate in house-plant soil to a harmful extent. If you have a water softener, install a tap in the waterline before it goes into the softener, so you will have unsoftened water for your house plants.

In parts of the country where the soil is very alkaline and the water is "hard," it is difficult to grow acid-loving plants. Generous use of acid peat moss and acid-reaction fertilizers will help offset the alkaline soil and water. Plants such as azaleas, gardenias and camellias will benefit from regular applications of an iron chelate to keep the foliage a healthy dark green. When new foliage of these plants is yellow, water them with a solution of one ounce iron sulfate in two gallons water. Repeat at biweekly intervals until growth has normal coloration.

Water temperature is important. Take the chill off water before you use it on house plants. Tropical plants are the most sensitive, but all may be harmed by having icy water applied either at the roots or on the foliage. Water should be barely warm or tepid—within ten degrees of the room temperature.

House plants' water requirements are indicated throughout this encyclopedia along with each genus entry. In general, *wet* indicates a plant that doesn't ever need to dry out. Spathiphyllum and aglaonema are excellent examples; they can virtually stand in water. *Evenly moist* means the plant will be wet immediately after you water it, but within a few hours, owing to properly drained soil, the dripping wetness will have gone, leaving a pleasantly moist, spongy growing medium not unlike a properly moist chocolate cake. *On the dry side* is a phrase commonly used for geraniums and succulents like kalanchoe and peperomia. You water them well, being sure that moisture drains quickly and that the pots do not stand for hours in saucers of water. You don't water again until the surface soil is dry. If this seems tricky to you, experiment with a geranium. You will quickly learn how much dryness is too much; if the leaves begin to wilt, you have waited too long, and the price you pay will be some leaves that turn yellow and drop off; others will have brown edges.

In spite of the necessity for faithful trips with the watering can, house plants are a lot easier to leave for a day, a weekend or even a week than cats or dogs. One method of staving off drought in plants left alone for a few days is thrusting into each pot a small plastic funnel with a narrow neck. The funnel's top is filled with water, which seeps slowly through the neck to moisten the earth. Another approach is to seal plants in plastic bags—one plant is put in each bag and the bag sealed. Plants should not be watered before they are bagged, for there would be danger of their remaining too wet.

Soil Mixes for Indoor Gardening

A container-grown plant depends on you to provide it with food and water. Start with a good potting soil to form the foundation on which you can build sound watering and fertilizing practices.

If you do not have a suitable place to prepare potting soils, time to do the work and a convenient source for the ingredients, use the commercially prepared mixes available at local garden centers, florists and hardware stores.

If you desire to mix your own medium for pot gardening, take advantage of the soil substitutes. Horticultural perlite is light as a feather and makes an excellent substitute for sand. Vermiculite, in place of leafmold, will lighten and condition heavy, sticky soil.

Potting—and Repotting

Just setting a plant into a pot, packing soil around the roots and hoping for the best will not necessarily produce the kind of plant you want. There is no great trick to potting, but it should be done carefully.

Clay pots with a drainage hole are by far the best, but plastic pots may be used. The hole should be covered with scraps of broken pot, called crock or shards. If you use a glazed clay pot without a drainage hole, provide at least a 1-inch layer of gravel or crock in the bottom.

Don't use a pot that is too large. Most plants—especially flowering

Top row: *Potting. Cover drainage hole, if pot has one, with scraps of crock or shards; when using containers without drainage hole, line with at least 1 inch of drainage material. Center sketches show planting procedure. Hold plant slightly above soil in the bottom of the pot, so roots will trail down and out; fill to within 1 to ½ inch of rim with loose soil; then firm. Sketches at right show correct proportions of pot to plant: Pot for a standing plant should be ¼ to ⅓ its height; for a spreading plant, let diameter of plant be about three times that of the container in which you place it.* Center row: *Repotting. Plant at left does not require repotting. When it is lifted from its container, soil crumbles away. Root-bound plant, center, does need repotting. Right sketch shows new pot with ⅓ new soil in bottom and positioning of plant. Fill around it with fresh soil.* Bottom row: *Root pruning. Trimming a pot-bound plant so it may be returned to its old container with fresh soil. Cut back plant in proportion to amount of root pruned.*

OTTING

RE-POTTING

ROOT PRUNING

plants—prefer to be a bit rootbound. When they get too large for the pot, they can easily be shifted to the next larger size pot.

When potting a small plant or seedling for the first time, fill the pot about half full of soil. Hold the plant slightly above the soil so that the roots trail down and out. Then sift in loose soil, press firm with the thumbs, and water. (Woody plants prefer a more compact soil than herbaceous plants.) When the job is completed, the surface of the soil should be ½ to 1 inch below the pot rim to allow space for watering.

Repotting is necessary when the roots form a tangled web on the outside of the rootball. This can be detected by turning the plant upside down, supporting the soil in one hand and knocking the pot rim on the end of a table. Lift off the pot and examine the roots. If only a few roots are visible, keep the plant in the same pot. Some plants need repotting once or twice a year; some need it only every two or three years. In general, flowering plants should be repotted less often than foliage plants.

To repot a plant, water it first. Knock the bottom or side of the pot to loosen the rootball. Fill the new pot about one-third with soil. (In most cases, the pot should be only one size larger than the old one; but for very fast-growing plants you can use two sizes larger.) Set the plant squarely in the center of the new pot and fill around it with soil. When leveled, soil should be about ½ to 1 inch below the rim.

After potting, water lightly and maintain a moderate temperature. Light shading may be advisable for a few days.

Some plants that have grown overly large, or that you don't want to move into a larger pot, can be safely root-pruned before repotting in the old pot. Trim off the excess roots on the outside of the ball with a sharp knife. If necessary, you can pare away some of the soil and roots. Replace with fresh potting soil.

Feeding House Plants

If plants start the indoor period in the best possible soil mixture, they will do well. Fertilizing is needed only in moderation, for this, like repotting, is not a cure-all for anything that may ail a plant. Fertilizing will not bring about healthy growth if light, temperature or humidity is wrong. Nor is fertilizer a substitute for sun during the cloudy days that may prevail from November to late February.

Fertilizer has its own place in stimulating bloom and in maintaining growth. For example, starting in November, feedings every two weeks are necessary to force the hold-over poinsettia into bloom. Fertilizing once a month provides a booster in late winter for laggards in bloom and growth. Easy to apply and nonmessy is liquid fertilizer diluted with water and applied to moist, but not dry, soil.

Healthy House Plants

An attractive plant is healthy and clean. Cleanliness means more than being pest-free. It means clean leaves too. I still favor the old method of cleansing foliage with water every two weeks during the house-plant season, rather than oiling or otherwise coating the leaves. Large-leaved philodendrons and other plants with bold foliage may be wiped clean with a damp cloth; gently dust woolly or plushy-leaved plants, such as African violets and geraniums. Move all other plants to a sink and spray their foliage with water at about room temperature.

Between the daily inspection for watering and the biweekly bath, insects should have little or no chance to gain headway. Insects, generally speaking, should be few and far between. Here, however, are some that may appear and some suggestions for extinguishing them:

Red spider. This mite is so tiny that only its results, not the creature, are visible. This is the mite that gives ivy leaves a yellow or gray tint and a fuzzy look beneath. Malathion is rated an effective control (isolate plants to spray them). Red spider is easier to prevent than to cure, and the best preventive is providing fresh, moist air and regularly showering the upper and under sides of the leaves with cool water.

Scale. This insect covers itself with a hard shell and is easy to see, usually along stems. Remove with a cotton-tipped toothpick dipped in alcohol. Regular showers are a preventive to scale insects. As with red spider, the house-plant insecticide aerosol bomb is effective.

Mealy bug. These look like a tuft of cotton along the stems or in axils of leaves. Like scale, they can be removed individually, though frequent spraying gives better control. Discard any plant severely infested.

White fly. A persistent pest that quickly spreads. Dispose of the plant that introduces it. These white flies are so active that they are hard to spray; but try malathion or wield the bomb.

Worms (larvae). Tiny white larvae sometimes appear on the surface of the soil during the cloudy months of winter. They'll disappear after an application of lime water. Put a heaping teaspoon of slaked lime in a pint of water, stir and then let it settle. The next day, pour off the clear solution and soak the soil with it. Repeat in a week, if necessary. This treatment is effective with all plants except those that must have acid soil. It also is good against grubs.

Any appearance of disease or mildew can usually be traced to poor ventilation, crowding of plants or lack of sun or light. Pick off yellowing or spotted leaves, for soft spots start rot. Above all, discard any plants that are severely affected by any insect or blight. (See also Chapter 14.)

Terrarium

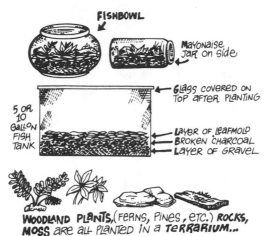

FISHBOWL

MAYONAISE JAR on Side

GLASS COVERED ON TOP AFTER PLANTING

5 OR 10 GALLON FISH TANK

LAYER OF LEAFMOLD
BROKEN CHARCOAL
LAYER OF GRAVEL

WOODLAND PLANTS, (FERNS, PINES, ETC.) ROCKS, MOSS are all PLANTED IN a TERRARIUM...

Woodland terrarium begins with gravel for drainage, covered with charcoal and leafmold. Charcoal keeps soil from turning sour. Planting materials come from woodland walks, and almost any of the low-growing wild subjects are suitable, from tiny blueberry bushes to rattlesnake plantain. Mosses and rocks are used to give a finished appearance.

CARROT

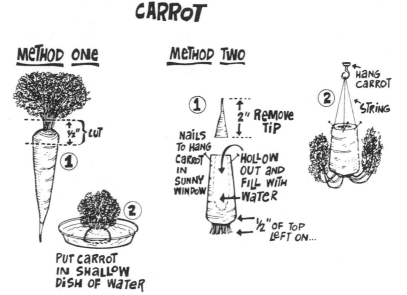

METHOD ONE

½" CUT

①

② PUT CARROT IN SHALLOW DISH OF WATER

METHOD TWO

① ↕ 2" REMOVE TIP

NAILS TO HANG CARROT IN SUNNY WINDOW

HOLLOW OUT and FILL WITH WATER

½" OF TOP LEFT ON...

② HANG CARROT
STRING

Carrots are eager to grow and, no matter what is done to them, seem willing to go on producing greenery. A favorite subject for children's kitchen gardens, they can be handled in several ways. The first method shown in this sketch involves only the top. Select a fresh firm carrot, cut away ½ inch of the top, remove the "fern" tips and set this small carrot stub in a shallow bowl with water. In a few days or so fresh ferny greens will develop. Method two makes a hanging basket. Cut away the bottom tip of the carrot and the "ferns" at the top, and hollow out the core of the carrot. Tie thread to nails stuck into cut end; hang in a sunny window; keep filled with water.

AVOCADO

①
TOOTHPICKS PUT THROUGH SEED--
FLAT SIDE OF SEED AT BOTTOM...
WATER LEVEL

SEED IS SUSPENDED IN GLASS OF WATER WITH END OF SEED JUST TOUCHING THE WATER...

②

WHEN TAP ROOT IS 3 TO 4 INCHES LONG--TRANSPLANT TO POT OF SOIL

③
SOIL
GRAVEL

Avocado seeds will root in either of the following ways: One method is to plant the seed, minus its brown paperlike covering, 3 to 4 inches deep in a regular clay pot and to water it until it sprouts. This can take several months, and children often prefer the method shown here: insert toothpicks around the middle of the seed and suspend it over a glass of water with the bottom of the seed (the flattish end) just touching the water, and watch roots grow. Transplant water-rooted seed to soil when root is 3 to 4 inches long and feed every six weeks.

Sweet potatoes and yams will sprout into lush healthy vines with a little help from the young gardener. Select a healthy fresh-looking sweet potato that has a distinctly tapered end. Place the tapered end inside a glass or jar with a slightly narrowed top and add enough water to cover the tip. Set the glass close to a sunny window but not directly in the sunlight. When the vines have sprouted, set the potato in soil in the sun.

SWEET POTATO

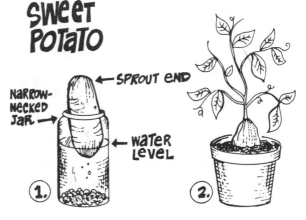

SPROUT END
NARROW-NECKED JAR
WATER LEVEL

①.

②.

IVY

TIE STAKES AT TOP
15" BAMBOO STAKES
GREEN STRING ON VINE
START 3 YOUNG IVY PLANTS AND TRAIN TO FRAME ...

①

②
FINISHED TREE COVERED WITH IVY

Ivy (Hedera) is a vigorous-growing vine that lends itself to training very easily. To make an ivy tree, start three young ivy plants in an 8-inch pot. Insert three strong bamboo stakes and tie them together at the top wigwam-fashion. As the young ivy shoots sprout, twist the woody stems around each of the stakes, one plant to each stake.

ABOVE: *A green-house that opens directly into a room of the house can be one of life's greatest pleasures, especially on a snowy morning. Note convenient work area, left, and attractive brick floor—which also helps control moisture for optimum growth. Begonias, orchids, bromeliads and climbing lilies are featured in this greenhouse.*
RIGHT: *If space or budget is limited, install a window greenhouse, heated and cooled automatically.*

16. Gardening Under Glass

As you work at your potting bench on a winter day, pausing to catch the fragrance of freesias, paper-whites and those first hyacinths, you will know that a greenhouse is one of life's greatest pleasures. January in my greenhouse brings the discovery of still more buds pushing up from amaryllis that bloomed in November, a pot of gold when crocus 'Canary Bird' blooms and the unmatched beauty of a rosebud reaching skyward. Toward the end of the month there will be azaleas, bougainvillea 'Barbara Karst' and a camellia joining the cyclamen in a display of Schiaparelli pink, but for relief from this shocking color, there will be daffodils mixing companionably with sky-blue ixias, and the species gloxinia, *Sinningia eumorpha*, covered with creamy slipper flowers.

How Much Does a Greenhouse Cost?

Cost varies, of course, from practically nothing for a makeshift lean-to over a basement window to several thousand dollars for a structure say 20 by 30 feet with an attached potting shed and garden house. Chances are you will find the greenhouse of your dreams at some point between these two extremes.

Plastic has done more than any other single factor to put a greenhouse into the realm of possibility for anyone. I have an acquaintance who enjoys a polyethylene-covered greenhouse 10 by 10 by 8 that cost initially only forty dollars. Now even those who rent or lease their homes can usually erect a small prefabricated greenhouse or a simple plastic-covered one on a portable foundation such as redwood timbers. At moving time the structure can be disassembled and transported to the new location.

How Large a Greenhouse?

While cost is an important factor, you will want to think at the same time about how large a greenhouse you really need. I progressed upward from 4 by 8, to 6 by 9, to 10 by 20 feet. I know now that it easier to keep the larger greenhouse neat, because there is more room to space out plants properly, but there is also more maintenance work.

How much time does it take to look after a home greenhouse? Naturally you have to take into consideration the size and the kinds of plant cultivated. My 10 by 20, which houses a variety of more or less common plants and a few rare kinds, does nicely on one to four hours every Saturday morning, plus an average of 15 minutes daily. This takes care of watering, transplanting, propagating and cleanup. Since my all-aluminum-and-glass structure requires no maintenance other than an occasional pane replacement and cleaning, I spend less time than if it had a wooden framework that required painting every year or two.

Most Greenhouses Need Sun

Before you start looking at catalogs and plans for home greenhouses, consider whether you have a good place on your property for such a structure. Except in the Deep South and sunny Southwest, greenhouses need to be located where they have full sun for at least half a day in the fall and winter. Filtered sun provided by tall, deciduous shade trees is fine for spring and summer.

I have known a number of home greenhouse gardeners in the South who have located greenhouses on the east, even north sides of dwellings, with bright open space all around, and they have had much success. They find that shading and cooling during warm months are much less a problem than for greenhouses that face south or west.

Home greenhouses are designed in two basic styles, even-span and lean-to. The even-span has two sides, two ends and a roof. The lean-to has one side, two ends and a roof. The even-span can be attached to a building, thus eliminating the need for one end. All lean-to greenhouses are attached to some other structure. When placed on the south of a building, a lean-to is much less costly to heat in the winter and makes a delightful addition to a living area. A lean-to can also be placed in the ell of a building, thus eliminating the need for one end, or in the U-shape formed by two wings of a house, with no ends required.

Before you buy a prefabricated greenhouse, or start a do-it-yourself project, check local building restrictions. If you live in the country, this will probably not be necessary, but in any organized urban or suburban area, you will probably need a building permit. Certain communities may have bylaws in homeowner associations that permit no buildings on

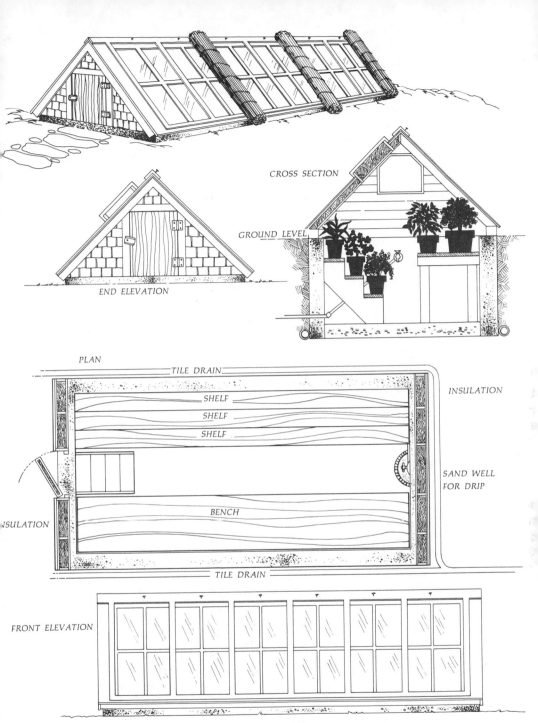

CROSS SECTION

GROUND LEVEL

END ELEVATION

PLAN

TILE DRAIN

SHELF

SHELF

SHELF

BENCH

TILE DRAIN

INSULATION

SAND WELL
FOR DRIP

INSULATION

FRONT ELEVATION

If you can dig a good sized hole, you are well on your way to having a sun-heated pit greenhouse. Using only the sun for heat, with heavy mats rolled over the windows to conserve heat at night and on cloudy days, an amazing variety of plants can be cultivated in a pit. Add a supplementary heating unit and you can grow almost anything.

a lot except the dwelling. This means that you will have to attach your greenhouse to the house as I did. A friend in Des Moines who wanted a detached greenhouse met a similar local restriction by attaching it to the house by means of a grape arbor. Now the breezeway between the greenhouse and house is refreshing with a bricked floor, a display of potted plants in summer and dappled shade cast by the grapevines.

Greenhouse Foundations

Once you decide on a greenhouse and place your order, the manufacturer will make available to you the foundation specifications. Except in mild climates where freezing seldom occurs, greenhouses require foundations that extend below the local frost line. These are usually made of poured concrete reinforced by steel rods. There are basically two types of foundation. One comes approximately to ground level, with the greenhouse having glass or plastic to the ground. The other has a foundation or wall of wood, stone, brick or concrete blocks that extends about three to four feet aboveground, meeting the glass or plastic at that point. It is this second type that is better in the far North, but glass to the ground is practical northward through USDA plant hardiness Zone 7 (winter temperatures to zero).

If you live on rented or leased land and want a greenhouse but do not want to invest in a concrete foundation, investigate the possibility of using redwood, cypress or cedar timbers, onto which the greenhouse sills will be bolted. If you do this in a severely cold climate, use polyethylene covering, not glass, as the heaving caused by alternate freezing and thawing could break the glass. However, this method works well even with glass in mild climates, provided that the site is solid and level.

Plumbing and Electricity

To be really enjoyable, every home greenhouse needs ample plumbing. I could not get along without hot and cold water, with a mixing faucet to which I attach a 25-foot length of dark green hose. This means that even on the coldest morning of the year I can give pleasantly warm water to tropicals.

Have the greenhouse wired for electricity. I use a 100-watt light bulb every four feet along the peak of my greenhouse roof. This gives plenty of illumination for enjoyment and work in the greenhouse at night. In addition, I have a plug-in at the potting bench for a desk lamp, to help me in transplanting seedlings. This is useful both at night and on cloudy, dreary winter days when there is work to be done.

Greenhouse Heating

How you will heat your greenhouse is determined largely by what is

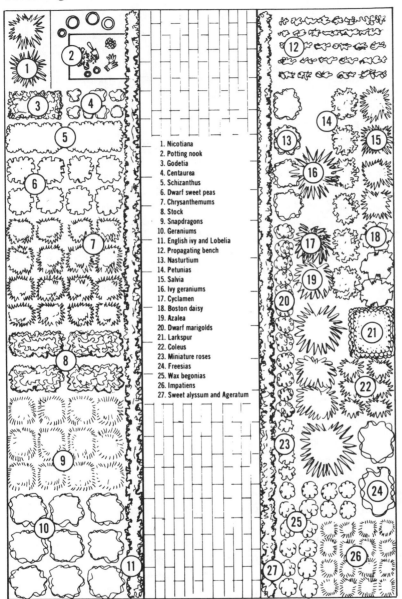

1. Nicotiana
2. Potting nook
3. Godetia
4. Centaurea
5. Schizanthus
6. Dwarf sweet peas
7. Chrysanthemums
8. Stock
9. Snapdragons
10. Geraniums
11. English ivy and Lobelia
12. Propagating bench
13. Nasturtium
14. Petunias
15. Salvia
16. Ivy geraniums
17. Cyclamen
18. Boston daisy
19. Azalea
20. Dwarf marigolds
21. Larkspur
22. Coleus
23. Miniature roses
24. Freesias
25. Wax begonias
26. Impatiens
27. Sweet alyssum and Ageratum

The plan here by Lord and Burnham, Irvington, New York 10533, suggests plant materials for a 10 x 16 greenhouse with a minimum nighttime temperature in winter of 55–60 degrees. The time is Labor Day. Depending on where you live and how you garden, you might obtain most of these plants from your own collection outdoors, or you could start seeds, obtain started plants from a local florist, or by mail from a specialist. You should have blooms all winter.

most practical locally. I use natural gas with the warm air circulated by a fan. If this stove fails, there are infrared heat lamps ready to place into the roof sockets and a small electric heater with circulating fan. If electricity goes out, I have two gas-line connections in the greenhouse, so that small heaters that do not require electric power to operate can be utilized. These precautions may seem too elaborate, but I have had to resort to both, and at times when the weather was so cold that I could have lost every plant.

As a general rule, gas or oil heat is the most economical in the North, with electricity best in the South, where very little heat is necessary except in the middle of winter. All gas or oil units need to be properly vented, otherwise plants may be damaged. Many small greenhouses, if attached to a dwelling, can be warmed by extending the existing heating system.

If yours is a severely cold climate with rough winter storms, check the greenhouse heating system daily. If heat should be lost and the temperature drop below freezing, raise it slowly, about five degrees per hour, and mist foliage frequently until the usual temperature has been reached. This procedure will save plants that might otherwise be lost. Install a battery-powered temperature alarm in a part of your residence where someone is likely to hear it at any time of day or night. If you have an alarm system already, check it out frequently.

Greenhouse Shading and Cooling

While heating may seem all-important, shading and cooling are just as vital to success. Even while the outside temperature hovers at zero on a sunny winter day, radiant heat may warm the greenhouse to the point that the ventilators open for brief periods through the midday period. From mid-spring until early fall, most home greenhouses require some kind of shading material to keep the sun from overheating the plants.

Shading may be as simple as planting grapevines around the greenhouse, or as complicated as whitewashing, using lath frames, roll-up bamboo curtains or a plastic shading cloth like Lumite Saran. The effect you desire is important here. Some people want the utilitarian and do not care how it looks. Others demand a good-looking shade material.

Heating and cooling controls for the home greenhouse can be manually operated, but the wisest investment the greenhouse gardener can possibly make is in automatic equipment. Be sure that thermostats for all units are located where the sun will not shine directly on them.

Besides shading, cooling and heating, a properly moist atmosphere is another key to successful greenhouse gardening. Automatic humidifying equipment for most prefabricated greenhouses is available at extra cost. A humidifier is a necessity if you plan to grow tropicals like orchids, philodendrons and gesneriads, but a boon for all kinds of plant, except possibly desert cacti.

In the absence of a humidifier, the best way to add moisture to the air is to wet down the walks, walls and floors every morning, except in cold, cloudy weather, and again at noontime, if possible.

Greenhouse Floors and Benches

A clean greenhouse floor is one big help in keeping a greenhouse nice to look at. I have a floor of patio blocks laid on a bed of sand tamped firm. Here and there the blocks have been removed to create pockets for special plants. Bricks and flagstones also make good greenhouse floors. Poured concrete is less desirable, because it does not have the moisture-holding qualities of the other materials.

After you have completed the greenhouse, with flooring, plumbing, wiring and heating in place, you will need benches—display areas for plants—and a place for potting. My first greenhouse was nearly all bench space with barely a turnaround left for me. My second consisted of about half bench area at waist height, and the balance in a slightly raised ground bed for tall plants, and a walkway. My present arrangement is similar, except there is space for a comfortable garden chair, where I take a break occasionally and enjoy the plants all around.

Greenhouse benches may be made of rot-resistant woods such as cedar, cypress or redwood, or you may choose corrugated or plain asbestos cement, or fiber glass. You want a material that will not rot or become unsightly after years of use. Benches need drainage holes so that excess moisture can escape. My own are made of redwood, 6 inches deep, about 3 feet wide, with an inch of space between each of the 1-by-6 boards in the bottom. Some of these are left open so that air circulation is free. In other sections I have lined the bench with heavy-duty polyethylene, cut a few drainage holes in it, then filled with a good soil mixture so that plants grow directly in the bench. It is in such an area that I have installed a thermostatically controlled heating cable to help in propagating plants from seeds and cuttings.

Shelves of beveled-edge plate glass will add prime growing space along the upper walls of your greenhouse. Trained vines and hanging baskets help complete the picture.

If possible, locate your potting bench in an adjoining room where space is not as valuable as in the greenhouse. In addition, this assures a neater greenhouse with more plants. If you have to pot inside the greenhouse proper, organize an attractive work center with containers for soil-mixture ingredients, space for labels, stakes, tying materials, hand shears and a pencil with small clipboard to make notes.

Cool or Warm?

The first decision to make about the operation of your greenhouse is the minimum nighttime temperature you will maintain in cold weather. A cool house is usually kept at 45 to 55 degrees at night, with a rise of 10 to 15 degrees in the daytime. A moderate to warm house varies from a 55- to 70-degree minimum nighttime temperature.

Fortunately, there are cool spots in most warm houses where cool-loving plants can be grown. And even in a cool house, there will be one place that is warm enough for a few tropicals. After a while you will know the general boundaries of these little climates so that they can be used to advantage. With the thermostat set in my greenhouse at a 55-degree minimum, I find that nighttime temperatures range in the winter from 50 to 65 degrees. Within the same 10-by-20 greenhouse I grow plants with such widely varied needs as cinerarias, chrysanthemums, fuchsias, calendulas, schizanthus, orchids, gesneriads, begonias, geraniums, amaryllis, beloperone, calamondin, coleus, crossandras, gloxinias and petunias. In one warm corner tomatoes thrive and bear all winter.

Seven Steps to a Flowering Greenhouse

(1) Invest in all-automatic equipment for ventilation, heating and cooling. Use a mixing faucet for hot and cold water. Place a temperature alarm somewhere in your home where you or a member of your family is most likely to hear it at any hour of the day or night.

(2) Install enough lights to provide plenty of illumination so that when you want to, you can put in an hour or two in the greenhouse before going to work in the morning, or at night. This enables you to keep up and avoids saving everything for the weekend—when it may turn out that you cannot possibly be in the greenhouse for a sufficient time to do the work necessary.

(3) Limit your plant collection to a few kinds well grown. Get over the urge to collect. Commonplace plants can be beautiful when they are grown well and thoughtfully displayed. The more you diversify, the greater will be the problems of culture, pests and disease.

(4) Grow as many carefree perennial greenhouse plants as you can. Annuals that require sowing and transplanting several times a year take a lion's share of time. On the other hand, some of the most colorful of all greenhouse plants are annuals—cinerarias, for example. Maybe you should grow ten dependable perennial plants and devote the time saved to two or three annuals that yield big dividends in floral display. The flowering greenhouse day by day depends on a selection of plants long-in-flower. Strictly seasonal bloomers—anemones, for example—will occupy a relatively small amount of total space.

(5) Use commercially prepared, pasteurized potting soil. In the long run this saves lots of time and trouble. I obtain two-bushel bags of a packaged planter mix that gives good results for practically all permanent plants in my greenhouse.

(6) If your time schedule is short and there is more to be done in the greenhouse than you can possibly accomplish, learn to decide what is most important and what can wait. If, for example, plants need feeding and pest control, you will be wise to take care of the pest control at once, tend to feeding the first chance later. And if you have time only for watering, but cannot take care of feeding or pest control for several days, you may be better off if you discard a plant infested with mealybugs; this requires almost no time, only a decision, but if you dash off and do not get back for several days, your pest problems may have multiplied until you cannot possibly throw out every infested plant. Another way to spot-check pests is to keep a house-plant aerosol on your supplies shelf. Aerosol spraying is not usually recommended for an entire greenhouse, but it can save the day when there is no time for complete spraying or fumigation.

(7) Develop a schedule of when to do what; this planning is the answer to a well-ordered greenhouse filled with thriving, flowering plants. Keep a clipboard with paper and pencil on your potting bench so that planting notes and good ideas will not be lost.

Window Greenhouses and Sun-Heated Pits

If a conventional greenhouse of any type is out of the question for you, consider a window unit. Prefabricated window greenhouses are available in a variety of standard sizes designed to be installed over house or apartment windows. When equipped with automatic ventilating and heating units, these function well with a minimum of attention.

If you own land with a sunny slope, but don't want the expense of heating a greenhouse in winter, you can construct a sun-heated pit. Essentially this is a deep hole in the ground used to store plants that need some protection in winter but do not have to be moved into a tropical climate. For example, large hydrangeas, oleanders, fuchsias and tree-form lantanas. The pit may need to be as much as 6 feet deep to keep plants below the frost line. Ideally it should be built with masonry walls and a dirt floor. An A-frame roof with glass sash toward the south and a well-insulated roof toward the north will enable you to enjoy the pit all winter. During severely cold nights and really bad days, cover the sash with straw mats, old blankets or other insulating material. Besides using a pit for storing large plants, you can bring on beautiful crops of such cool-weather flowers as pansies, violas and primroses, and a supply of early leaf lettuce, radishes and parsley.

17. Tools for a Better Garden

How far you go in acquiring garden tools is strictly a matter of personal convenience. You can do very well with just a few, but there is no doubt that much work can be taken out of gardening by having the specialized tools and gadgets suited to your needs as a gardener. Whatever you buy should be of the very best quality. Cheap materials and workmanship cost money in the long run and will always be a source of annoyance.

Here are some of the most useful types of tools, their purposes and other facts you should know about them.

Clean-up Tools
Leaf rake: Bamboo variety breaks more easily than steel, but is lighter, doesn't bend and sweeps better. *Wood rake:* Only for raking hay and coarse debris. Teeth break easily but are replaceable. *Magnesium rake* of similar design is available at twice the cost.

Cultivating Tools
Level-head rake: Head is directly connected to handle, not by steel bows; is therefore stronger. The usual wide rake is good for general use; a narrow one for cleaning up closely planted beds. *Garden hoe:* Get a heavy one that swings right, has a good feel. *Scuffle hoe:* For cutting off weeds, mulching. There are two types to choose from: one cuts only on the push stroke; the other cuts both pushing and pulling. *Warren hoe:* Heart-shaped, for making furrows. *Italian grape hoe:* Short-handled, with a sharply sloping blade. Very heavy, akin to a mattock. *Short-handled cultivator:* A three-pronged scratcher for hands-and-knees work. Wire prongs are best. *Long-handled cultivator:* Three- or four-pronged

OPPOSITE: *An individual garden sometimes calls for individual tools. As this one was being dug out of clay, and plants set in their pockets, a light-weight pick was needed. This mountain climber's pick was perfect. Long narrow English trowel is also useful.*

The pleasure of gardening is increased when you have the proper hand tools and power equipment, stored neatly in a convenient place. Every gardener acquires, over a period of time, a supply of tools and other equipment uniquely suited to his individual circumstances. After you move to a new property or you start a new garden, it is a good policy to purchase the first season only the basic necessities; later, you can assess your requirements. Next, plan tool storage. LEFT, TOP: Pegboard organizes this garden work space. LEFT, CENTER: Redwood and corrugated fiber-glass make a simple, inexpensive storage and potting center. LEFT, BOTTOM: Window-cleaning bottle filled with clean water makes a handy mister for house-plant care. ABOVE: Perfect combination— lath house for baskets of shade plants, potting bench and storage space. BELOW: This well-designed cabinet in a carport provides space for sacks, shelves for pots, racks for hoses.

varieties available. Easier on the knees than the short-handled types; does the same job. *Marcross cultivator:* Three or five heavy prongs, staggered. Long handle. For deep cultivating, especially in the vegetable garden. *Wheel-hoe cultivator:* Needed only if you have a large vegetable garden. Should have small wheel, low-set handle.

Cutting Tools

Ax: If you need one, get a 4-pound head. *Ax mattock:* has two wide blades, one horizontal, one vertical. Ideal for cleaning out woodlands, chopping roots. *Pruning saw:* Has five or six teeth to the inch. Several types available. A pole pruning saw is needed for high overhead work. *Tree-top pruner:* A shearing tool, the knife being operated by a rope. A 12-foot length is about right. *Pruning shears:* The pattern pruner with two sharp blades is preferred by some gardeners; others say the snap-cut variety makes a cleaner cut and doesn't bruise the wood. If you are undecided, try a shear of each type, then make your choice. *Lopping shears:* For pruning hard-to-get-at branches too large for ordinary pruning shears, too small for sawing. Get the heavy-duty type. *Hedge shears:* The larger and heavier the better. *Sickle:* For cutting tall grass. Heavier weight does the better job. *Grass whip:* Has a flat, two-edged blade attached to a long handle like a golf club. A lazy man's sickle, but effective. *Scythe:* Heavy bush scythe cuts both weeds and brush. *Grass scythe,* for cutting long grass and hay, is a tool for real experts. *Edging knife:* A sharp half-moon. Does the best edging job. *Asparagus knife:* A long steel shank with a V-pronged, sharp blade. Originally designed to cut asparagus, but widely used for digging out deep-rooted weeds, such as dandelion.

Digging Tools

Round-pointed spade: Long-handled type is easier to handle. *Square-pointed spade:* Used for most garden work—digging and transplanting, for example. A good substitute for an edging knife. *Fork:* A wide-pronged spading fork does all the work—digging, turning, leaf and hay tossing. You don't really need a pitchfork. *Trowel:* Wood-handled variety is best, even though heavier than stainless steel. Much easier on the hands. *Pick mattock:* Has one horizontal wide blade, a sharp pick. Best all-round mattock. *Pick:* Sharp-pointed front and back. For heavy digging, prying out stones.

Lawn Tools

Spreader: For distributing seed or fertilizer. Get one that is sturdily made, but remember that if you don't keep it clean, even the best won't last very long. Width of 18 inches is satisfactory for most purposes.

Aerator: Small roller, with sharp-toothed disks, spikes holes in the lawn when you roll it back and forth. A power-driven aerator does a better job by far. *Roller:* Water-filled type is the only one to consider, but don't overestimate your strength. A 14- by 24-inch size weighs 180 pounds filled; 18- by 24-inch size weighs 275 pounds; 24- by 24-inch size weighs 440 pounds. *Tamper:* Not essential for firming a surface but you'll use it often if you have one. *Grass shears:* Easiest type to use has a spring which opens the blades when a cut is made.

Miscellaneous Tools

Sprayer, duster: Study the units on display at your garden center or hardware store. Select one large enough to do your work, and light enough to carry around easily. *Wheelbarrow:* Wooden type with removable sides has a large capacity, is excellent for moving soil and manure. Relatively lightweight, dish-shaped metal type will last longer, can be converted to a large leaf carrier by placing a wire basket on it. In either case, be sure the wheelbarrow has a good-sized rubber tire. *Ladder:* Aluminum (or, better yet, magnesium alloy) extension ladder is lightweight but sturdy. Don't look for a bargain if you don't want a broken neck. *Crowbar:* Needed only if you live in rough country and have a yen for prying out boulders and stumps and building stone walls.

Power Tools

In many cases you have a choice between gasoline-driven and electric tools. Gasoline-powered are generally preferable because you can operate them anywhere, don't have to soil and store a long cord. The most recent equipment in this field is battery-operated; edgers and hedge trimmers have proven to be excellent performers.

Rotary mower: Leads in popularity because it is lightweight, less expensive, cuts grass no matter how high it is and mulches leaves. But it is one of the most dangerous machines ever invented if it is not well designed and operated properly. *Reel mower:* Gives the best, cleanest, most even cut. It is recommended for use on large, flat, luxuriant lawns. All models are self-propelled. *Trimmer:* Small mower for trimming edges. Some types can also be used to cut the edges. *Lawn renovator:* Tool with revolving knives digs dead grass (thatch) out of lawns and helps to aerate the soil. *Garden tractor:* Small-size tractor with up to 12 hp. Though most gardeners originally buy tractors to simplify the lawn-mowing job, they soon find out that the machines can be used for countless other purposes. A wide array of attachments is available. *Chain saw:* Fastest tool for cutting down trees, lopping off large limbs, cutting firewood. *Hedge trimmer:* One type operates like a small chain saw; another like barbers' clippers.

Watering Tools

Watering pot: Ordinary pots come in 4- to 16-quart sizes. The 8-quart pot is about the right size for most people to handle easily. English watering pots have extra-long spouts. Both types should have two sprinkler heads: a small, fine one for seedlings; a large, coarse one for general work. *Hose:* Rubber hoses are heavy to handle and are subject to damage by exposure to sun, but they resist kinking and have about the right degree of flexibility. Plastic hoses are lighter to handle, generally less expensive and take up less space in storage. But most clear types are very inflexible except in hot weather, and lightweight, reinforced types kink easily. In either case, don't buy smaller than ½-inch size. *Soaker:* A porous canvas hose that gets water directly to the roots of plants without waste. *Sprinklers:* If your water pressure is uneven and not too good at best, buy a simple perforated, nonmoving type. If you have excellent water pressure, automatic, oscillating or revolving sprinklers are recommended because they cover more territory.

Once you have bought good tools, it is your duty to keep them in good condition. Don't leave them out in the rain or store them when still wet. Remove caked-on soil. Wipe with a damp, oily rag. If rust accumulates, rub with steel wool and wipe with oil. A clean tool is much easier to work with than a dirty, rusty one, because soil doesn't cling to it.

Straightening bent tools is difficult because they are made of tough steel. But the job can be done by putting them in a vise and bending gently.

If the steel of a spade or hoe becomes pitted by corrosion, file down the rough edges and sand with emery cloth.

To sharpen spades and hoes, clamp in a vise and file toward the edge of the blade at a 45° angle. Grinding on a small electric wheel may take the temper out of the steel.

Sharpen pruning shears on a carborundum stone. Take the shears apart first.

Sharpen scythes, sickles and grass whips with a scythe stone swept slowly along and slightly against the blade.

Remove broken handles by putting the head of the tool in a hot fire and burning out the wood. Then cut the rivet. New handles are easily set in and secured with a rivet or bolt. Avoid heating the whole implement or you will destroy the temper of the metal.

Store tools at all times in a dry place. For long-term storage, spray with a light film of oil (available in aerosol cans). Drain power tools completely of gasoline (run motor to use up last drop from carburetor). Scrape off encrusted dirt and clean with a damp cloth. Touch up nicked paint. Remove spark plug, squirt a little oil into the hole and turn motor over by hand to distribute oil on inner surfaces. Keep manufacturer's directions for operating and maintaining all power tools, and follow them faithfully.

Abies. *See* Firs
Achimenes, in basket, 210
Acidity, soil, 14–17
Aconitum, 195
Aerators, 312
Aechmea, 286; container-grown, 204; forcing, 126
African violets, leaf cuttings of, 69
Ageratum, seedling of, 134
Air (atmosphere): greenhouse, 304–5; for houseplants, 290; pollution, 274
Air layering, 54, 55
Alfalfa hay mulch, 89
Alkalinity, soil, 14–17
Alpine madwort. *See* Alyssum
Alkanet. *See* Anchusa
Althaea. *See* Hollyhocks
Aluminum foil mulch, 90
Alyssum: maintaining, 139; seedling, 134; shearing back, 136
Amaryllis, forcing, 122
Ammonia, 15
Ammonium nitrate, 10, 11, 14
Ammonium sulfate, 11, 14
Ananas. *See* Pineapple
Anchusa, seedling of, 134
Anemone coronaria, forcing, 125
Angelica, 195; harvesting, 197
Annuals, 129–40 (*See also* specific plants); for containers, 206; early sowing, indoors, 133; maintaining, 136–40; propagating (*See* Propagation); seeding in the garden, 133–36; uses of, 130–32
Antirrhinum. *See* Snapdragons
Aphid lions, 263
Aphids (plant lice), 172, 221, 270, 273
Apples, in forcing bromeliads, 126, 127
Apple trees, 189 (*See also* Espaliers); grafting, 72–73; pruning, 106

Apricot trees, 189; pruning, 106–7
Arborvitae: pruning, 105; topiary, 239
Armeria. *See* Statice
Artemisias, for herb garden border, 195
Asexual propagation, 49–79
Ashes, 11
Assassin bugs, 263
Asters, 144–46 (*See also* Michaelmas daisies); seedling, 134
Atmosphere. *See* Air
Avocado seeds, growing, 297
Axes, 311
Azaleas: forcing, 119; pruning, 104

Baby blue-eyes, seedling of, 134
Baby's-breath, seedling of, 134
Bachelor's-button, seedling of, 134
Bacillus thuringiensis, 221
Bacteria, soil, 10
Bagasse mulch, 90
Balsam. *See* Impatiens
Balsam fir, bonsai, 117
Bamboos, propagating, 52, 57
Banks, 22, 254
Barber Preplant 50-D, 268
Barberry, hedge of, 87
Bark mulch, 90
Bark-ringing, 108, 109
Barrel, strawberry, 212
Basil, 196
Basket gardening, 209–10
Beans, marigolds with, 221
Beaucarnea, 204
Bees, 263
Begonias, 62, 213 (*See also* Strawberry-begonia); leaf cuttings, 68–70
Belgian endive, 77; forcing, 120
Bells-of-Ireland, seedling of, 134
Benches, greenhouse, 305
Berberis, 87

Berries (*See also* Fruits; specific kinds): keeping birds from, 278
Biennials, 141–42, 143; cultural directions, 141–42; propagating (*See* Propagation)
Birds: attracting, 262; discouraging, 278, 279; for pest control, 221
Blackberries, 187; pruning, 109, 111
Black-eyed Susan vine, seedling of, 134
Black spot, 172
Blanket flower. *See* Gaillardia
Blocking, 45
Blood, dried, 11, 14; and deer, 277
Blueberries, 188–89; pruning, 109, 110
Bonsai, 117, 200, 230–36; chrysanthemum, 242–43
Boston daisies, container-grown, 213
Boxwood, 190
Boysenberries, 187; pruning, 111
Bramble fruits, 187–88 (*See also* specific kinds); pruning, 109
Brick, 28. *See also* specific uses
Bridge graft, 75
Bromeliads (*See also* specific plants): forcing, 126, 127; potting mixture for, 21; training, 243
Broom, cuttings of, 64
Browallias, 213
Buckwheat: for green manure, 219–20; hulls as mulch, 88, 90
Budding (bud grafting), 72, 73, 76, 77
Buds (*See also* Budding; specific plants): pinching, 104, 113–14, 115; and pruning, 98–99
Bugloss. *See* Anchusa
Bulbs (*See also* specific plants): as annuals, 30;

depth of planting; height of bloom, 150–51; forcing, 120–26; propagation by, 59–62; to plant in fall, 149; to plant in spring, 149
Burning bush. *See* Euonymus
Bush fruits, 186–87
Butterfly palm, 285; container-grown, 204
Buxus, 190

Cabbage worms, 221
Cacti, grafting, 78
Caladiums, 213; forcing, 125
Calcium, 14, 15
Calla-lilies, propagating, 62
Camellias, forcing, 127
Cannas: preserving flower, 161; propagating, 49–53, 62; storing tubers, 152
Cardinal flower. *See* Lobelia
Carrots, in basket, 296
Caterpillars, 271
Cattle manure, 219; liquid, 220
Celosia. *See* Cockscomb
Centaurea. *See* Bachelor's-buttons
Charcoal, 21
Chelated iron, 17
Cherry trees, 189; pruning, 107
Chicken manure, 219
Chicory. *See* Endive; Witloof chicory
Chives, with roses, 221
Chloramine, 291
Chlorine, 291
Chlorophytum. *See* Spider plant
Chloropicrin, 45
Christmas begonia, leaf cuttings of, 68–70
Chrysalidocarpus. *See* Butterfly palm
Chrysanthemums (*See also* Costmary): propagating, 51; staking, 156; training, 242–43
Cissus, 281
Cleft grafting, 75, 76, 78

Clematis: container-grown, 203; pruning, 113
Cleome, seedling of, 134
Clivias, 286; container-grown, 204
Cockscomb, seedling of, 134
Cocoa-bean hull mulch, 90
Cold frames, 41–43 (*See also* Cuttings; etc.); construction, 246, 247; in landscaping, 27; seed propagation in, 47–48
Coleus, seedling of, 134
Companion planting, 221, 223
Compatible plants, 222
Compost piles, 9–10; how to make, 214, 215–18; in landscaping, 27
Concrete, 28. *See also* specific uses
Construction, 244–61
Container-gardening, outdoor, 200–13
Convallaria. *See* Lily-of-the-valley
Corms, 62; as annuals, 130
Corncob mulch, 89
Cornstalk mulch, 89
Cosmos, seedling of, 134
Costmary, 195
Cottonseed meal, 11
Cover-cropping. *See* Green manure
Cow manure, 219 (*See also* Manure); liquid, 220
Crocuses, container-grown, 200
Crowbars, 312
Cultivators, 309–11
Curly endive, 177
Currants, 186–87; pruning, 109, 110, 111
Cuttings, 51, 59–62, 63–72 (*See also* Slips; specific plants); deciduous hardwood, 65–66; evergreen, 66–67; leaf, 68–70; leaf-bud, 70–71; root, 71–72; softwood, 67–68
Cyrtomium. *See* Holly fern
Cytisus, 64

Daffodils, forcing, 123–26
Dahlias: propagating, 59–62; seedling of, 134
Daisies: container-grown, 213; staking Michaelmas, 157
Damsel bugs, 263
Daphne, 64
Daylilies, 142; propagating, 52
Damping-off, 45
DBCP, 268
DD, 268
Deer, 277
Delphinium (larkspur), 144, 145; for herb garden border, 195; seedling of, 134
Dewberries, 187; pruning, 109, 111
Dianthus (*See also* Sweet William): seedling, 134
Digitalis. *See* Foxgloves
Dill, harvesting, 198
Disbudding, 114, 127
Disease, 265. *See also* Pests and diseases
Division, 49–53, 58ff. *See also* specific plants
DMTT, 268
Dogs, and deer, 277
Double digging, 17–19
Drains and drainage, 18–19; construction, 246–49; grading and, 25, 91–92; pool, 258–60; for pots, 211
Drills, seeds in, 42
Driveways, 26; weeds in, 276
Drop-pruning, 99
Dust mulch, 89
Dusters, 269–70, 312

Earwigs, 172
EDB, 268
Edgings, lawn, 29, 30
Elecampane, 195
Electricity (*See also* Lights): greenhouse, 302
Endive, 177. *See also* Belgian endive
English ivy: espaliers, 230–31; topiary, 238
Entrance courts, 26
Entrance walks, 27–28

Erysimum. *See* Wall-
flowers
Escarole, 177
Espaliers, 224, 225–30;
fuchsia, 243; tomato,
178
Ethylene dibromide, 268
Euonymus, preserving, 161
Euphorbia, 204. *See also*
Snow-on-the-mountain
Evergreens (*See also*
Espaliers; Hedges; spe-
cific plants): cuttings,
66–67; fertilizing broad-
leaf, 12; preserving, 161;
pruning, 102–6; topiary,
238–39

Fences, constructing, 249
Fern ball, 210
Ferns, propagating, 48–49
Fertilizers, 9, 10ff. (*See
also* specific plants):
basics, 11–14; house
plant, 271–72, 294; lawn,
12, 14, 96; organic, 218–
20
Fescues, 96; pruning, 115
Fiber-glass mulch, 90
Ficus, 286; container-
grown, 204
Figs. *See* Ficus
Firs (Abies): bonsai, 117;
pruning, 105
Firethorn (Pyracantha):
container-grown, 203;
espalier, 228
Fish emulsion, 219
Flagstone, 28, 37. *See also*
specific uses
Flat graft, 78
Flats (*See also* Cuttings;
etc.; specific plants):
indoor propagation by
seeds, 43ff.
Floss flowers. *See* Ageratum
Flowers, 128–60 (*See also*
specific kinds): con-
tainer-grown, 206–9;
forcing, 126–27; green-
house (*See* Green-
houses); in modular
garden, 36; for pot-
pourri, 198–99; preserv-
ing, 161–64; propagating
(*See* Propagation);

seedlings identified,
134–35; weeds in beds,
275
Fluorine, 274
Foliage (*See also* House
plants; Leaves; specific
plants): perennials for,
160
Foliage plant. *See* Coleus
Forcing, 118–27; bulbs,
120–26; flowers, 126–27
Forks, 311
Formaldehyde, 268
Four-o'clocks, seedlings
of, 134
Foxgloves, seedlings of,
134
Fragrance. *See* Scent
Freesias, forcing, 125
Front door, planning
walks to, 27–28
Fruit trees (*See also* Es-
paliers; specific kinds):
grafting, 76–79; prun-
ing, 106–8
Fruits, 183–89 (*See also*
Fruit trees; specific
kinds): discouraging
birds from, 279
Fuchsias, training, 243
Fumazone, 268
Fungi, soil, 10
Furrows, seeds in, 42

Gaillardia, seedling of, 134
Garbage, 26–27
Gas, house plants and, 290
Gates, fence, 249
Geraniums: container-
grown, 200, 213; for
potpourri, 199; stand-
ard, 240
Gibbing, 127
Gladiolus: propagating,
62; storing corms, 153
Globe amaranth, seedling
of, 134
Gloxinia, propagating, 62
Gomphrena. *See* Globe
amaranth
Gooseberries, 186–87;
pruning, 109, 110
Grading, 25–26, 91–92
Grafting, 72–79
Grape-ivy, 281
Grapes: and grafting, 73;
pruning, 109–12

Grass (*See also* Lawns):
cuttings as mulch, 89
Greenhouses, 298–307;
cost of, 299; founda-
tions, 302; heating, 302–
4; how large, 300; night-
time temperatures in
cold weather, 306; seed
propagation, 47; shad-
ing and cooling, 304–5;
and sun, 300–2; window
greenhouses, sun-heated
pits, 301, 307
Green manure, 19, 20,
219–20
Grit mulch, 158
Guano, 220
Gypsophila. *See* Baby's-
breath

Hardwood cuttings, 65–66
Hatrack, container-grown,
204
Hay mulches, 89
Heating (*See also* House
plants): greenhouse,
302–4
Hedera. *See* Ivy
Hedges, 132; planting, 86,
87; pruning, 100–2
Hemerocallis. *See* Day-
lilies
Herbs, 190, 191–99; con-
tainer-grown, 206, 207;
growing indoors, 195–
96; harvesting, 196–97,
198; in modular garden,
36; for pest control, 222;
for potpourri, 198–99;
surround for garden,
194–95
Hilly land, 25–26. *See also*
Banks
Hippeastrum, forcing, 122
Hoes (hoeing), 41, 309;
care of, 313
Holly, espalier of, 228
Holly fern, 285; container-
grown, 204
Hollyhocks, seedling of,
134
Hops, as mulch, 90
Hormones, root-inducing,
66ff.
Horse manure, 90, 220
Hoses, 313
Hotbeds, 246, 247

House plants, 281–97; air, 290; climate, 281–90; feeding, 294; keeping healthy, 270–73, 295; light for, 282–89; potting, repotting, 292–94; for semishade, 284; for semisun, 286–87; for shade, 282–83; soil mixes for, 292; for sun, 288
Houseleek, propagating, 57
Howea, 286
Hoya, container-grown, 204
Huckleberries, pruning, 110
Humidity. *See* Air
Humus, 9–10, 217
Hyacinths: forcing, 122, 123, 124; propagating, 59
Hydrangeas, forcing, 119
Hydrogen, 14

Impatiens, 213; seedling of, 134
Incompatible plants, 222
Inlay graft, 74
Insects. *See* Pests and diseases
Inula, 195
Ipomoea. *See* Morning-glories
Irises, propagating, 50, 53, 58
Iron, 14, 15, 17
Ivy (*See also* specific kinds): espalier, 230–31; preserving, 161; topiary, 238; training, 297

Japanese beetles, 172
Japanese holly, espalier, 228
Jar-on-side seed propagation, 46
Jars, strawberry, 212
Junipers, pruning, 105

Kalanchoe, propagating, 72
Kentia palm, 286
Kentucky bluegrass, 96
Kniffin system, 111

Knives, 311
Knot gardens, 190, 239

Ladders, 312
Ladybugs (lady beetles), 221, 263
Landscape design, 22–37; advantages of hiring help, 23–24; designing lawn, 29–30; do-it-yourself, 25; hilly land, 25–26; modular approach, 35–37; preparing questionnaire, 24–25; recreational areas, 27–28; service areas, 26–27; surfacing materials, 28–29; traffic patterns, 26; with trees, 30–34; work areas, 27
Larkspur. *See* Delphinium
Larvacide, 45
Lath house, 310
Lathyrus. *See* Sweet-peas
Laundry facilities, 27
Lavender potpourri, 199
Lawns, 12, 14, 91–97; first feeding, 95–96; first mowing, 95; good seed mixture, 96; how to grade land, 91–92; kinds of grasses, 95–96; in landscaping, 28–30; mulching to encourage, 94–95; soils for, 92–94; sowing, 96–97; tools, 311–12; weeding, 276; when to start, 91
Layering, 53, 54–55
Leaf-bud cuttings, 70–71
Leaf cuttings, 68–70
Leaf mulch, 89
Leafhoppers, 172
Leaves (*See also* Foliage; Leaf . . .); preserving, 161; propagation by, 56 (*See also* Leaf cuttings)
Lemon-verbena, for potpourri, 199
Lettuce, 176
Lights, 289 (*See also* House plants); for herbs, 195–96
Ligustrum. *See* Privet
Lilacs: grafting, 73, 79; propagating, 57

Lilies (*See also* specific kinds): for herb garden border, 195; propagating, 38, 59, 61, 62; staking, 156
Lily-of-the-valley, forcing, 123
Lime: for lawns, 93; test, 8
Linaria, seedling of, 134
Lippia. *See* Lemon-verbena
Liquid manure, 220
Loam. *See* Soil
Lobelia, seedling of, 134
Lorette pruning, 108
Lovage, 195
Love-in-a-mist. *See* Nigella

Magnesium, 14, 15
Manganese, 14, 15, 17
Manure, 9, 218–20 (*See also* Green manure); for mulch, 90
Marigolds: with beans, 221; seedling, 135
Mattocks, 311
Mealybugs, 270, 273, 295
Mexican bean beetle, 221
Michaelmas daisies, staking, 157
Miller Mico-Fume 25D, 268
Mimosa, forcing, 120
Mirabilis. *See* Four-o'clocks
Misting, 63–64
Mites. *See* Pests and diseases
Modular gardens, 35–37; materials, 36–37
Moles, 277–79
Molucella. *See* Bells-of-Ireland
Monkshood, for herb garden border, 195
Morning-glories, seedlings of, 135
Moss, rose. *See* Portulaca
Mowers, power, 312
Mowing bands, 91, 92
Mulching, 87–90 (*See also* specific plants); to encourage lawn, 94–95; in organic gardening, 220–21; perennials, winter, 158; weeds, 275

Muriate of potash, 11
Mylone, 268

Narcissus (*See also* Daffodils): forced, 118, 121; storing bulbs, 153
Nasturtiums, seedlings of, 135
Nectarines (*See also* Espaliers): pruning, 106–7
Nemagon, 268
Nemophila. *See* Baby blue-eyes
Newspaper mulch, 90
Nicotiana, seedling of, 135
Nigella, seedling of, 135
Nitrate of soda (sodium nitrate), 10, 11, 14
Nitrogen, 10ff.
Nymphaea. *See* Waterlilies

Oats, for green manure, 219
Offsets, 55–57
Orchids, dividing, 58
Organic gardens, 214–23; compost, 214, 215–18; feeding, maintaining, 218–23
Oriental-poppy, root division of, 71–72
Ozone, 274

Palms, 285, 286; container-grown, 204
PAN, 274
Pandanus. *See* Screw-pines
Pansies: mulching beds, 89; seedlings of, 135
Papaver. *See* Poppies
Paper mulch, 90
Paths. *See* Walks and paths
Peace-lily, 283; container-grown, 204
Peaches, 187 (*See also* Espaliers); and grafting, 73; pruning, 106–7
Peanut-shell mulch, 90
Pears, 189 (*See also* Espaliers); pruning, 107
Peat moss, pH of, 14
Pebbles, as mulch, 90
Pelargonium. *See* Geraniums

Peonies, dividing, 146
Pepper, hot, for pest control, 221
Perennials, 142–60 (*See also* specific plants); for border, 147–54; for containers, 206; double digging, 18; maintaining border, 154–56; to plant in spring, fall, 149; propagating (*See* Propagation); sources, 158–59; for specific uses, 159–60; staking, 156, 157; structure of, 144–47; water and fertilizer for, 157–58; winter mulching, 158
Periwinkle. *See* Vinca
Pests and diseases, 262–79 (*See also* specific plants); air pollution, 274; beneficial insects, 264–65; controlling, 265–73; dusters, 269–70; grafting and resistance to, 73; granular applicators, 270; house plants and, 270–73, 295; moles, 277–79; organic gardening and, 221–22, 223; rabbits and deer, 276–77; soil fumigants, 267–68; spray or dust, 266–67ff.; sprayers, 268–69; weeds, 274–76 (*See also* Weeds)
Petunias: cutting back, 113; maintaining, 139; seedling of, 135
pH, 14–17
Phlox, 144–46; seedling of, 135
Phosphoric acid, 11, 12
Phosphorus, 11, 12, 14, 15; and lawns, 93; test for, 8
Picks, 308, 311
Pinching, 104, 113–14, 115 (*See also* specific plants); espaliers, 229–30
Pine bough mulch, 89
Pine needle mulch, 89
Pineapple, rooting, 56
Pines: bonsai, 233; pruning, 105–6

Pinks. *See* Dianthus
Plant lice. *See* Aphids
Plectranthus, 204
Plumbing, greenhouse, 302
Plums, 189; grafting, 72; pruning, 107
Polygonatum, 58
Ponytail, container-grown, 204
Pools, 257–61
Poppies: root division, 71–72; seedling, 135
Portulaca, seedling of, 135
Potash, 11, 12, 14, 15
Potassium, 11. *See also* Potash
Potassium nitrate, 10, 11
Potatoes (*See also* Sweet potatoes): fertilizing, 12
Pot-in-pot seed propagation, 46
Pots, 292–94 (*See also* Container-gardening; Cuttings; Forcing; etc.; House plants); indoor propagation by seeds, 43–44, 46
Potting and repotting, 292–94
Potting soils, 20–21. *See also* specific uses
Powdery mildew, 172
Praying mantises, 263
Preserving flowers, 161–64
Preserving herbs, 196–97
Privet, planting hedge of, 86
Propagation, 38–79 (*See also* specific plants): by parts of plants, 49–79; by seeds indoors, 43–47, 61; by seeds outdoors, 39–43, 47–48, 61; by spores, 48–49
Pruners, 311
Pruning, 98–117 (*See also* Espaliers; Topiary; specific plants): bramble fruits, 109; broadleaf evergreens, 102–5; flowering bushes, 102, 103; fruit trees, 106–8; fruits, small, 109–12; garden climbers and creepers, 113; hedges, 100–2; needle evergreens, 105–

6; pinching, 104, 113–14; root, 114–17
Pyracantha. *See* Firethorn
Pyrethrum, 221

Rabbits, 276–77
Ragweed, and good tilth, 19
Railroad ties, 22
Rakes and raking, 41, 309
Ramps, and changes of lawn level, 93
Raspberries, 187, 188; pruning, 109, 110, 111
Recreational areas, 27–28, 253
Red fescue, 96
Red spider. *See* Spider mites
Redtop, 96
Renovators, lawn, 312
Rex begonia, leaf cuttings of, 67, 68
Rhizomes, 58, 146. *See also* Division; specific plants
Rhododendrons, 53; grafting, 73; leaf-bud cuttings, 70–71; pruning, 104
Rock gardens, 144
Rollers, lawn, 312
Root cuttings, 71–72
Root pruning, 114–17; of house plants, 293
Rose chafers, 172
Rose daphne, cuttings of, 64
Rose geraniums, for potpourri, 199
Rose midges, 172
Rose slugs, 172
Roses, 164–73; chives with, 221; container-grown, 213; and grafting, 73, 76, 77; for herb border, 195; mulching, 88, 89; for potpourri, 199; pruning, 103, 112–13
Rotenone, 221
Runners, 55, 57
Ryania, 221
Rye, 19, 20, 220

Saddle grafting, 76, 79
Sage, seedling of, 135
Saintpaulia. *See* African violets

Salt-marsh hay mulch, 89
Salts, and injury to house plants, 272
Sand box, 253
Sawdust mulch, 90
Saws, 311, 312
Saxifraga, 55
Scabiosa, seedling of, 135
Scale disease, 270, 273, 295
Scales, propagation by, 59, 61
Scent: annuals for, 138; gardens for, 190, 191–92; and pest control, 222; potpourri, 198–99
Scion grafting, 76–79. *See also* specific types
Screw-pine: container-grown, 204; pest-free, 273
Scythes, 311; care of, 313
Seedlings, 41ff. (*See also* Seeds; specific plants); flower, identified, 134–35
Seeds (*See also* Annuals; specific plants): harvesting herb, 198; indoor propagation, 43–47, 61; outdoor propagation, 39–43, 47–48, 61
Sempervivum, 57
Sensitive plant. *See* Mimosa
Service areas, 26–27
Sewage sludge, 220
Shade (*See also* House plants; etc.; specific plants): for newly planted seedlings, 155
Shallots, for pest control, 221
Shears, 311, 312; care of, 313
Sheep manure, 220
Shrubs (*See also* Bonsai; Cuttings; Espaliers; Evergreens; Hedges; Pruning; specific plants): in landscape design, 30; to plant in spring, fall, 149; planting, 81ff.; weeding borders, 276
Sickles, 311; care of, 313
Side grafting, 74, 76, 79

Sieve, 44
Slips, 58–59
Slugs, 172, 271, 273
Snapdragons: maintaining, 139; seedling, 135
Snow-on-the-mountain, seedling of, 135
Soakers, 313
Sodium nitrate (nitrate of soda), 10, 11, 14
Softwood cuttings, 67–68
Soil, 8–21 (*See also* House plants; etc.; Propagation; specific plants); fertilizer basics, 11–14; fumigants, 267–68; for healthy turf, 92–94; how to make garden loam, 17–19; indoor garden mixes, 292; maintaining garden loam, 19–20; pH, 14–17; recipe for potting mixes, 20–21; sterilizing, 44–45
Soil Fumigant M, 268
Solomon's seal, propagating, 58
Southernwood. *See* Artemisias
Spades (spading), 41, 311; care of, 313
Spathiphyllum, 204, 283
Spider flower. *See* Cleome
Spider mites (red spider), 172, 295
Spider plant, 283; container-grown, 204
Spindle tree. *See* Euonymus
Splicing (splicing graft), 75
Spores, 48–49
Sprayers, 268–69, 312
Spreaders, 311–12
Sprinklers, 256–57, 313
Staking. *See* specific plants
Standards (*See also* specific plants): training, 240–43
Statice, seedling of, 135
Steps, 22; constructing, 249–50, 254
Sterilizing soil, 44–45
Stolons, 53–55
Stone. *See* specific uses
Stones, as mulch, 90
Storage, 27, 310, 313

Straw mulch, 89
Strawberries, 182–86; barrel for, 212; keeping birds from, 278; mulching beds, 89; propagating, 55; in terraces, 175
Strawberry-begonia, 55
Strawflowers, seedlings of, 135
Succulents, potting mixture for, 21
Suckers, 56, 57–58. *See also* specific plants
Sugarcane mulch, 90
Sulfate of potash, 11
Sulfur dioxide, 274
Sunflowers (*See also* Tithonia): seedlings of, 135
Superphosphate, 11, 14, 93
Surfacing materials, in landscape design, 28–29
Swedish-ivy, container-grown, 204
Sweet-peas: maintaining, 140; seedling, 135
Sweet potatoes: slips, 58–59; vines, 297
Sweet William, seedling of, 135
Syringa. *See* Lilacs

Tagetes. *See* Marigolds
Tampers, 44, 312
Tansy (Tanacetum), 195
Taxus. *See* Yews
Tear gas, 45
Terraces, 28; constructing, 250–52; weeds in, 276
Terrariums, 296
Thrips, 172
Tithonia, seedling of, 135
Toadflax. *See* Linaria
Toads, 221
Tobacco: flowering (*See* Nicotiana); stems as mulch, 90
Tolmiea, propagating, 72
Tomatoes, 177–79; container-grown, 207
Tongue (whip) grafting, 74, 76–79
Tools, 27, 308–13 (*See also* specific uses); clean-up, 309; cultivating, 309–11; cutting, 311; digging, 311; lawn,

311–12 (*See also* Lawns); miscellaneous, 312; power, 312; watering, 313
Topiary, 132, 236–40
Tractors, garden, 312
Traffic patterns, 26
Transplanting. *See* specific types of plants
Trees (*See also* Bonsai; Cuttings; Espaliers; Evergreens; Grafting; Pruning; specific kinds): container-grown, 201–6; fertilizing, 12, 13; in landscape design, 30–34; mowing bands to protect, 92; to plant in spring, fall, 149; planting, 80ff.
Trenching, 17–19
Trichogramma, 221
Trimmers, power, 312
Tropaeolum. *See* Nasturtiums
Trowels, 42, 308, 311
Tubers (*See also* specific plants): as annuals, 130; propagation by, 62
Tulips, forcing, 123–26

Urea, 11, 14

Vapam, 268
Vegetables, 175–82 (*See also* specific kinds); for containers, 206, 207; forcing, 119–20; to plant in early spring, 180; to plant in late spring, 182; to plant in mid-spring, 181; weeds in gardens, 275–76
Veneer grafting, 76, 79
Verbena (*See also* Lemon-verbena): seedling of, 135
Vinca, seedling of, 135
Vines (*See also* specific plants): container-grown, 203
Viola (*See also* Pansies): seedling of, 135
Virgin's bower. *See* Clematis
Viviparous plants, 72
V.P.M., 268

Walks and paths, 22, 27–28; constructing, 250–52, 253, 256; weeds in, 276
Wallflowers, maintaining, 139
Walls, 22, 26; constructing, 252–55; for modular garden, 36
Wasps, 263
Water and watering, 255–57 (*See also* Drains and drainage; Pools; specific plants); greenhouse plumbing, 302; indoor gardens, 290–92; tools, 313
Water-lilies, 72, 261
Wax plant. *See* Hoya
Wedge grafting, 76, 79
Weeds, 274–76 (*See also* Mulching); and good tilth, 19
Wheat, as green manure, 220
Wheelbarrows, 312
Whip grafting, 74, 76–79
Whips, grass, 311; care of, 313
Whiteflies, 270, 295
Window boxes, annuals for, 137
Window greenhouses, 307
Wisteria, forcing, 126–27
Witloof chicory, 177; forcing, 120
Wood, 245–46 (*See also* specific uses); ashes, 11; chip mulch, 90
Work areas, 27, 256–57. *See also* Tools
Worms, and house plants, 295

Yams, for vines, 297
Yews: pruning, 105; topiary, 239
Youngberries, 187; pruning, 111

Zantedeschia. *See* Calla-lily
Zelkova, for bonsai, 117
Zinnias: preserving, 162; seedling, 135